IMAGES
of America

COOS BAY

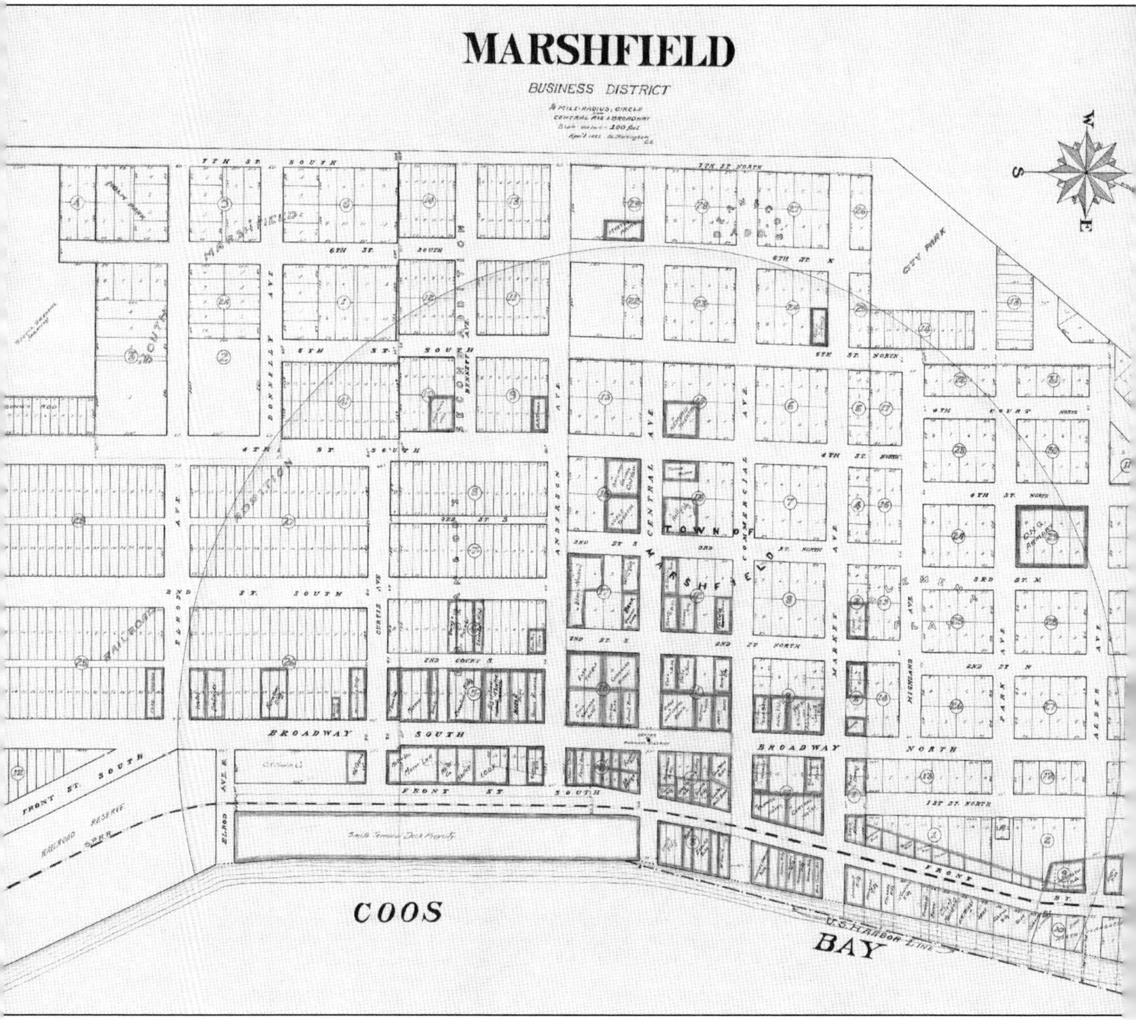

For over 50 years, Front Street reigned as the business district of Marshfield. After the devastating fire of 1922, the business district began to take shape off Broadway Street and Central Avenue. The surrounding area soon took hold as the center of Marshfield's business district. (Coos Historical & Maritime Museum 987-m38.)

On the Cover: Coos Bay Pirates Jim Baker and Moe Littrell are seen capturing personnel from the First National Bank of Portland, Coos Bay, North Bend, and Coquille branches. The Coos Bay Pirates were a civic group that promoted Coos Bay and North Bend. They were known for their colorful pirate costumes and high jinks in capturing civic members for a time of folly. (Coos Historical & Maritime Museum.)

IMAGES of America

Coos Bay

Andie E. Jensen and the
Coos Historical & Maritime Museum

ARCADIA PUBLISHING

ISBN 978-0-7385-8917-6

Published by Arcadia Publishing
Charleston, South Carolina

Printed in the United States of America

Library of Congress Control Number: 2011933817

For all general information, please contact Arcadia Publishing:
Telephone 843-853-2070
Fax 843-853-0044
E-mail sales@arcadiapublishing.com
For customer service and orders:
Toll-Free 1-888-313-2665

Visit us on the Internet at www.arcadiapublishing.com

Contents

ACKNOWLEDGMENTS

Authoring a book is not the work of one person. Many contributors have provided their knowledge and family photographs to make this book a reality. First and foremost, one must acknowledge the Coos Historical & Maritime Museum. If not for their vast collection of photographs, an undertaking such as this would have far more difficult to present. I thank Vicki Wiese, interim director and collections manager of the Coos Historical & Maritime Museum, for her skills in collecting and researching photographs and keeping me on track. I also thank Steve Greif, president of the Coos Historical & Maritime Museum, for his time in editing this book.

Many more individuals have provided their family photographs and knowledge of the area to enhance the quality of this book. I give my thanks to the following people: Jim and Jan Hillar, Tom Greaves, and Frank Walsh for their knowledge of Empire; Besse Guthrie, Gordon Ross, and Jack Beebe for their knowledge of Eastside; and Jesse Beers, cultural director of the Confederated Tribes of Coos, Lower Umpqua, and Siuslaw Indians, for his expertise on the Coos tribe. Thanks to Coos Bay city manager Rodger Craddock, executive assistant Jackie Mickelson, and economic revitalization administrator Joyce Jansen for their research and knowledge of the City of Coos Bay.

Plus, special thanks to Arcadia Publishing and editors Donna Libert and Shayne Ross for their guidance and skills in preparing this book. Additional thanks to Tom Baake, secretary of the Oregon Coast Historical Railway; Benjamin Brayfield and Lou Sennick from the *World*; Steven Broocks from the Coos Art Museum; Dick and Judy Wagner; and John Whitty.

A photograph credit appears at the end of each caption. Abbreviations include CHMM for Coos Historical & Maritime Museum; "Confederated Tribes" for the Confederated Tribes of Coos, Lower Umpqua, and Siuslaw Indians; and CCB for the City of Coos Bay.

Introduction

Not always known as Coos Bay, the city had a humble beginning in the winter of 1853 as Marshfield. The dream of a city was the vision of James C. Tolman, a member of the Coose Bay Company, who came to settle the new frontier seeking profitable investments. Exploring the bay, Tolman noted the advantages of the different points on the bay and selected the area he developed as Marshfield. Tolman considered the area, the point designated by nature, as the future emporium of the bay. Marshfield was not named for the marshy land from which it was built but for Marshfield, Massachusetts, the hometown of Daniel Webster, who Tolman greatly admired.

Coos Bay became a city after a ballot measure was passed on November 7, 1944, to change the city name from Marshfield to Coos Bay. The name change was confirmed in a special election on December 28, 1944, with a 101-vote victory. With the victory, Coos Bay became the reigning queen of the bay, and Marshfield faded into history.

The name change was deemed historically significant and more appealing and provided a better image for potential growth of the city. It was felt that Marshfield connoted a swampy marsh area. Additionally, the name "Marshfield" hailed from New England, thus providing no ties to the original terrain on which the city was built. Hence the name Marshfield lacked originality, with no ties to the southwestern Oregon area. The change to Coos Bay provided the city with a tie to the bay on which it is located.

Coos Bay is situated on the Pacific coast of Oregon, about 180 miles south of the Columbia River and 445 miles north of the San Francisco Bay. Coos Bay is considered the most important harbor between San Francisco and the Columbia River and is one of the few natural harbors along a stretch of 800 miles extending from San Francisco to the Canadian border. Coos Bay is Oregon's largest estuary.

The name Coos has been a topic of debate that continues to this date. Some assert that Coos was derived from the Hanis stem *gus*, meaning "south" as in *gusimídžic* (southward). Another idea is that it is derived from a southwestern Oregon Athabaskan word *kus* (bay). Two additional Indian meanings for Coos are "lake" and "place of pines."

What makes the meaning so difficult to understand is that the natives were a people of oral tradition, and thus, it was easy for the white settlers to confuse their language. Throughout the early history of the region, several names surfaced identifying present-day Coos Bay and the native tribesmen. Some of the names included Koos, Koos-koos-kee, Koos-koos-ka, Koos-koos-ky, Cook-koo-oose, Kouse, Cowis, Cowes, Cowan, Kowes, Coose, and finally the spelling we have today—Coos. One white man's interpretation came from Coose Bay Company founder Perry Marple, who stated that "Coose" was an Indian corruption of the English word *coast*.

Throughout the years, Coos Bay has continued to grow and prosper. Annexations and mergers have successfully grown the city. The first annexation of a community occurred in 1874, when Marshfield annexed the community of Ferndale. Ferndale was located in the area near the Red

Lion Hotel at 1313 North Bayshore Drive, extending west to about Ninth Street, south to about Date or Elm Streets, and then north to Koos Bay Boulevard.

In 1964, the City of Coos Bay annexed the community of Englewood, adding 1,307 people to Coos Bay's population. Originally named Eastport, Englewood was an import coal-mining community. The following year, the City of Empire merged with Coos Bay. At a special election on December 7, 1964, Empire citizens voted for the surrender of their city charter and asked to be merged with Coos Bay, with 463 in favor and 387 opposing. On January 8, 1965, with a vote of 1,329 in favor to the 181 opposed, the voters of Coos Bay approved the merger with Empire. Empire ceased to exist as its own city effective February 8, 1965. The merger added an additional 3,917 people to Coos Bay's population. With the merger, Coos Bay replaced Astoria as the largest city on the Oregon coast.

On December 29, 1983, the City of Eastside merged with the City of Coos Bay. The original plan was to consolidate three cities: Coos Bay, North Bend, and Eastside. However, North Benders overwhelmingly opposed the consolidation with Coos Bay.

For years, Coos Bay has had an eye on merging with North Bend. After the failed ballot measure in 1944 to consolidate Marshfield and North Bend, there have been five more attempts to consolidate the two cities. The first attempt occurred in 1962 and was followed in 1968, 1983, and 2002. The final attempt occurred in 2004. Each time, the citizens of Coos Bay have voted in favor of the merger; however, North Bend's residents rallied to defeat the measures.

Coos Bay has a city flower, tree, and song. The city wanted plants that were indigenous to the community, and on October 22, 1984, the Pacific dogwood was selected as the city tree and the Pacific rhododendron was adopted as the city flower. The city song was written and composed by local Melody Caldera. The song was adopted by the city on November 25, 2006.

For many years, Coos Bay flourished as the world's largest lumber port. However, the wealth generated by the lumber industry came to a crashing halt in the late 1970s and early 1980s. The first mill to close in 1979 was Coos Head. Additional mill closures soon followed until the prosperous days of the lumber industry nearly vanished. The failure of the mills was attributed to rising interest rates and the fluctuation of the US dollar in foreign markets. The export of raw lumber also played a major role in the closures of the mills.

Despite the loss of the timber industry, Coos Bay has opened its doors to tourism as a major contributor to the commerce of the city. Coos Bay serves as the gateway to the best recreational opportunities the Oregon coast has to offer.

One

THE COOS PEOPLE

Undisturbed for centuries, the people who inhabited the area of Coos Bay were given the name "Coos" due to a misappropriation of the several names that were used at the time for the Kusan people. The Coos or Kusan comprised a small language family formed by two tribes in a narrow coastal strip between the Coos and Coquille Rivers. Several villages were located around the bay. Nikawaha was located at Giromy, a flat in southern Empire. Further north, Hanasich was located near the Empire boat ramp, where natural springs provided the village's drinking water. The next village up the bay was Ntisæ'ich (Intesedge). Near the old Empire cemetery was the village of Wu'alach.

Initially, the natives and whites lived peaceably and coexisted. However, the settlers wanted to own the Coos lands. In 1856, war broke out with the Indians on the Rogue River. The Rogue River War worried the settlers near Coos Bay, who feared that the Coos would join the war. As a preemptive strike, the Coos Indians were rounded up and held at an encampment south of Empire City. In 1860, the Coos were forcibly transported by ship and later marched to the Siletz Reservation. In 1861, the Coos were forced to relocate again to the Yachats (Alsea) Reservation, next to the Siletz Reservation. In 1871, there were 136 Coos on the Alsea Sub agency of the Siletz Reservation. The closing of the Alsea Reservation in 1875 allowed the Coos to return to their homeland. However, most of the livable land was taken by the white setters.

The Coos tribe adopted its first constitution and bylaws in 1938. In 1941, on six acres of donated land in Empire, the Bureau of Indian Affairs built a hall for the general use of the tribe. However, it was not until October 17, 1984, that restoration of the tribe was granted. This was due to the Indian termination policy in 1954. Today, the Confederated Tribes of the Coos, Lower Umpqua, and Siuslaw remain in touch with a rich, traditional culture and value system of living harmoniously with the earth.

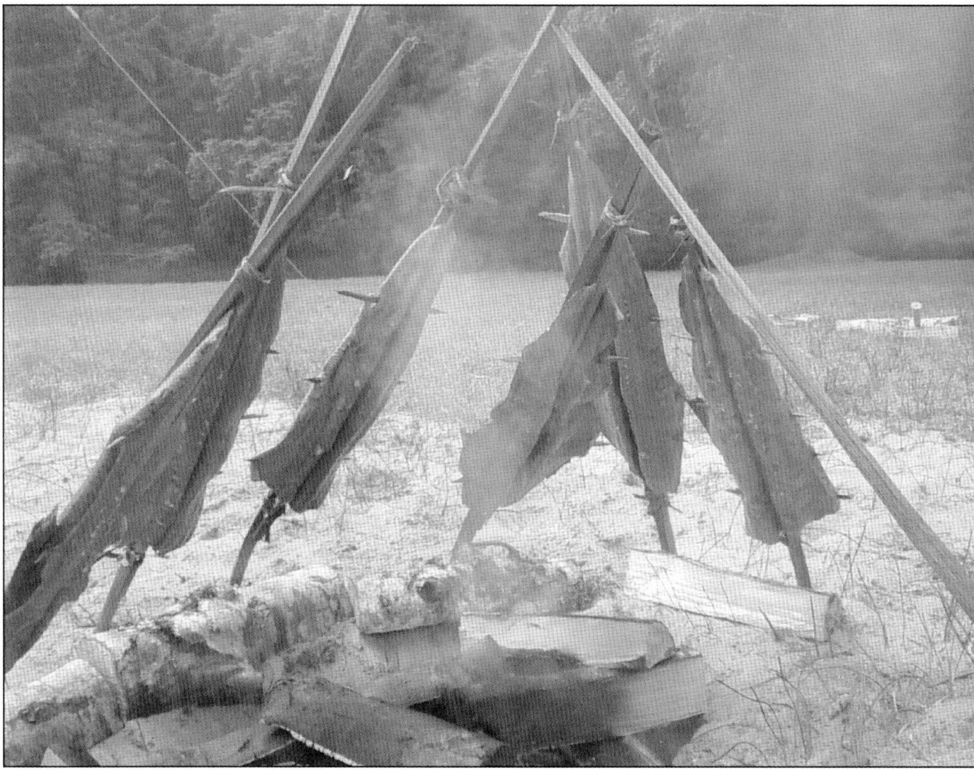

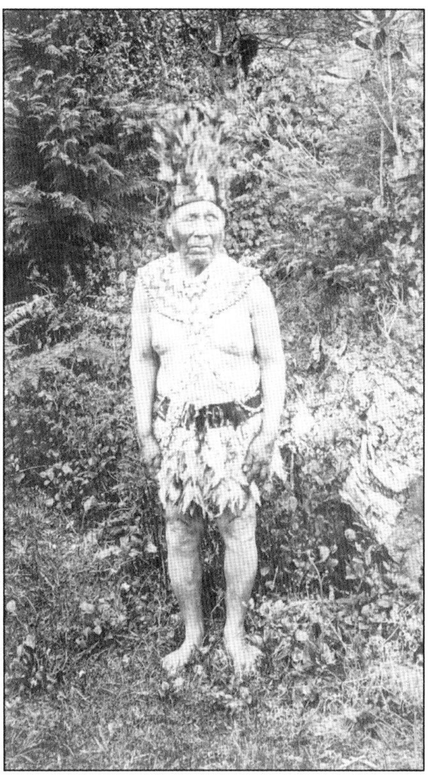

An annual Salmon Ceremony is held on the first Sunday in August. Cooked outdoors in the traditional way, the ceremony honors the salmon. After the meal, a ceremony is preformed, returning the salmon remains to the ocean as an act of respect and gratitude to the creator. (Confederated Tribes.)

Coos chief Daloose Jackson displays his native attire. Another spelling is Doloos, a name play on the word *diluutl*, meaning "young man." Daloose Jackson as a younger man was chief but, at some point, was not regarded as a chief. As an old man, people offered to recognize him as chief again, but he declined, saying something like "when alder gets old, it is rotten." (CHMM 975-73L a.)

Blended with Anglo clothing, two Native Americans display their baskets, headgear, and clothing. Traditionally, clothing was made from materials including elk and deer hides along with a wide variety of plant fibers. Women wore capes and skirts made from many local materials. Cedar bark provided day skirts, whereas sedges made good skirts for working around water. (CHMM 959-246 s.)

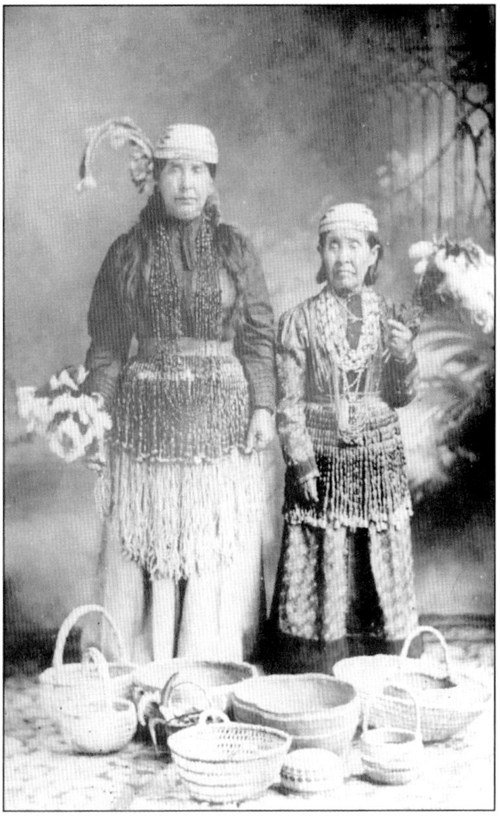

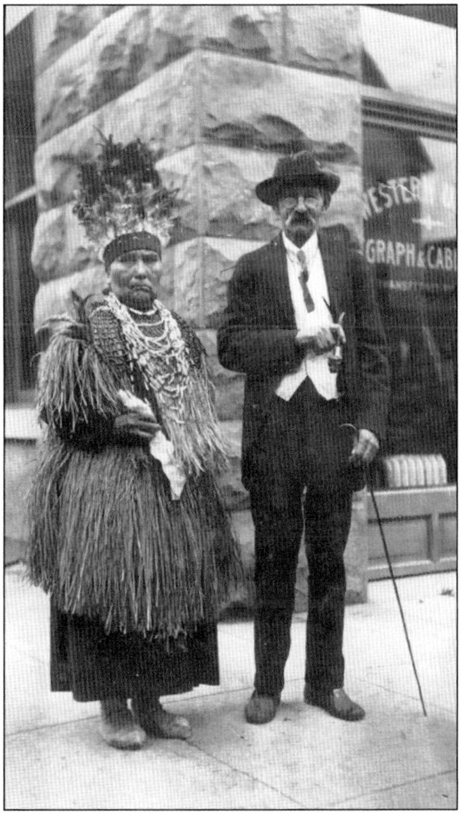

In 1916, Miss Coast and Mr. Williamette participated in Marshfield's Railroad Jubilee. Miss Coast dons the traditional cedar-bark clothing and wears the feathered headdress usually worn for ceremonial occasions. Headdresses decorated with red feathers from the pileated woodpecker were valued. Mallard feathers were also used but were not considered as valuable. (CHMM 968-135.)

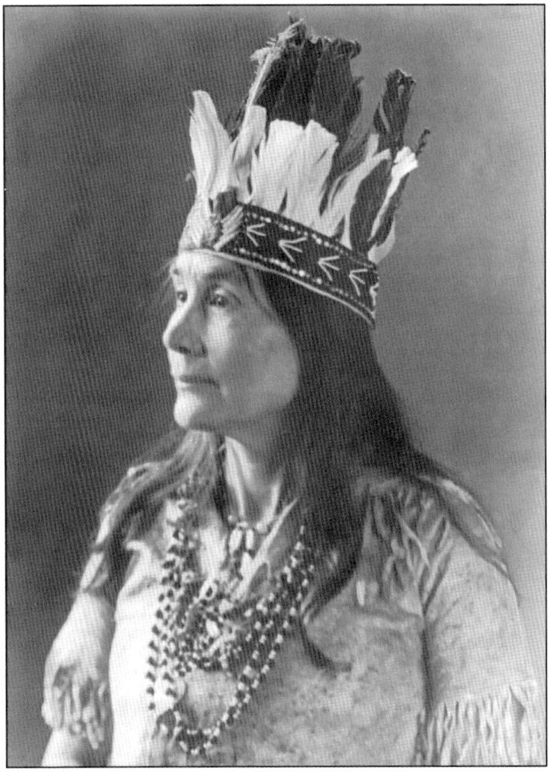

Annie Miner Peterson was perhaps the most published local Native American. In 1933–1934, Annie dictated hours of traditional oral literature and songs in the Hanis (Coos proper) and Miluk dialects to University of Washington anthropologist Melville Jacobs. Peterson's native name was "Hets'miixˇwn," which translated "she's tricky like coyote." Annie Miner Peterson was the last person known to speak the native Miluk language. (CHMM 989-P209.)

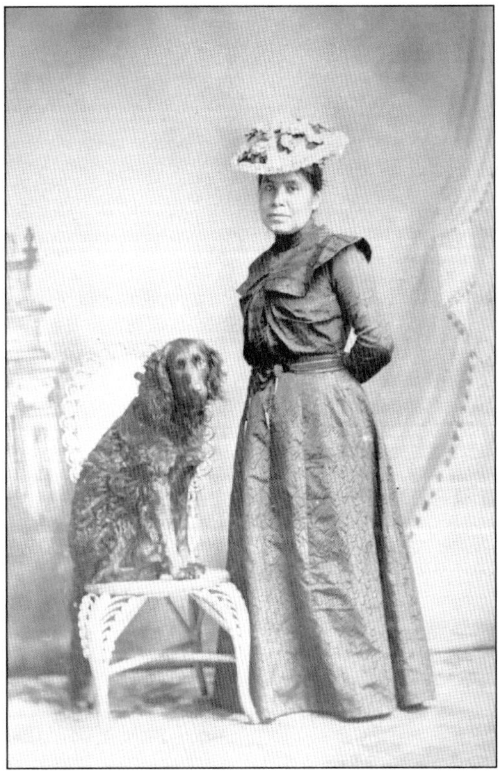

Referred to as the "Indian Princess," Lottie Evanoff was the daughter of Daloose Jackson and a survivor of the march to Fort Umpqua in 1856 and the relocation to Yachats in 1859. Evanoff also served as a linguistic informant. Evanoff was said to be the last full-blooded member of the Coos tribe. Evanoff died at Ross Inlet on March 11, 1944. (CHMM 009-16.4971.)

"Old Blind Kate" proudly displays her native accessories. Along with the apron and headband, she is adorned with many dentalium necklaces. Highly prized, dentalia were used as currency from Northern California to Alaska. Longer dentalium shells were sometimes decorated by incising geometric designs on the shell. Not only made into necklaces, dentalia shells were widely used for earrings and sewed on clothes and hats. (CHMM 995-D184.)

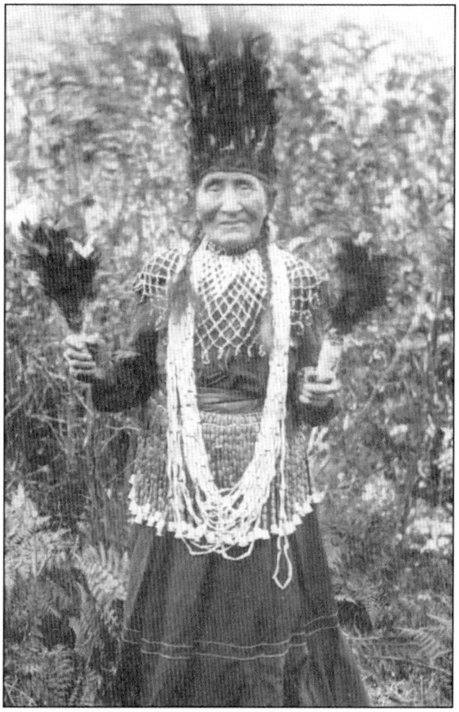

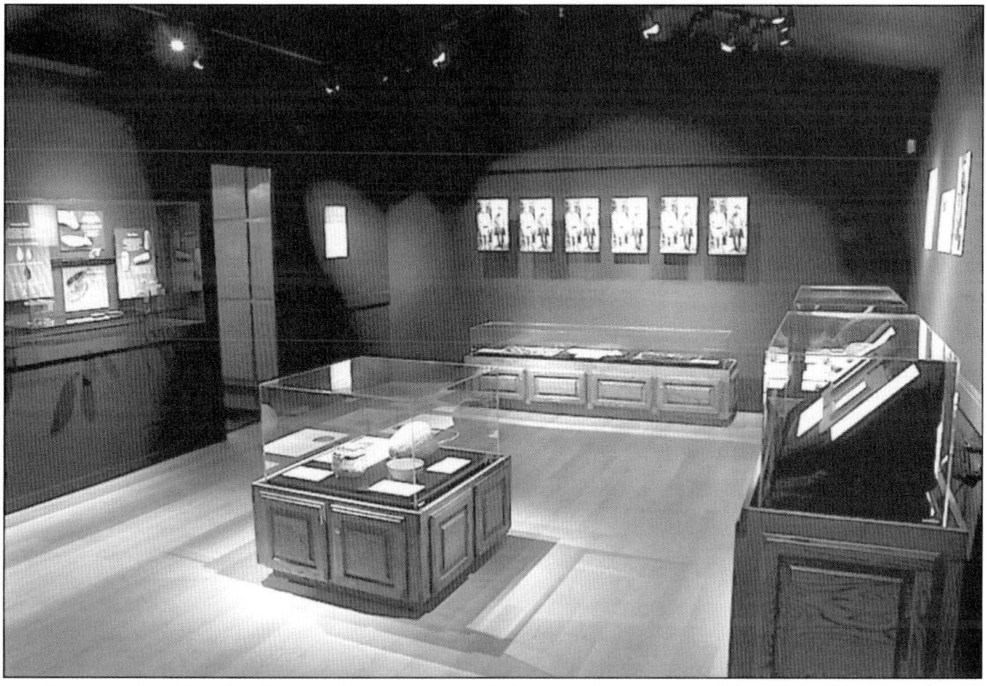

On January 9, 2010, the Coos tribe announced the grand opening of the Tribal Hall Cultural Center's Laquawiyat'as Gallery. The Return of the Heart was the first exhibition of 2010. The gallery is located at the Tribal Hall in Empire. There is also a gallery at the administration building. Located at this gallery is a kiosk in which one can hear the native language spoken. (Confederated Tribes.)

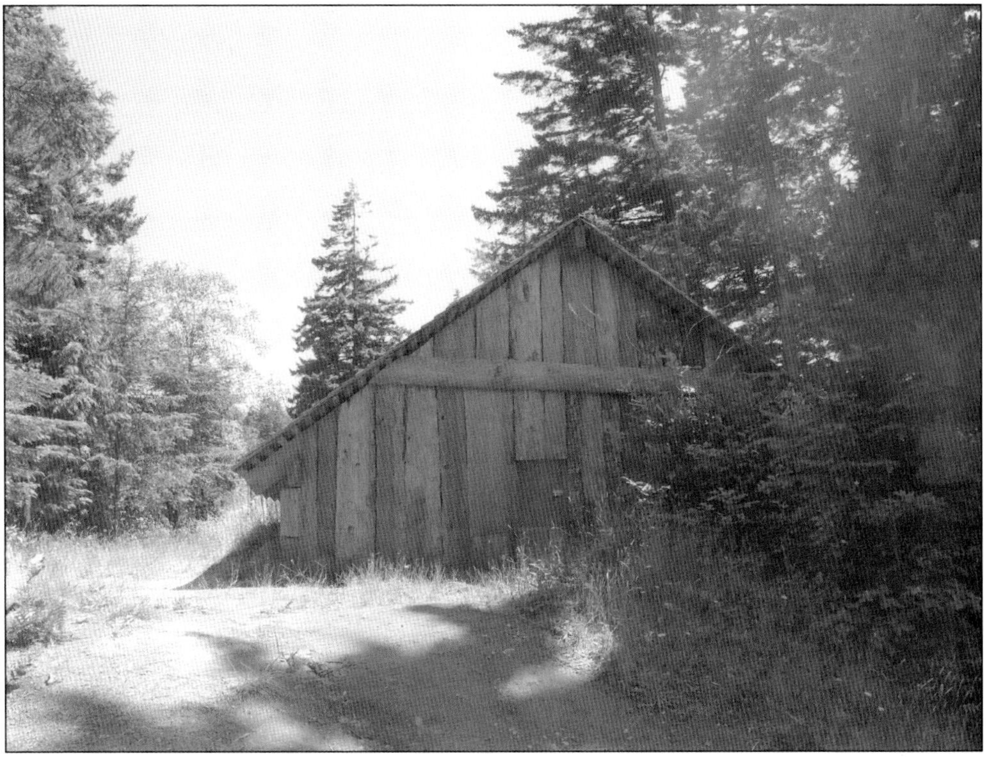

The building of this plank house was a long process for the Coos tribe and was a cooperative process by the Coos, Lower Umpqua, and Siuslaw tribes. Reminiscent of their ancestors' buildings, the plank house is subterranean structure made of cedar. The plank house is a gathering place for the tribe and is used for ceremonies, such as sacred dances. The plank house is located on tribal property adjacent to the Tribal Hall. (Confederated Tribes.)

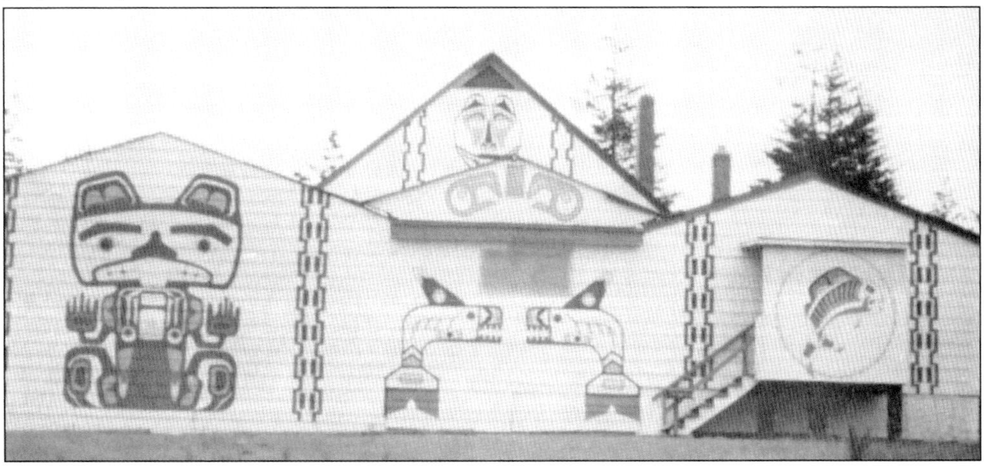

The Tribal Hall, located in Empire, is considered a simplified version of a Cape Cod Colonial–style building. The building was typical of many federally sponsored architectural projects of the 1930s and early 1940s. Built in 1940, the building is historically significant due to the fact that it is the only known surviving New Deal Indian community building left intact in Oregon. On February 7, 1998, the building was added to the National Register of Historic Places. (Stephen Dow Beckham.)

Two

The Empire Years

In 1965, the city of Empire merged with Coos Bay. With the merger, Coos Bay gained a rich heritage dating back to the formation of Coos County. In 1853, the Coose Bay Company arrived on the bay and established the town of Empire City. After the county was established in December 1853, Empire City was adopted as the county seat, and it remained as such until July 1897. Empire City not only served as the governmental hub, it was also the seat of commerce.

As Euro-Americans began settling the area, a sawmill was erected in 1854 by Henry Heaton Luse. Luse also established a shipyard and general store. The post office was established on March 27, 1855. In 1856, Empire City became the Southern Oregon port of entry for the US Customs. By 1860, the population of Empire City was 176. In 1877, Empire City boasted a population of 300. Empire City had a church, school, Odd Fellows lodge, and a weekly newspaper called the *Coos Bay News*. Described as the official newspaper of the county, the paper was published every Wednesday by Jacob M. Siglin and Joseph W. Bennett, both Democrats.

On April 11, 1885, by an act of legislation, Empire City was formally incorporated. Even though Empire City was the initial key shipping port, the population stayed low. North Bend and Marshfield primarily became the focus of building on the bay as the settlers spread out from Empire. By 1894, "City" was dropped from the formal name of Empire.

Until a devastating fire in June 1924, the heart of Empire's business district was located on the tidal flats. After the fire, the city began to focus on building on higher ground, and Empire began to branch out and spread. Substantial growth occurred between 1940 and 1950. The influx in population was due to employment at the Cape Arago Lumber Company, Coos Bay Pulp Corporation, and Coos Head Timber Company. After the lumber boom, Empire primarily remained a residential community.

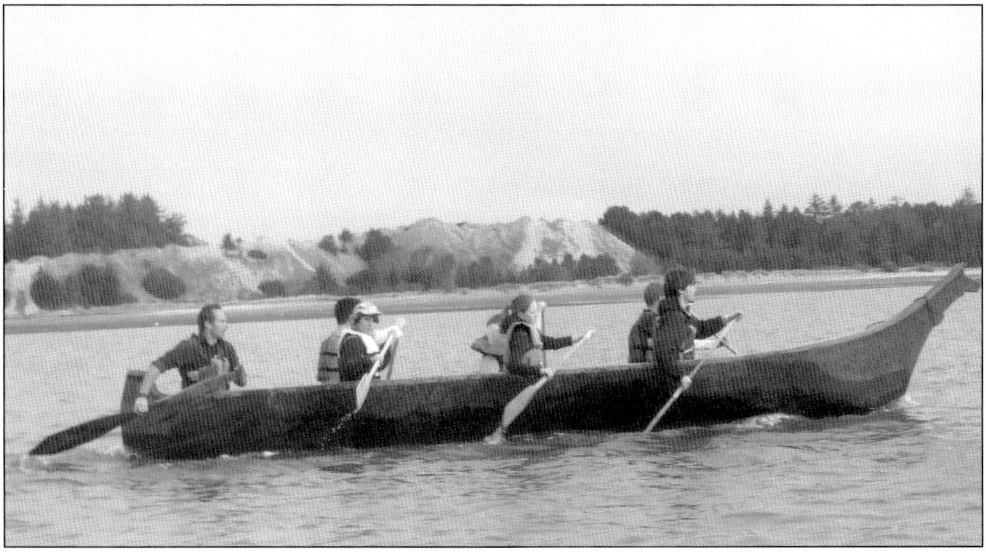

The first ferry in the county was established by William H. Harris at the site of what became known as "the Hollering Place." White settlers followed the Native Americans custom of hollering across the bay so they could be ferried from the North Spit to the mainland. The natives had yelled "*kelideichil*" (pronounced as "keh-lid-day-chil," stressing the first and third syllables), which meant "Ferry me across." (Confederated Tribes.)

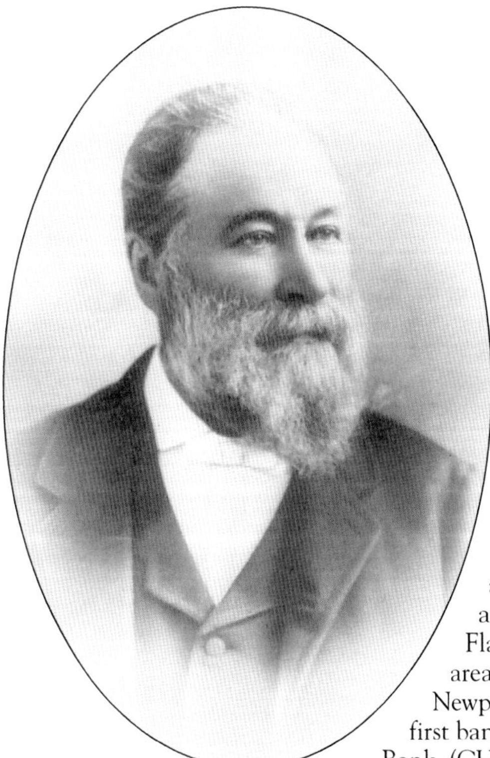

The *Captain Lincoln* was a military transport bound for Port Orford from California that was forced to proceed north due to weather conditions. It ran aground on the North Spit where, the crew established a camp until they could be rescued. It was this wreck that brought attention to the region. When word spread of the wreck of the *Captain Lincoln*, Patrick Flanagan, an Irish immigrant, was one of the first to arrive and settle the region. With capital and credit, Flanagan successfully mined coal in the Coos Bay area for 30 years, serving as the superintendent of the Newport Coal Company. In 1889, Flanagan founded the first bank in Coos County—the Flanagan and Bennett Bank. (CHMM 988-P299.)

In the autumn of 1853, Benjamin Franklin Ross, who followed the first group from Jacksonville, built the first hotel in Empire City. Along with the first cabin built by William H. Harris, the Eagle Hotel housed the early arrivals to Empire City. Ross was one of the original members of the Coose Bay Militia and was one of the earliest county commissioners. (CHMM 989-P56.0.)

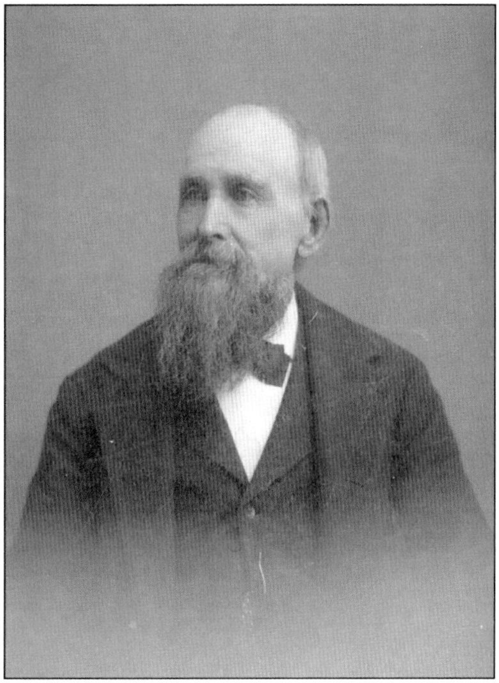

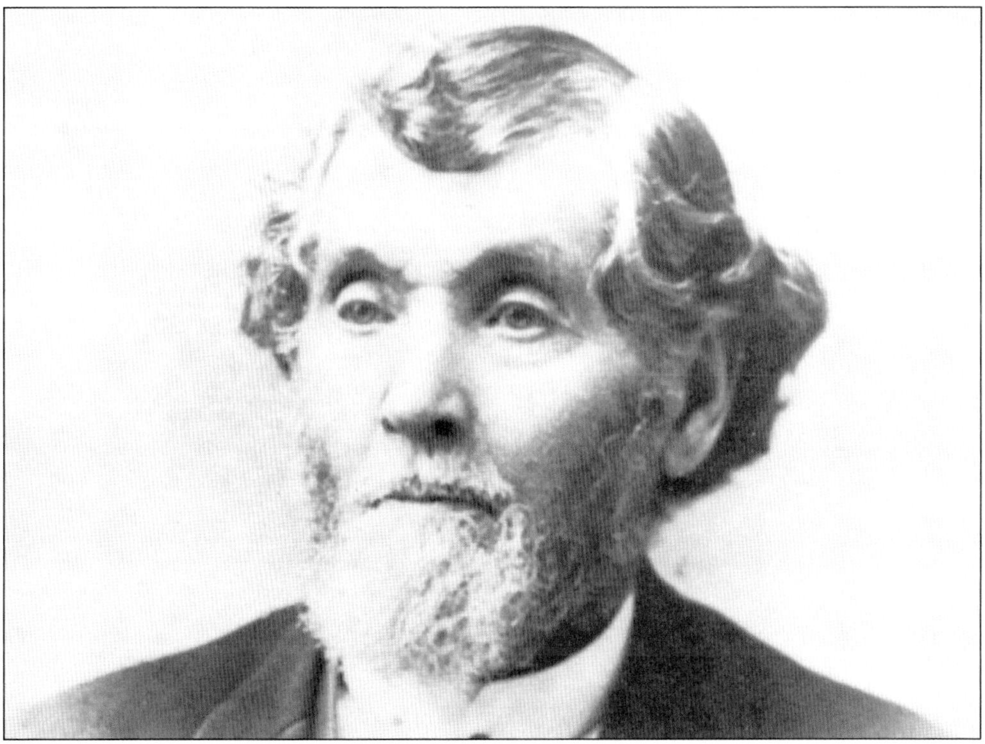

In 1856, Henry Heaton Luse, a native of Pennsylvania, arrived on Coos Bay to build the first steam sawmill, which had a capacity of 20,000 feet per day, in Empire City. Luse also opened one of the earliest shipyards at Empire City. After building two successful businesses, Luse sold them and relocated to San Francisco, California. (CHMM.)

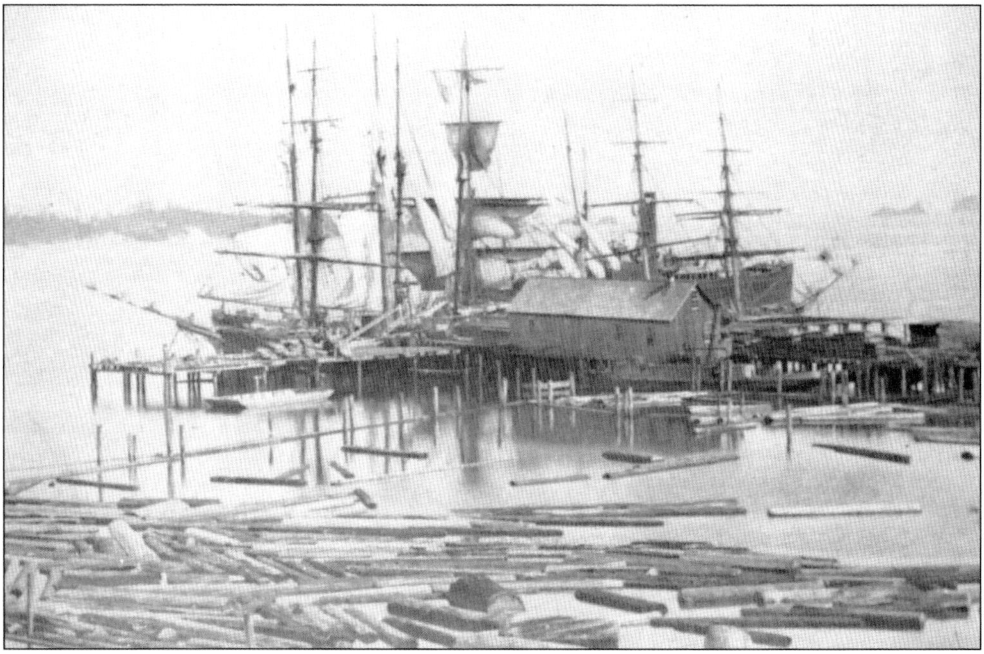

Henry H. Luse arrived at Coos Bay in 1856, and shortly afterward, he built a sawmill. His efforts gave Empire City a lively growth. He began shipbuilding in 1868 by constructing the steamer *Alpha*. In conjunction with the mill and shipyard, Luse also operated a general store. (CHMM 992-8-0752.)

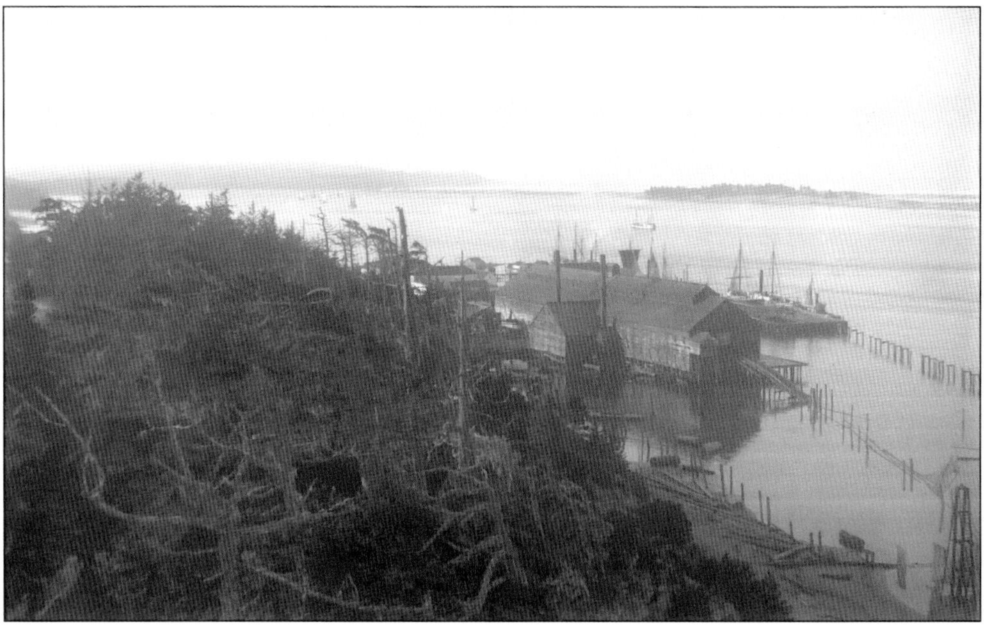

The old Luse mill went through many owners and physical changes. The Southern Oregon Improvement Company built a larger mill and operated it for 10 years before changing the name to the Southern Oregon Company. In 1928, the Empire Development Company rebuilt the mill and called it the Empire Western Lumber Company. (CHMM 987-S1217.).

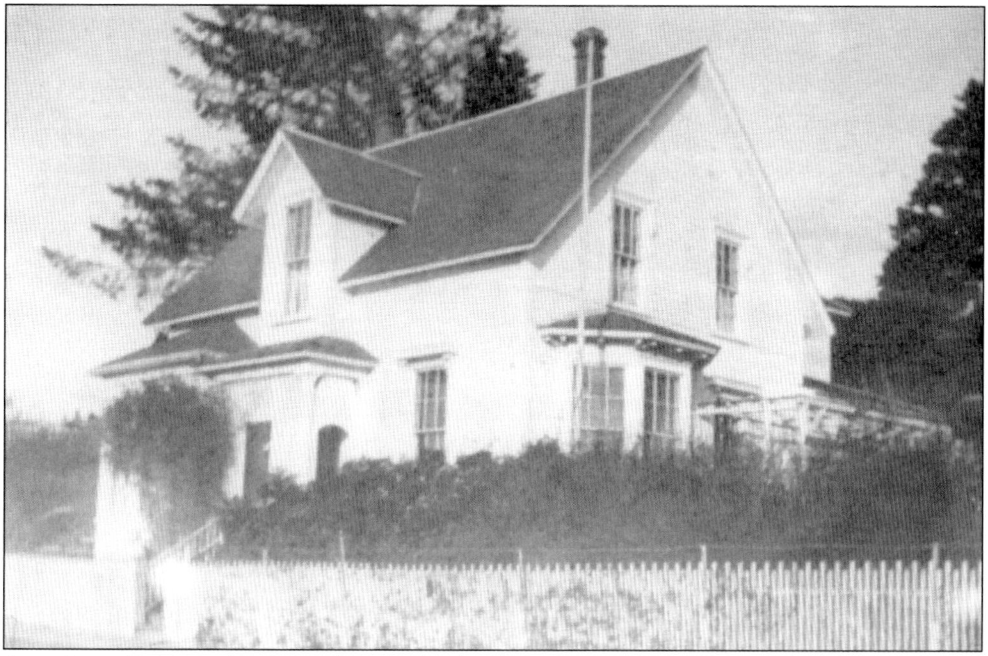

Capt. James B. Magee has been identified with the shipping interests of the Pacific Coast, having been a master of boats that he owned. He was sent to Coos Bay in 1867 to assist in building a sawmill and three vessels, including the tugboat *Escort*, for John Pushbaker at Marshfield. His home in Empire was built in 1873 and is still occupied as a family residence. (CHMM 974-64.)

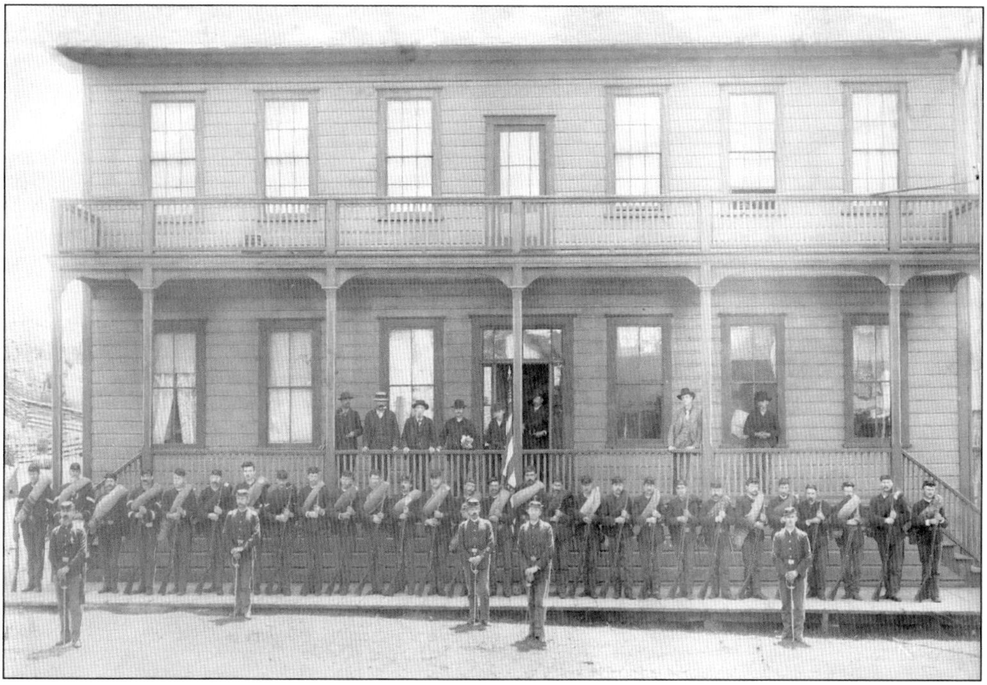

There had always been a military presence in Empire dating back to the formation of the county. Pictured is Company K, 1st Infantry of the Oregon National Guard. The photograph, from the Spanish-American War, was taken in front of the Darcat Pioneer Hotel. (CHMM 988-P483.)

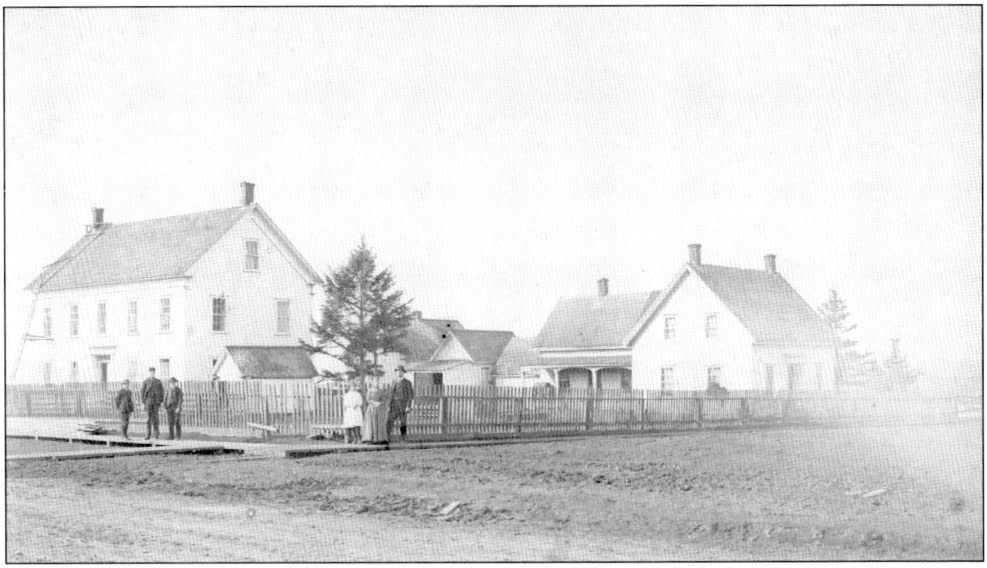

From 1853 to 1897, Empire City reigned as the seat of Coos County. The county erected a courthouse for $4,000 in 1872. In 1888, a vault was built on the south side of courthouse. After the courthouse was razed, the vault served as a gas station for Tom Wasson. To the far right is the residence of Isaiah Hacker, who served as sheriff and later county judge. (CHMM 959-280H2.)

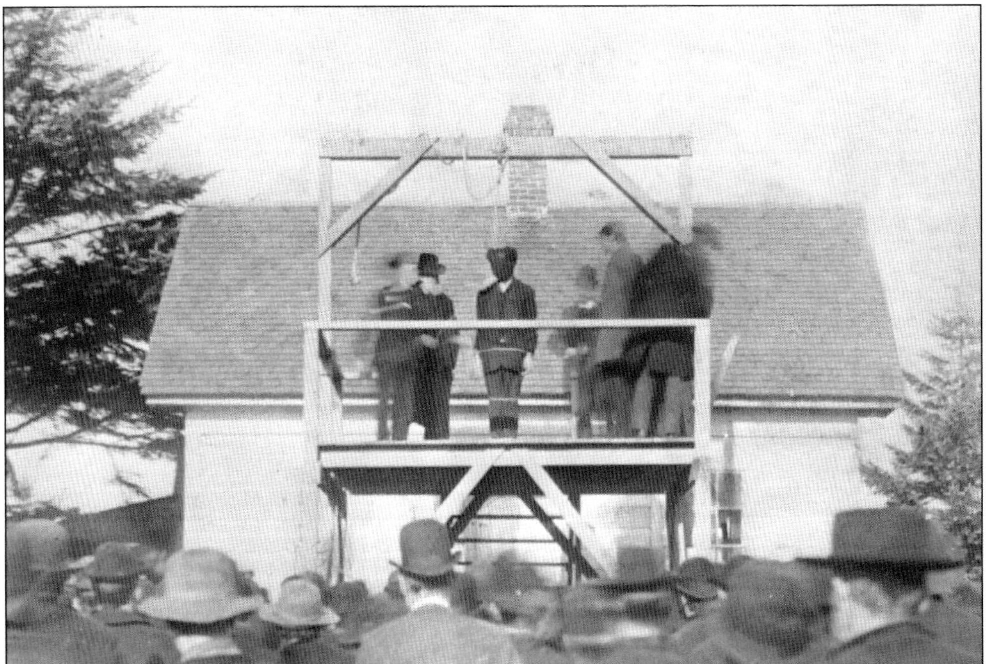

Three executions by hanging were conducted at the jail located next to the county courthouse. The second execution, shown here, occurred on Friday, December 13, 1889. John Gilman was convicted of the double murder of his tenant Elizabeth Eationhover and her five-year-old son William in Coquille, and he was hanged. It was not until 1903 that county executions were banished. (CHMM 986-N788.)

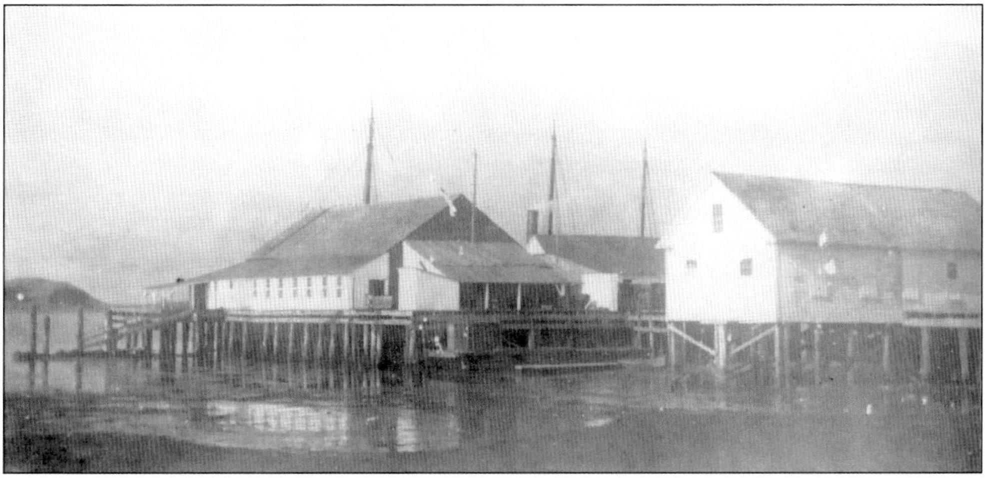

The one salmon cannery at Empire City remained idle from 1890 through 1892, as the fisheries were not given so much attention as in past years. The fisheries of Coos Bay and Coos River produced 50,000 pounds of salmon that were sold fresh for local use or shipped to San Francisco. (CHMM 007-25.287.)

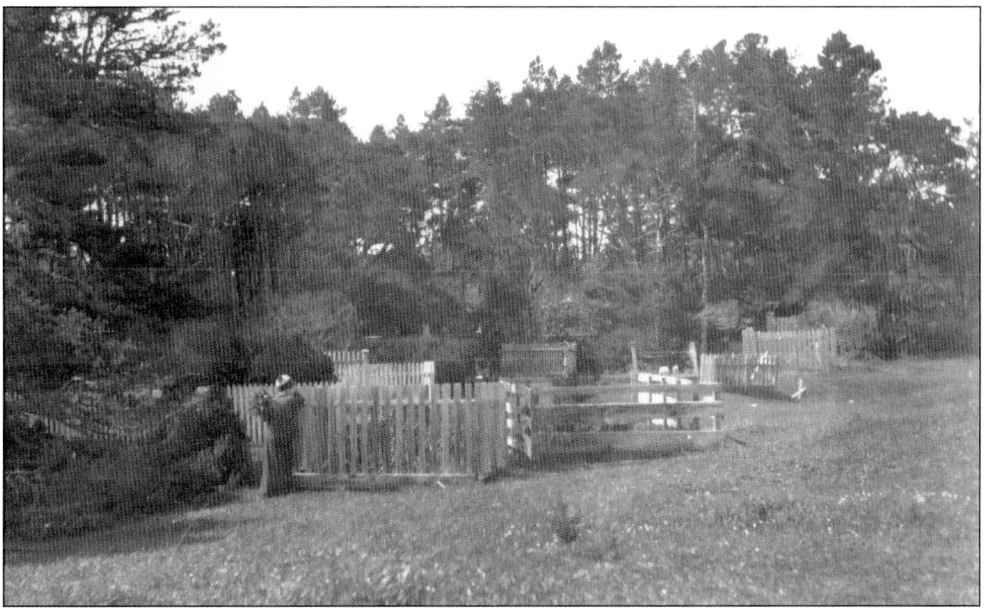

The oldest cemetery in the county was located on the north side of Empire City. Many of the original settlers were buried there, and it was not uncommon for those buried near the bay to be dislodged as the sandy banks of the bay eroded. The cemetery has long since been abandoned and is now owned by the Confederated Tribes of the Coos, Lower Umpqua, and Siuslaw. (CHMM 992-8-0775.)

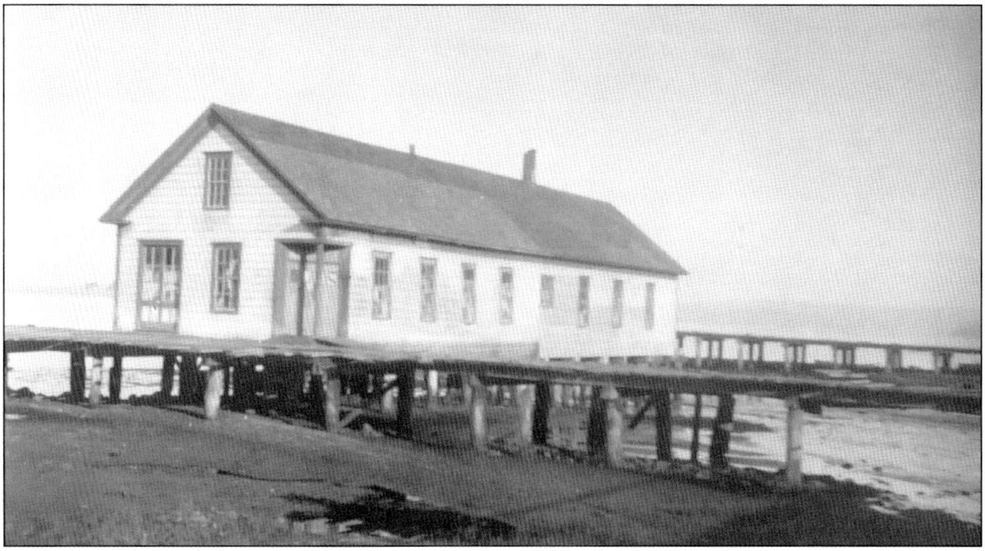

As a port town, Empire City provided liquid refreshment to the multitude that arrived by boat. At one time in its early years, Empire City boasted as many as 13 saloons. By 1898, Empire City only had three saloons remaining. One of the remaining ones was the Clipper Saloon, shown here on the waterfront in 1915. (CHMM 992-8-9772.)

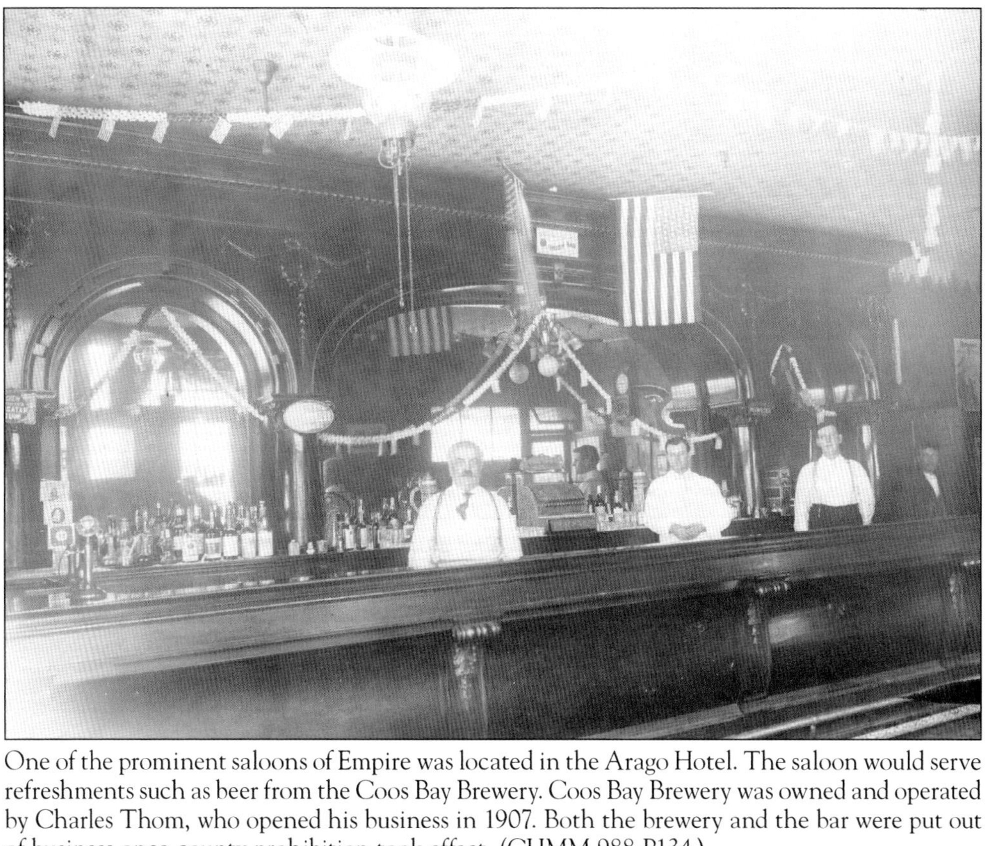

One of the prominent saloons of Empire was located in the Arago Hotel. The saloon would serve refreshments such as beer from the Coos Bay Brewery. Coos Bay Brewery was owned and operated by Charles Thom, who opened his business in 1907. Both the brewery and the bar were put out of business once county prohibition took effect. (CHMM 988-P134.)

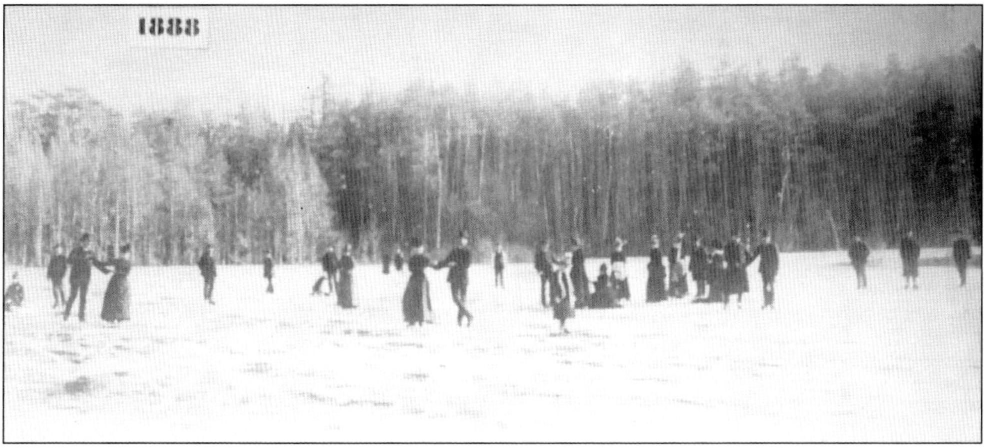

The Coos region is normally known for a temperate climate, but occasionally the weather would become extreme. The Empire Lakes became a playground of unusual sorts in the winter of 1888, when a cold snap froze the lakes, thus providing a natural skating rink. (CHMM 988-P94.)

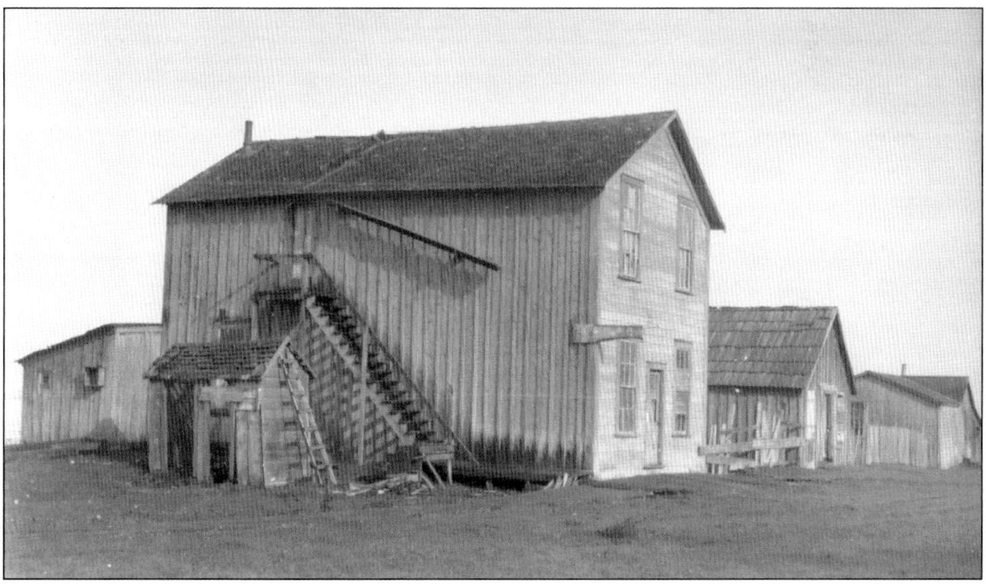

Even though the city of Empire remained a small community, it did have a diverse population. In 1915, a separate section of town was known as Chinatown. The Chinese of the city provided services to the community such as laundry and domestic help. (CHMM 992-8-0771.)

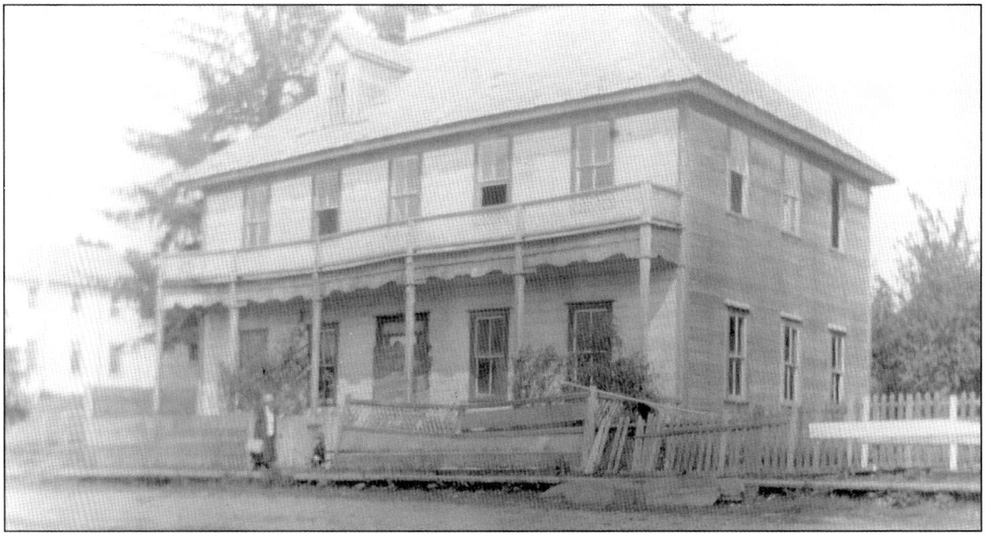

Hotel life in Empire City was not uncommon. What was uncommon was when the Tenbrook Hotel temporarily served as a school after the town's schoolhouse was destroyed by fire on May 8, 1919. Classes were held on the lower floor of the hotel until a new schoolhouse was built. (CHMM 988-P523.)

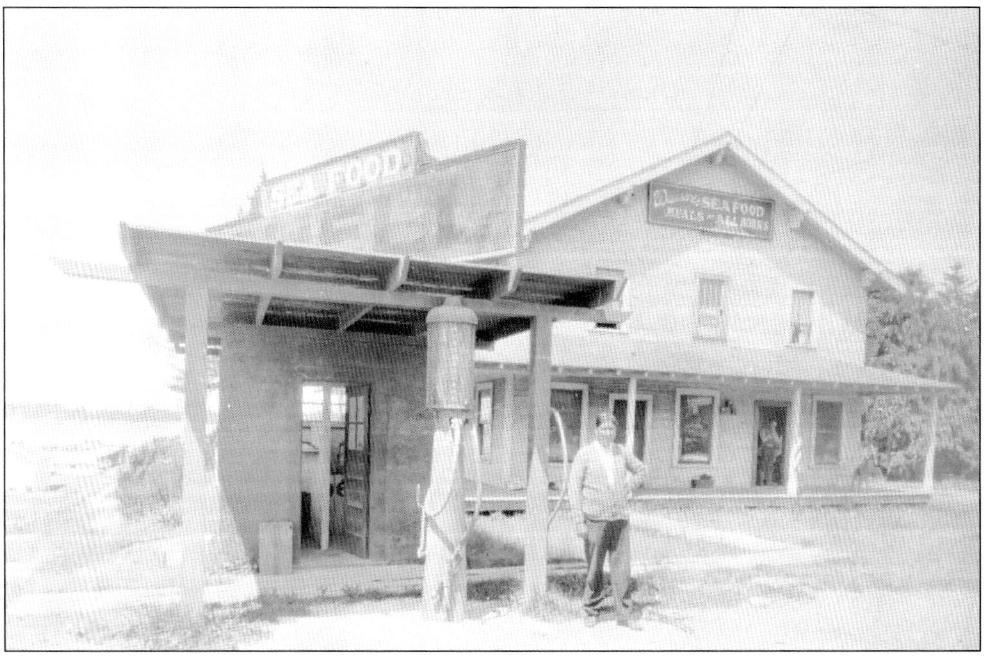

Tom Wasson's Shell service station was located at the corner of Newmark Avenue and Empire Boulevard. Located to the rear was his wife Pauline's seafood restaurant. Described as the best restaurant in the area, the Wasson has demonstrated the resourcefulness of the local Native Americans. (CHMM 992-8-0767.)

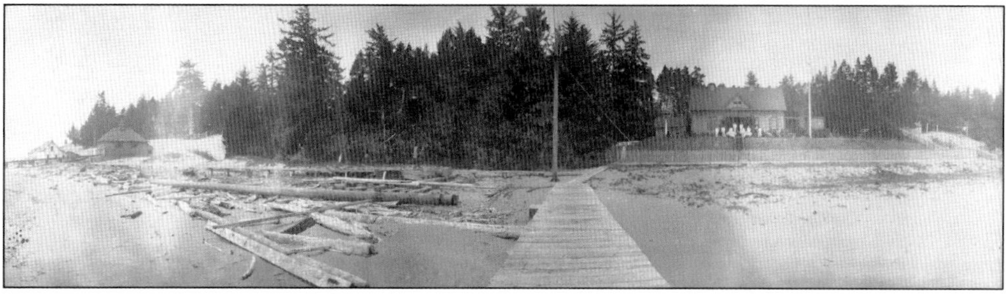

On July 1, 1941, the Navy turned over its medium-frequency radio direction finder (radio compass) stations to the Coast Guard. The only station manned by the Coast Guard in the state of Oregon was located in Empire. By August 4, 1944, operational control of the stations was transferred to the Coast Guard. (CHMM 008-28.7.)

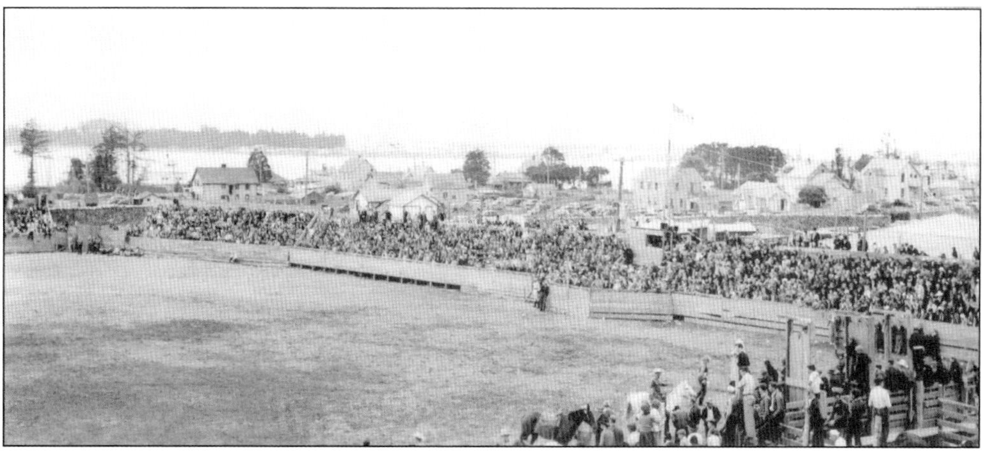

Prior to Myrtle Point serving as the seat of rodeo entertainment, from 1928 to 1941, Empire was home to the Coos County Rodeo. Providing all the entertainment associated with a rodeo, the annual three-day event was held during the Fourth of July. (Hillar family collection.)

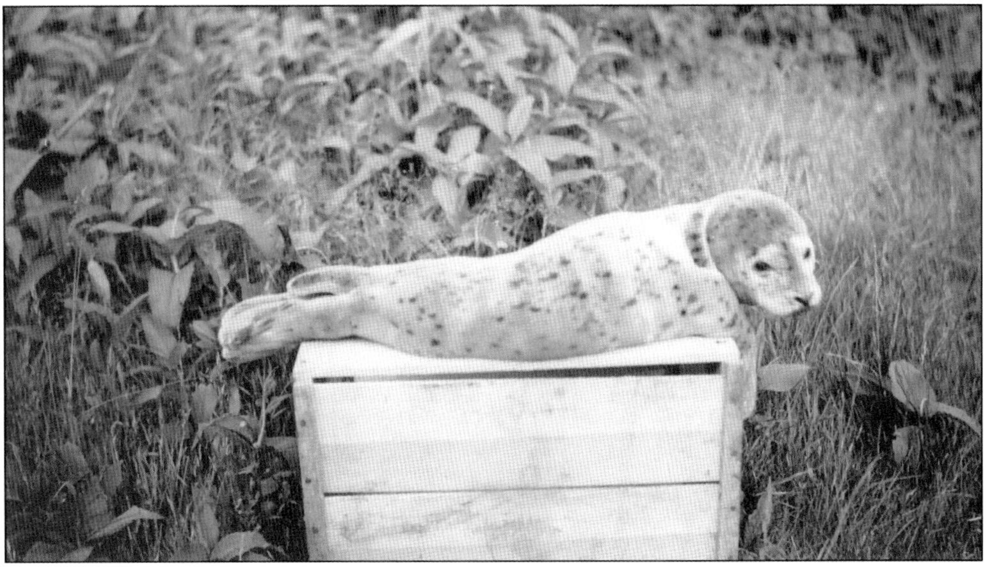

One year during the rodeo in Empire, something special was sought to entertain the children—a baby seal. W.H. "Bill" Hillar was selected to find a seal. Finding a baby seal along with its dead mother, Hillar rescued the seal and named him Oscar. Oscar was a rousing success. After the rodeo, Oscar was cared for by the marine biology school in Charleston and lived a long life. (Hillar family collection.)

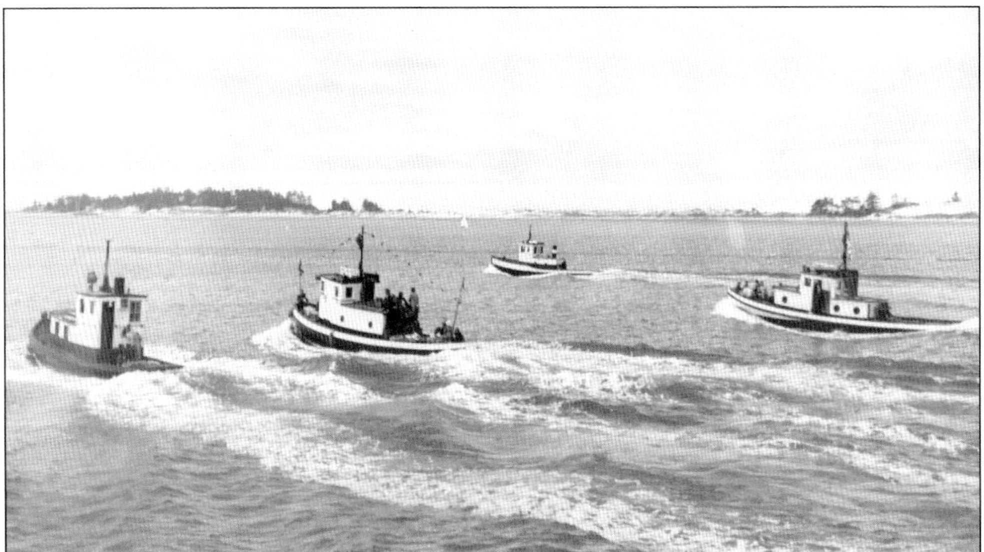

Vessels on the bay were much more than workhorses. They occasionally provided entertainment. During the Fourth of July festivities of 1940, tugboat races were held at Empire. Tugs *Alice H*, *Wm. Vaughn*, *Coos King*, and *Hercules* all competed. *Hercules* won the race. (Hillar family collection.)

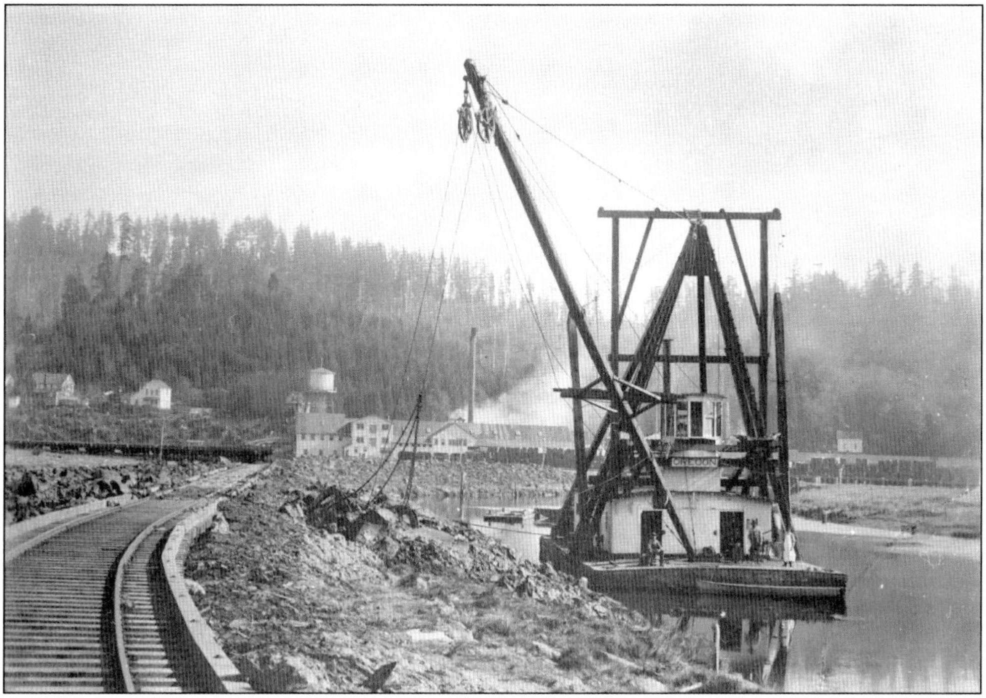

The dredging of Coos Bay dates back to an act of August 18, 1894, which appropriated $13,000 for the construction of a dredge for operation on the bay. The name of the dredge is unknown; however, the dredge *Oregon* was designed and built by Herman Larson in 1904 at the Heuckendorff shipyard in Marshfield. (CHMM 992-8-0548.)

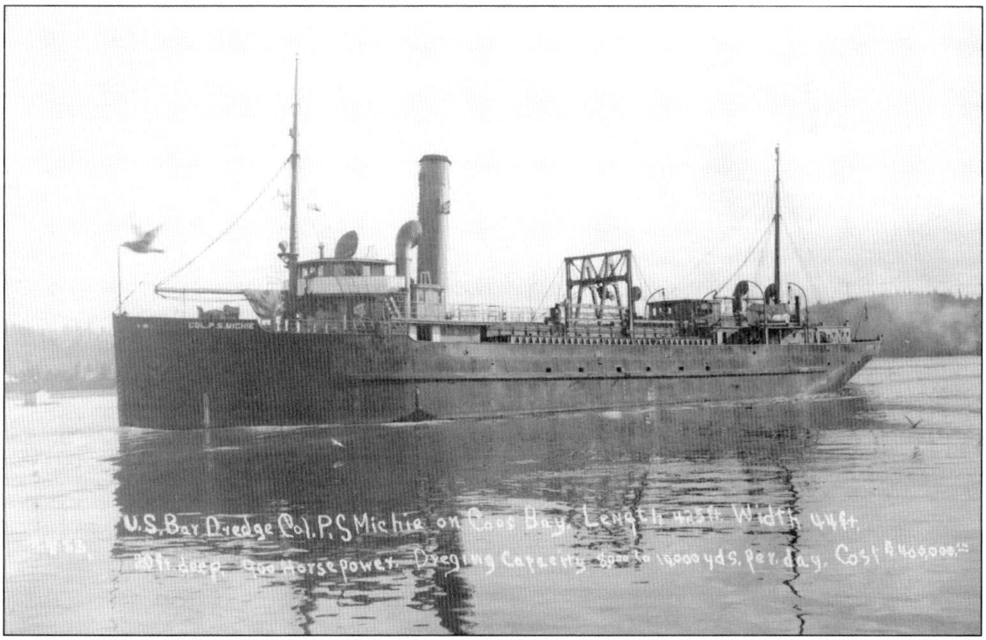

The government dredge *Col. P.S. Michie* was built for Coos Bay to maintain a bar depth from 36 to 40 feet. A hopper dredge, the *Michie* arrived on January 20, 1914. She was designed in the Office of the Chief of Engineers of the US Army in Washington, DC. (CHMM 961-33.13.)

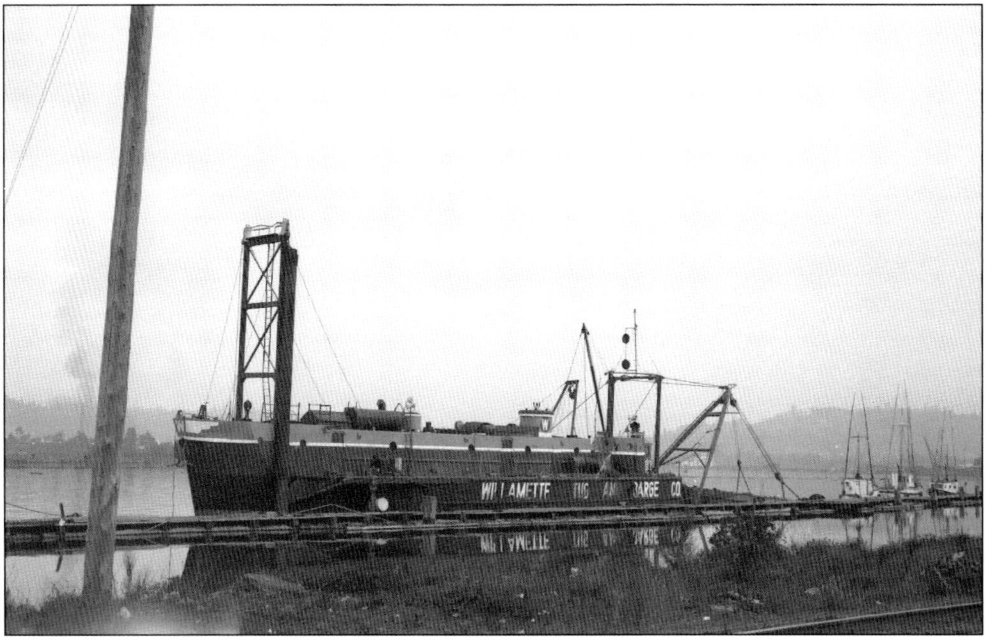

In 1919, shipwrights from Kruse and Banks of North Bend and Coos Bay Shipbuilding of Marshfield broke away from their employers to create the Scandia Shipbuilding Company. The company was never able to compete with the larger shipbuilders. Its only large-scale undertaking was the US grapple dredge *Coos*, for which a contract was given for the hull and house. (CHMM 009-16.3281 b.)

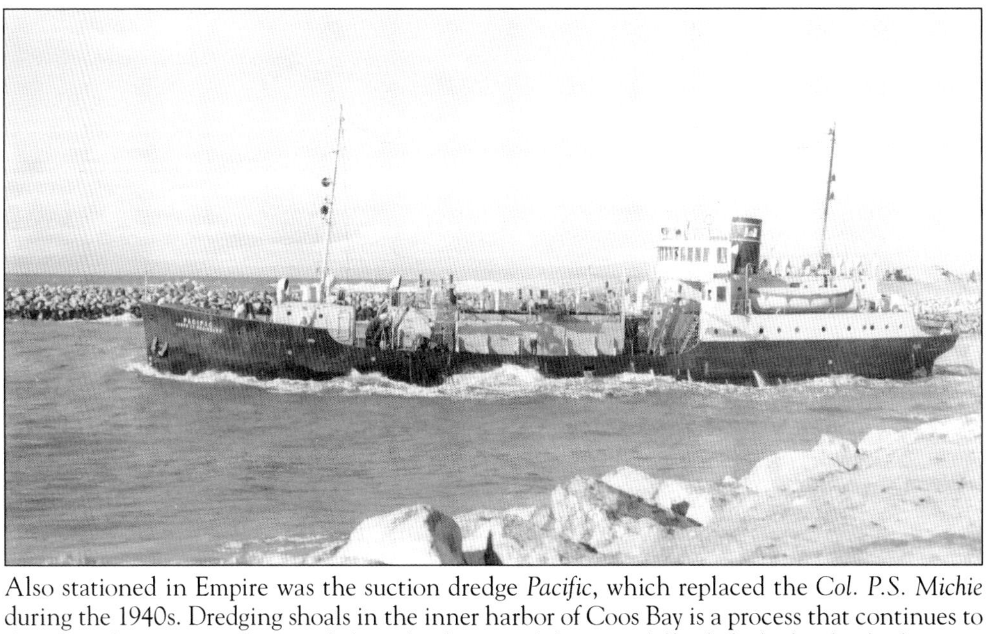

Also stationed in Empire was the suction dredge *Pacific*, which replaced the *Col. P.S. Michie* during the 1940s. Dredging shoals in the inner harbor of Coos Bay is a process that continues to this day. The Coos Bay bar was believed to be one of the most difficult for hydraulic dredging on the Pacific Coast. (Hillar family collection.)

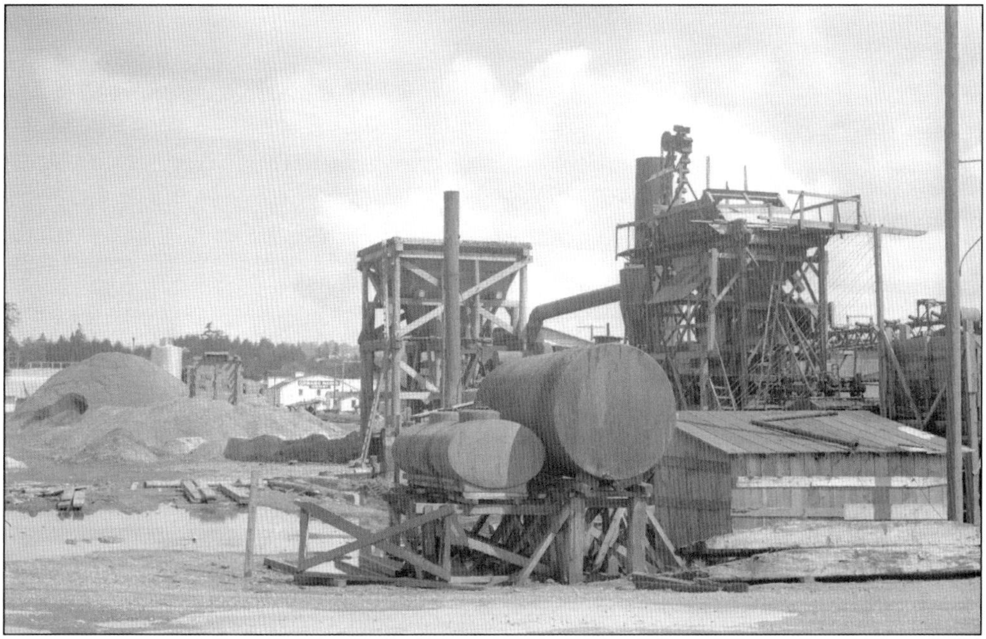

With the dredging of the bay to maintain proper channel depths, something had to be done with the spoils gathered. Thus the Coos Bay dredge plant was erected in Empire. The plant was key to the disposal of all the bay dredge materials. (CHMM 986-N523.)

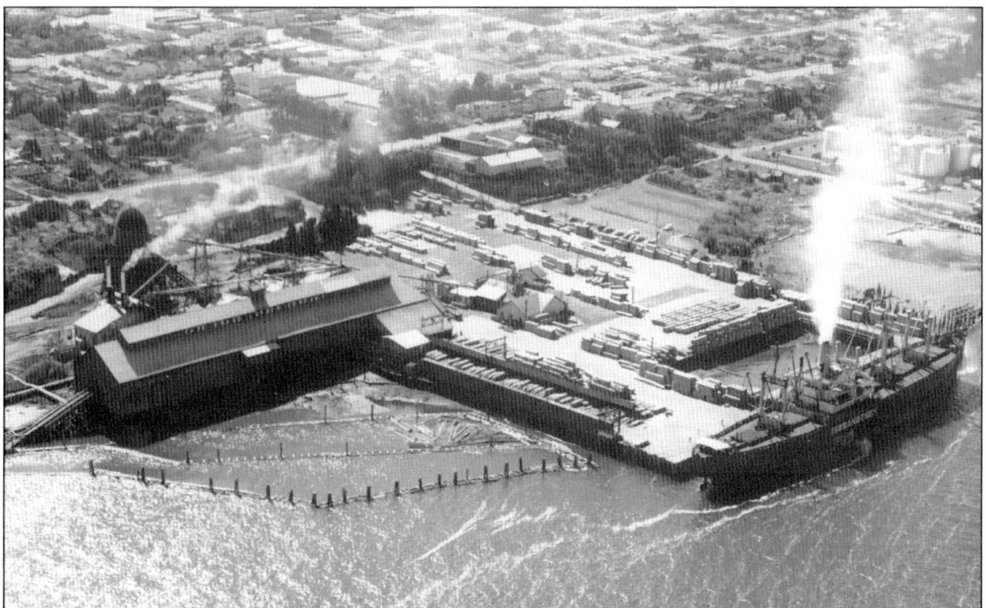

The Cape Arago Lumber Company was opened in 1941 by the Moore Mill and Lumber Company of Bandon, Oregon. Set up as a cargo operation to supply lumber to the East Coast market, the mill employed more than 70 workers on a shift. The mill eventually closed in 1980. (CHMM 991-2.23.)

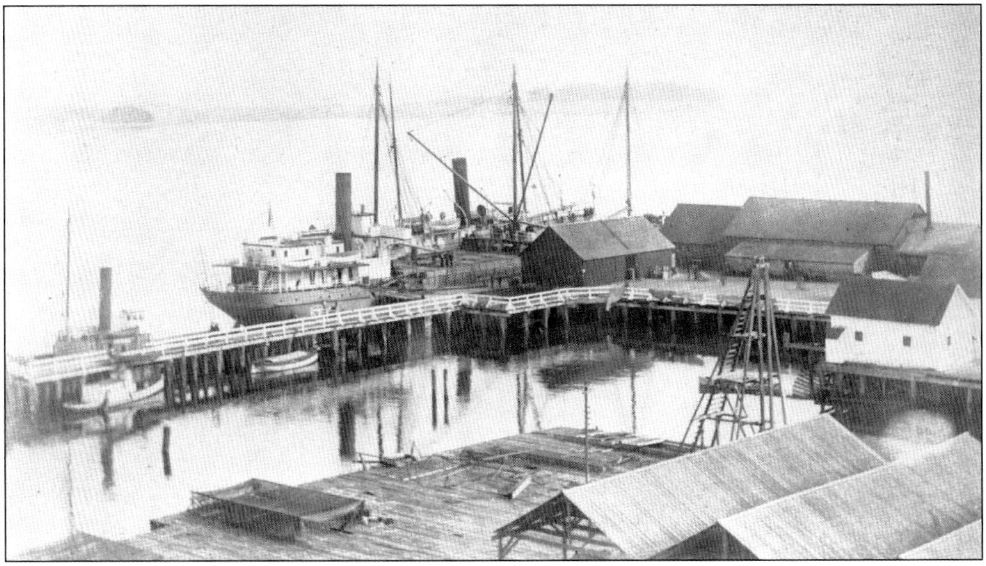

The Cape Arago Mill Dock was only one dock in Empire, which ensured a busy waterfront. Other docks included the River Terminal Dock and the Coos Head Timber Company with a 200-foot dock. (CHMM 992-8-0773.)

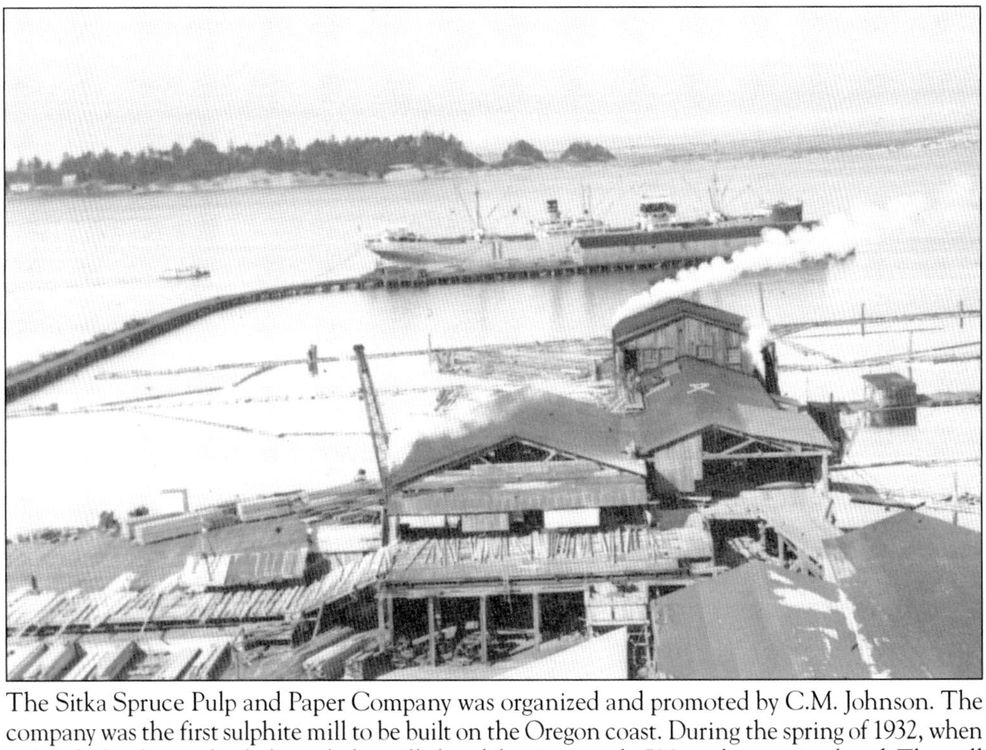

The Sitka Spruce Pulp and Paper Company was organized and promoted by C.M. Johnson. The company was the first sulphite mill to be built on the Oregon coast. During the spring of 1932, when orders for lumber and pulp lagged, the mill closed, leaving nearly 500 workers unemployed. The mill reopened in the summer of 1935 as the Coos Bay Pulp Corporation. (Hillar family collection.)

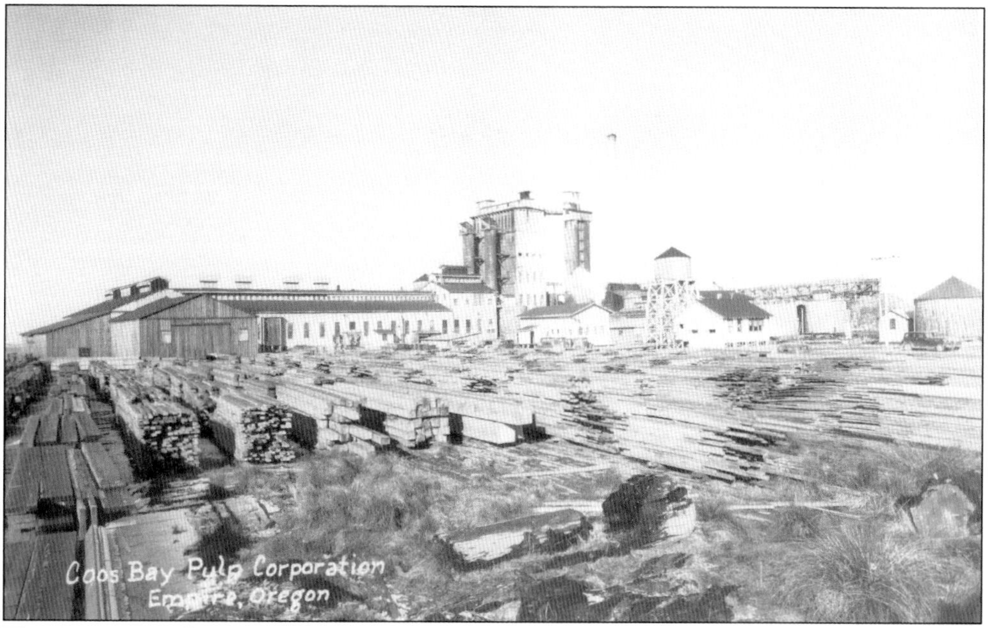

The Coos Bay Pulp Corporation was almost totally dependent on the export of pulp to Japan. However, by January 1938, the corporation found itself without a market when the Japanese suddenly cancelled all orders. Operations remained dormant until the fall of 1939, when the war in Europe created a new market for pulp exports. (CHMM 010-2.19.)

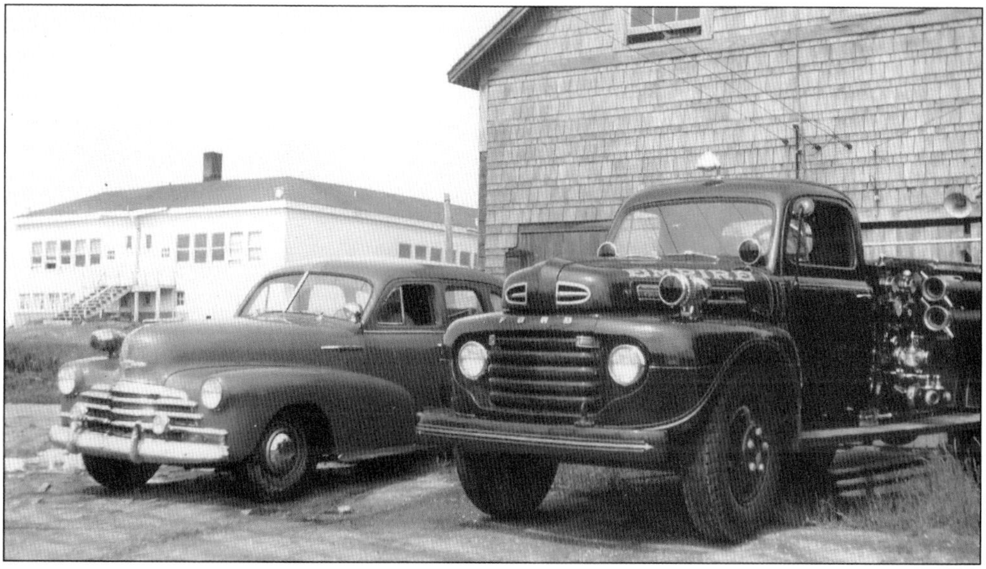

It was not until 1948 that Empire purchased its first factory-built fire engine. The fire engine was built on a Ford chassis by the Coast Apparatus Company. Pictured with the fire engine is Empire's first police car, a 1949 Chevrolet. (CHMM 006-12.4.)

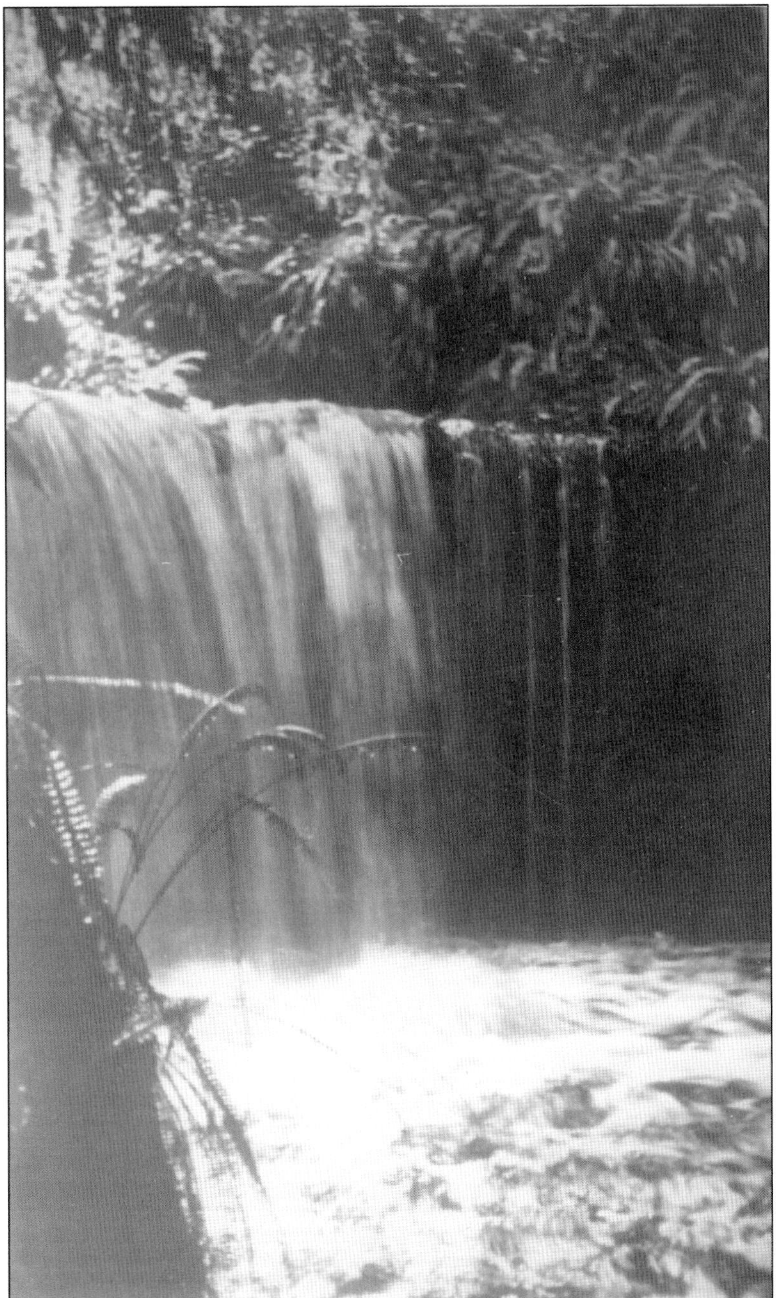

Empire was not only known for its two lakes, located in John Topits Park. It was also known for Empire Falls, which was located on Chickses Creek near the Coos Bay pump station on North Schoneman Street. Young people used the swimming hole below the falls up until at least the 1940s. Today there is no trace of the falls. However, old-timer Bill Goodman, an Empire native, stated there were some smaller falls above where the creek starts at Lower Empire Lake. There are five access points to John Topits Park, home to the Empire Lakes trail system. The trail system is centered on the natural beauty of the two lakes and stabilized dunes. The Empire Lakes are home to a variety of fish (bass, bluegill, perch, and catfish) and birds. (CHMM 959-119.)

Three

The Marshfield Years

Prior to the name change to Coos Bay in 1944, the city was originally called Marshfield. Even before Marshfield, the native village Atsixis (pronounced "ahts-ee-khees") was located on the land. In March 1854, James C. Tolman filed a land claim and built a double log house with the goal of building the town of Marshfield.

About August 1, 1854, due to an illness of his wife, Tolman returned to Jackson County, never to return. On June 10, 1855, Tolman sold his interest in the Marshfield claim to J.S. Hatch, who entered into partnership with George C. Furber. In the fall of 1856, Socrates Schofield, under the direction of Hatch, Furber, and Davis, platted a village upon the claim taken up by Tolman. A saloon was built in 1866 and occupied by Henry Heaton Luse. Soon after, in 1867, a sawmill was built at Marshfield by John Pershbaker. In the same year, John's brother Charles opened a store and Capt. George Hamilton opened a tavern. By 1870, the population grew to 428, and on October 24, 1874, the town of Marshfield was duly incorporated.

For the first 50 years, the wooden structures of Front Street boasted the frontier life with saloons, hotels, and shops of all types. The frontier lifestyle came to an abrupt end on July 23, 1922, when a fire devastated a major portion of Front Street. After the fire, concrete and brick buildings emerged, providing a new look and feel to the city. Central Avenue and Broadway Street became the new hub of the city. The forced transition, along with the automobile, brought the city into the new standards of the 20th century.

By 1930, the city of Marshfield boasted a population of 5,287 and rallied around the slogan of "The Metropolis of Southwestern Oregon." The primary industries included fishing, lumber, dairy, and produce. Around 2,100 men and 500 women were employed with an annual income of $3.6 million. By the 1940s, the city adopted a new slogan, "The Treasure Chest of Oregon."

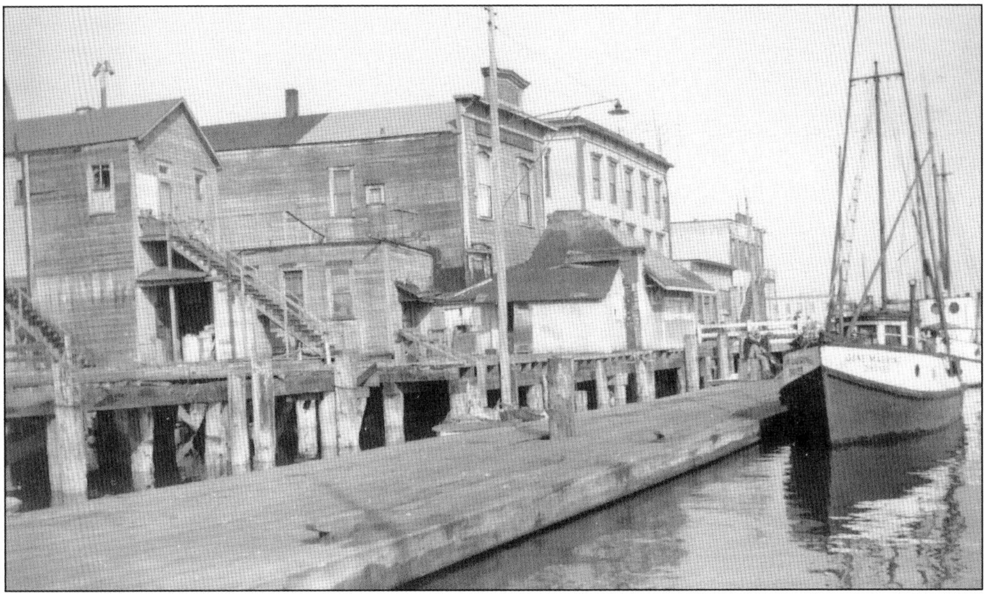

The waterfront of Marshfield was the key to development and paramount to the prosperity of the city. Many of the businesses were connected to the waterfront. Docks and wharves lined the bay, providing a hub of activity for the city. The entire eastern portion of the bay business district was built upon pilings. (CHMM 001-10.5 d.)

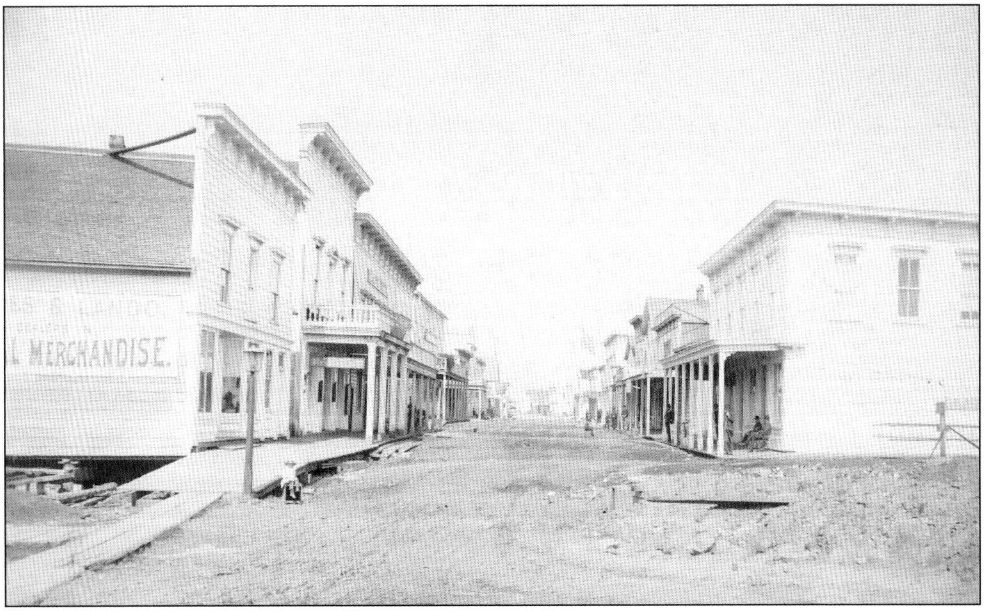

The primary business district of Marshfield bordered the bay and initially consisted of three blocks known as Front Street. Four hotels—the Central, Blanco, Eldorado, and Garfield—along with many saloons occupied the west side of the street. The city hall, the jail, and other businesses occupied the east side of Front Street. Initially there were only dirt streets, which often made travel along Front Street difficult in the winters. (CHMM 975-143 g.)

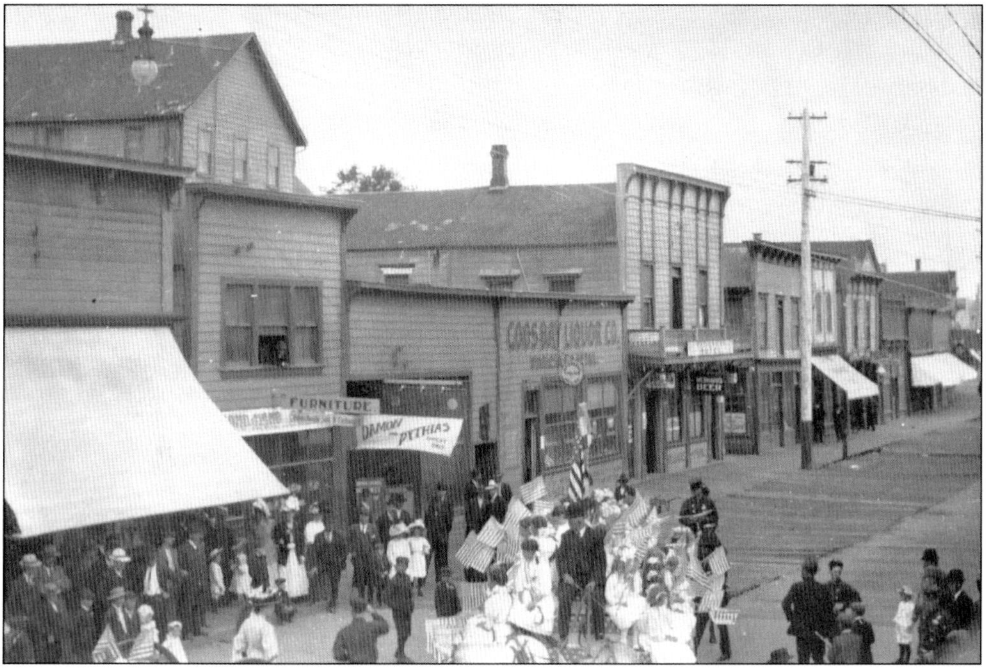

The Front Street business district was constructed of wood, and the dirt streets of Marshfield were eventually planked with wood. Front Street was a hub of activity and was the sight of many parades. By 1924, there were a total of eight miles of wood-planked roads and six miles of hard-surfaced roads in the city. (CHMM 992-8-1068.)

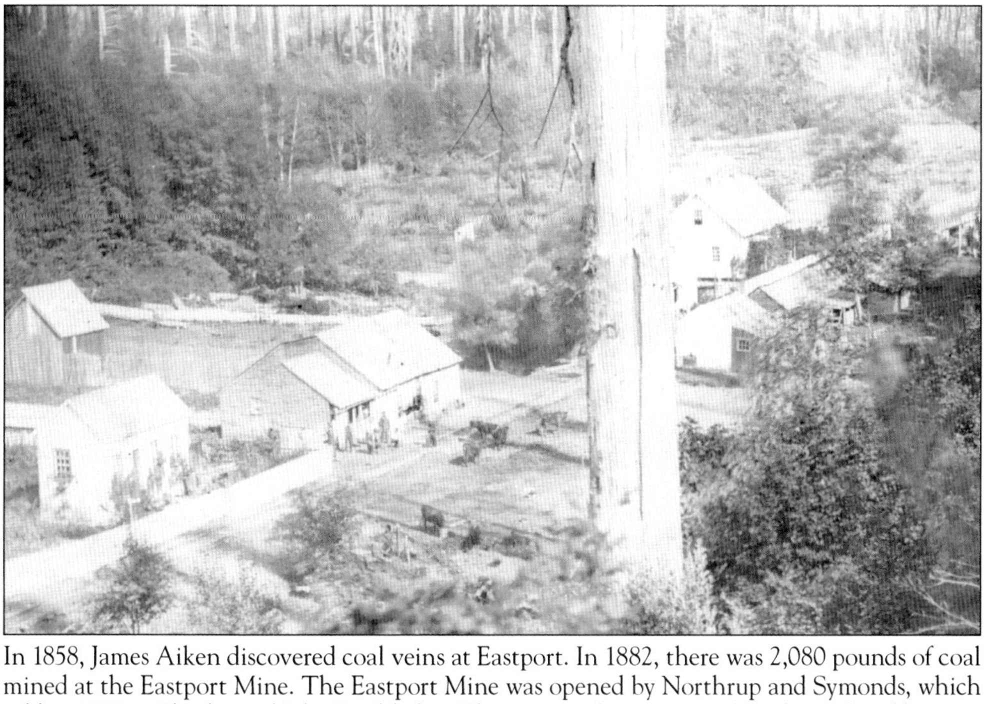

In 1858, James Aiken discovered coal veins at Eastport. In 1882, there was 2,080 pounds of coal mined at the Eastport Mine. The Eastport Mine was opened by Northrup and Symonds, which sold in 1868 to Charles and John Pershbaker. The area was later renamed Englewood and became a part of Coos Bay. (CHMM 981-149 p.)

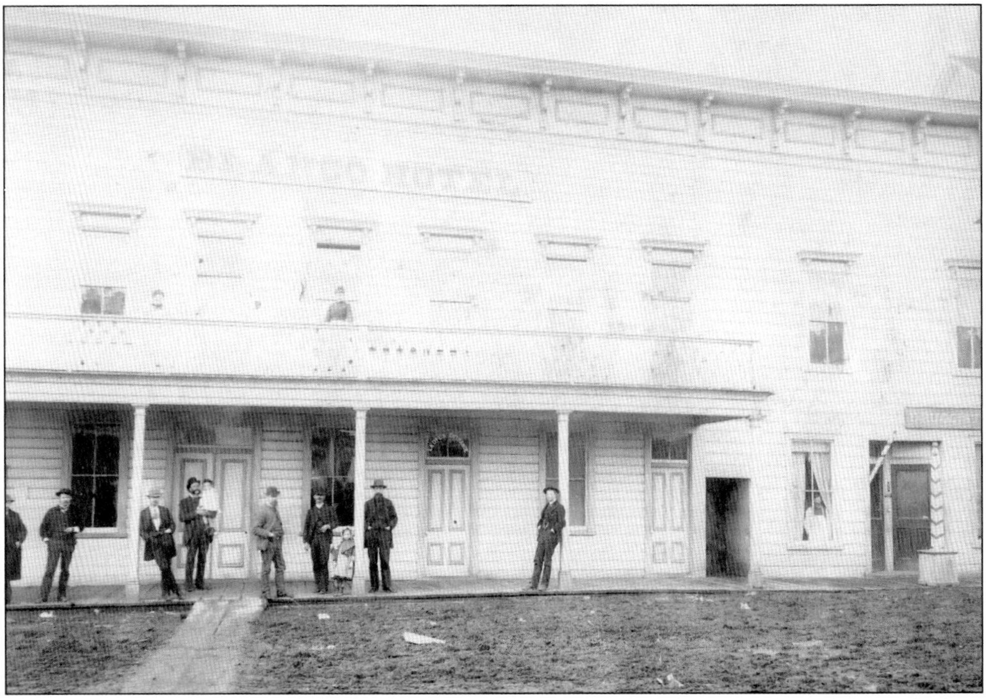

In 1869, the Blanco Hotel was erected by George Stauff. It soon became distinguished as the best hotel in Marshfield catering to traveling businessmen. It would retain this title for 40 years until the construction of the Chandler Hotel. In 1942, the city condemned the Blanco Hotel, and the lumber from the hotel was used to build the Sumner Grange Hall. (CHMM 971-38 b.)

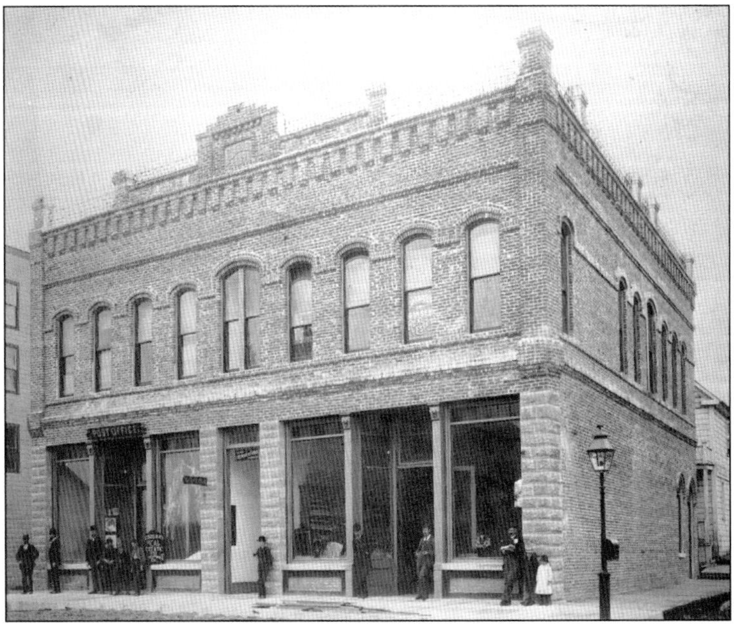

The Eldorado was another of the Front Street frontier hotels. Before the days of a city hall, rooms six and seven served as the seat of city government. The Eldorado building also served as the post office. Hotel life was not just for those visiting Marshfield. Several working residents made the various hotels their homes. (CHMM 992-8-0985.)

Advertised as "the traveling man's resort," the Central Hotel was built in 1870 by William Noble. Like the other hotels, the Central Hotel would provide other entertainment, such as hosting weddings. On May 31, 1892, a major fire erupted. Fortunately, the Central Hotel was empty excepting one room used as a barbershop by Al Devaul. (CHMM 998-P398.)

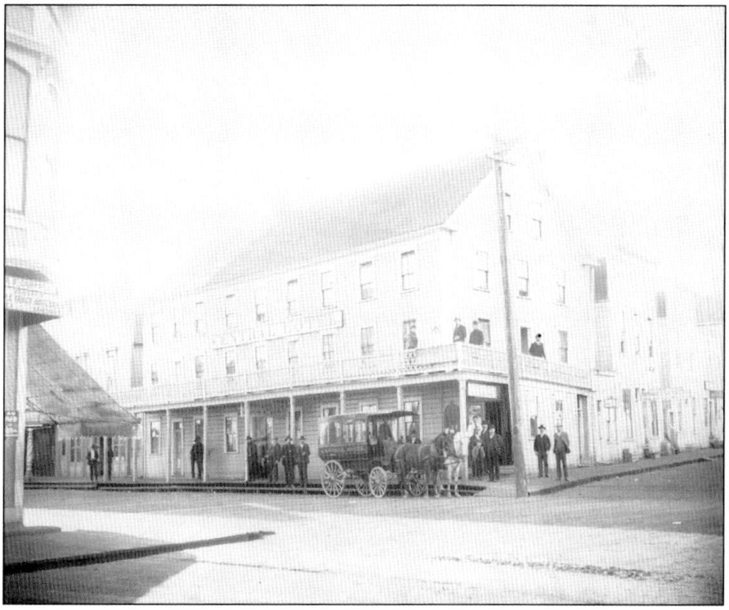

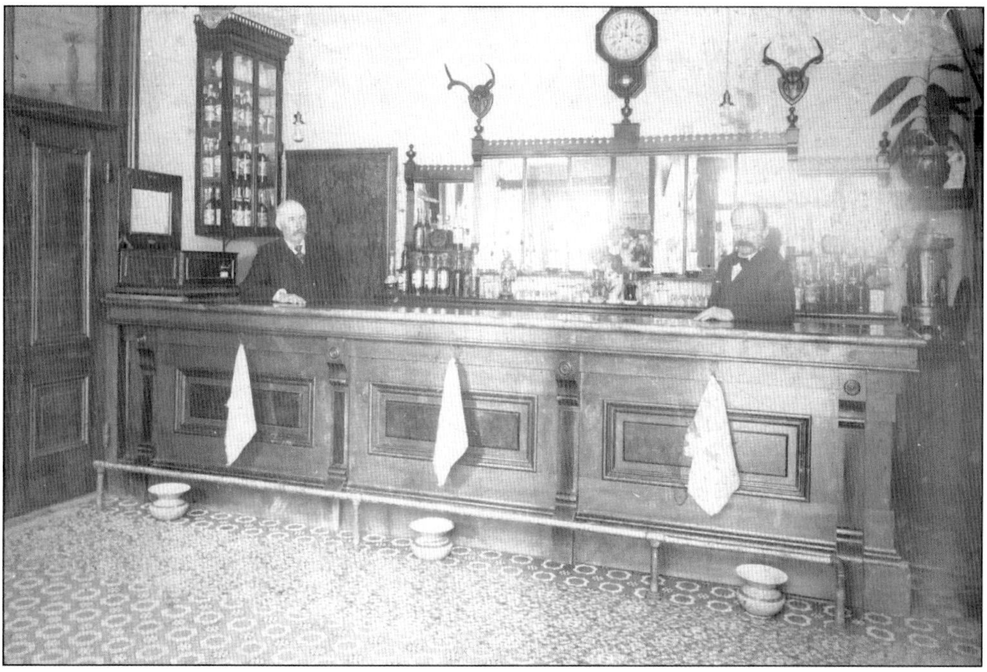

The bar in the Central Hotel was a common gathering place for the hard-working men in and around Marshfield. Yet on January 1, 1916, well before national Prohibition, the county "dried up." Only physicians were allowed to stock a monthly quantity of two quarts of whiskey and 24 quarts of beer to prescribe to their patients. (CHMM 992-8-1022.)

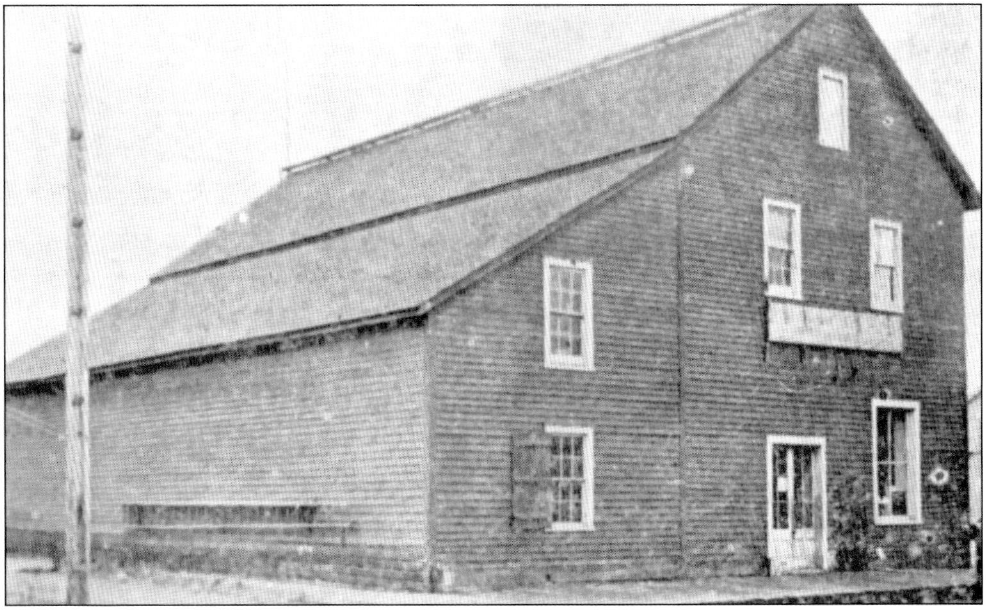

In 1873, E.B. Dean and Company began operating a steam-powered mill in Marshfield. Within a year, the company had become stiff competition for the Luse Mill in Empire and the Simpson Mill in North Bend. In 1885, when the City of Marshfield complained of smoke created by open burning by the mill, it was relocated to East Marshfield. (CHMM 009-16.4823.)

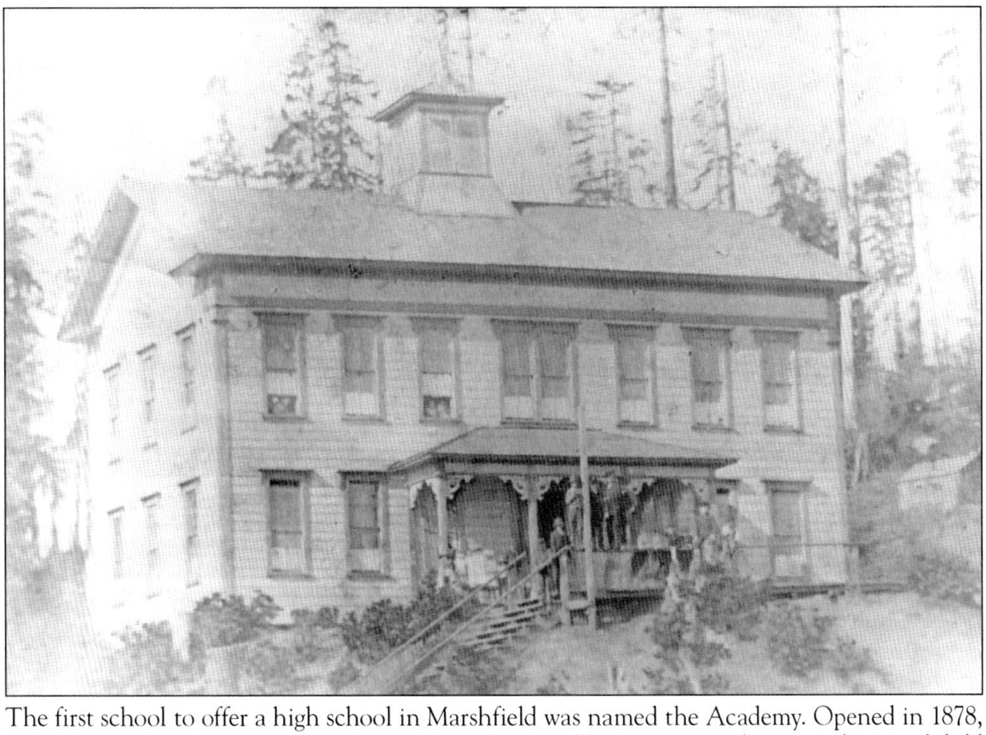

The first school to offer a high school in Marshfield was named the Academy. Opened in 1878, the Academy was a private school that charged a monthly tuition. At the time, the Marshfield Academy was the westernmost educational concern of a high order in America. T.J. McCormac was the Academy's first principal. (CHMM 977-101.97.)

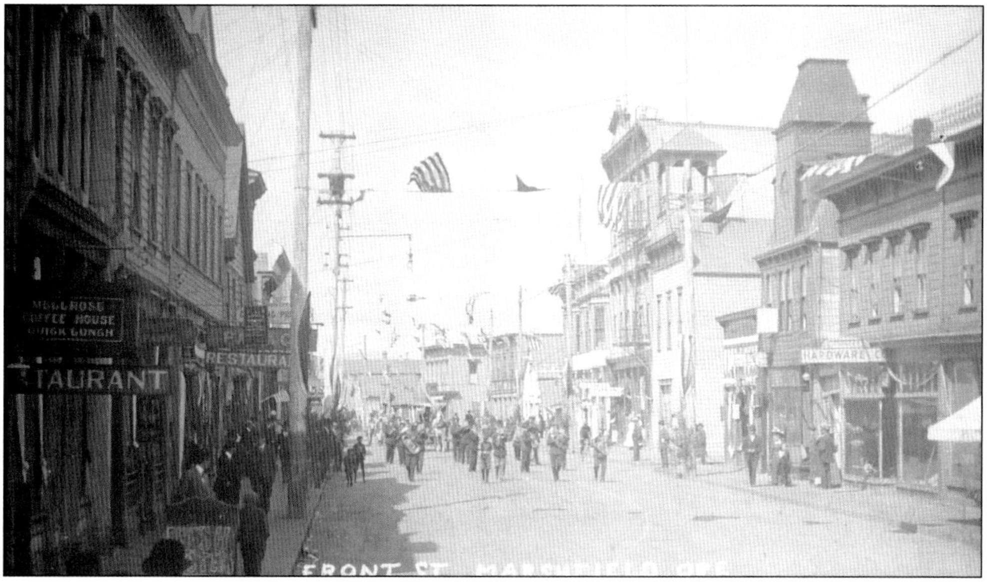

The city hall building became a reality 18 years after Marshfield's incorporation. It was a wooden two-story structure built on pilings on the bay side of Front Street. The building had space for the fire apparatus, sleeping rooms for the firemen, a recorder's office, and a council room. A tower for a fire gong was erected on the building. (CHMM 992-8-1045.)

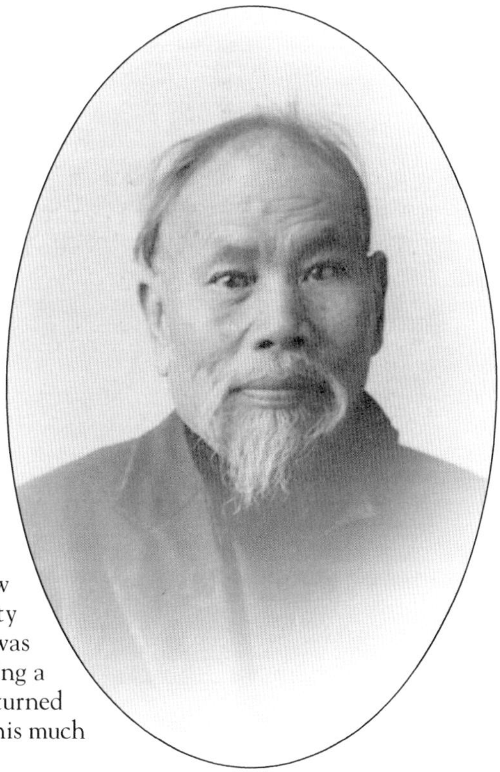

Best remembered as a vegetable merchant, Gow Why exemplified the success of the minority immigrant. As a successful merchant, Why was able to build his business to the point of opening a general store in the early 1900s. Gow Why returned to China around 1930, leaving his business to his much younger wife. (CHMM 988-P427.)

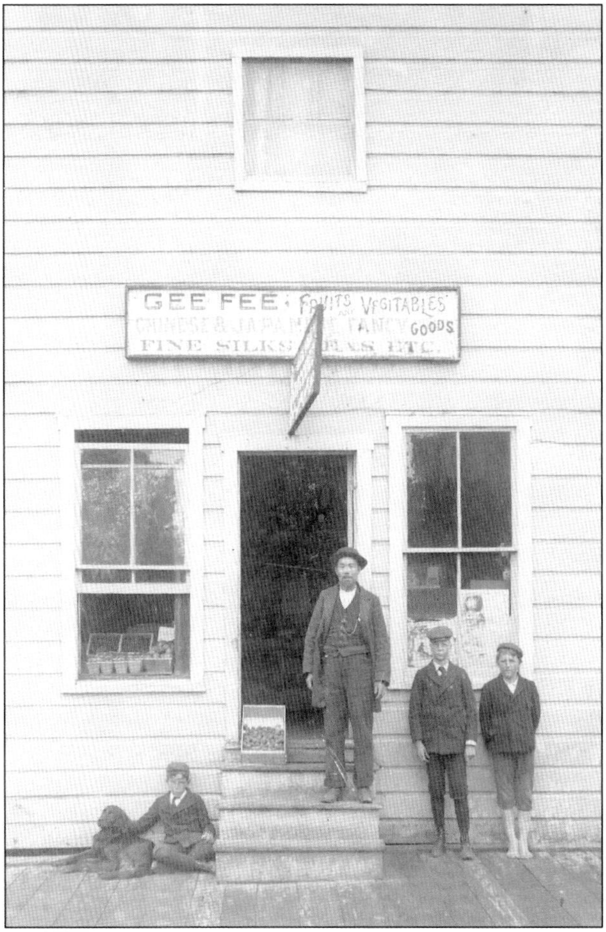

Like Gow Why, another successful Chinese businessman was Gee Fee, who during the 1880s operated his grocery store on the tidal mudflats before Market Avenue was filled. The fruits and vegetables sold were grown locally by the Gee family. Fee is pictured with three boys in front of his store. (CHMM 968-154 c.)

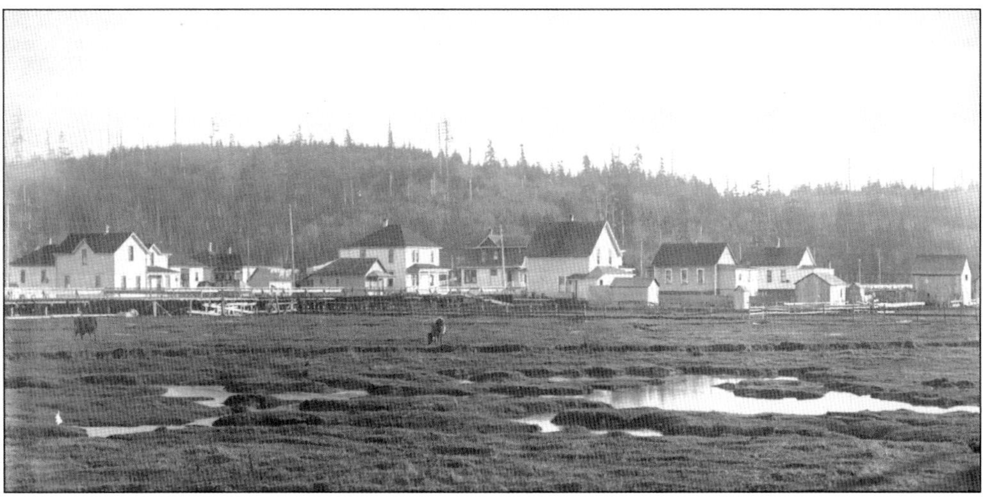

In the early days, Marshfield was divided by Mill Slough, which ran up from the bay about where Anderson Street is now. This view of South Broadway Street in 1909 reveals the true appearance of the tidal area prior to filling with dredge spoils. Marshfield experienced the greatest change in physical appearance between 1910 and 1920. (CHMM 992-8-1132.)

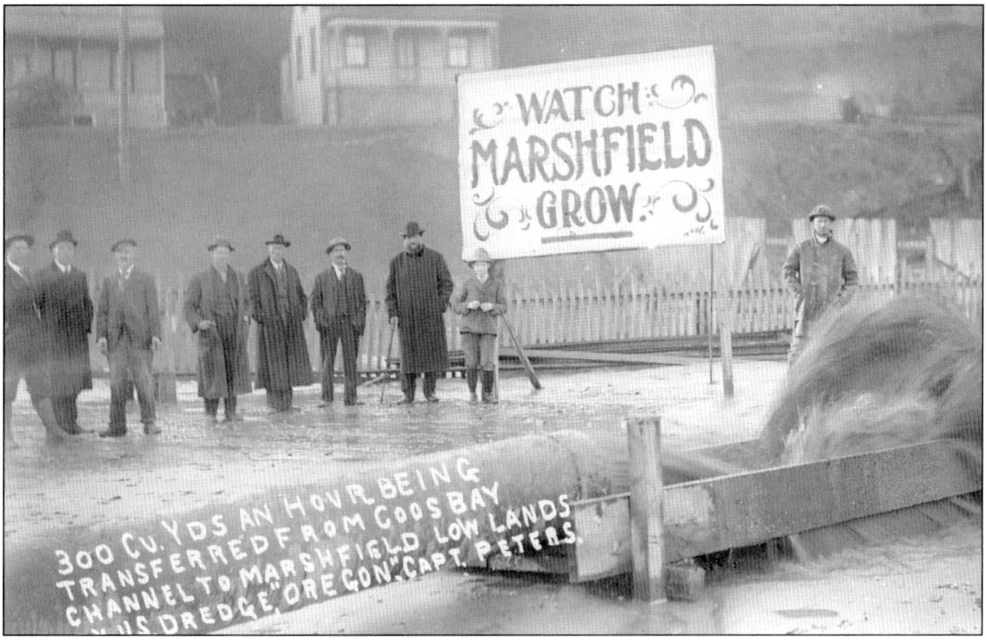

The sign "Watch Marshfield Grow" was not referring to population growth but to land mass growth. Not only did dredging provide a navigable way in the bay, the spoils of the dredging also provided land mass for the city. The dredge *Oregon*, built in 1909, transferred the spoils from the bay directly to the low-lying areas of Marshfield. (CHMM 995-D126.)

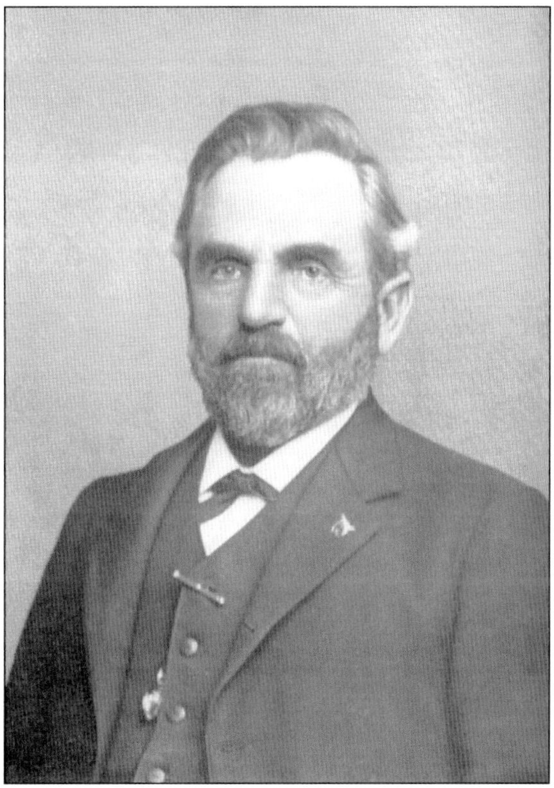

Charles H. Merchant became one of the most prominent citizens. Merchant was copartner with E.B. Dean and David Wilcox, doing business under the firm E.B. Dean and Company. They engaged in conducting a sawmill and general store. Some have referred to Merchant as the "Father of Marshfield," which may have been coined by Percy Levar, the last editor of the *Coast Mail*. (CHMM.)

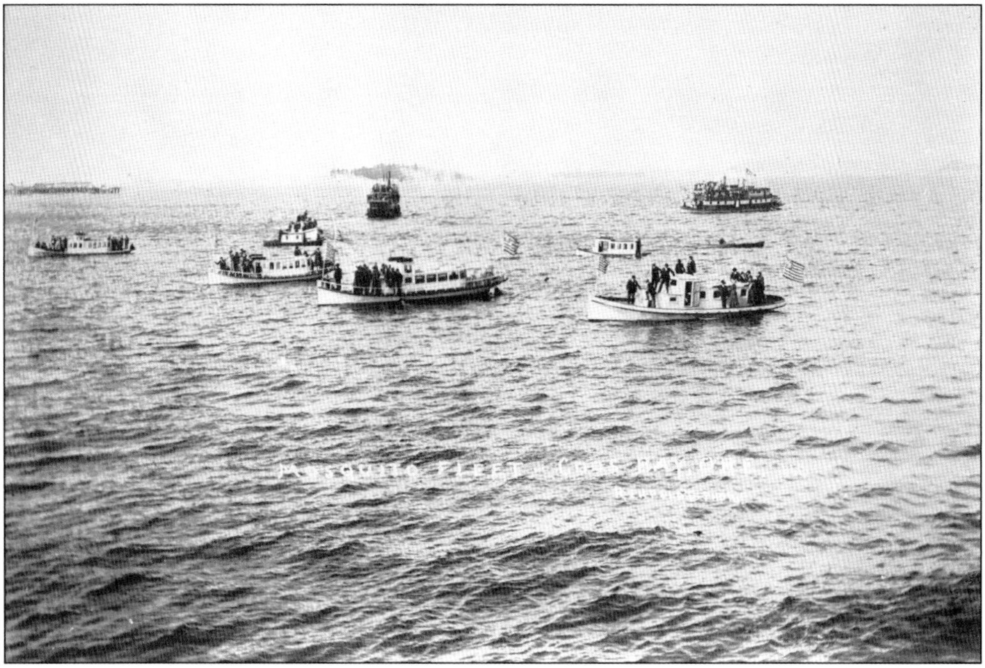

The employment of motorboats on the Pacific Coast for fishing, freight carrying, and other commercial purposes rapidly increased after the advent of gasoline-powered engines. A large number of small steam tugs were rapidly replaced by the more economical and handy gasoline-powered craft. "The Mosquito Fleet of Coos Bay" was a name coined by William Holland, a Pacific Coast boat builder. (CHMM 992-8-0617.)

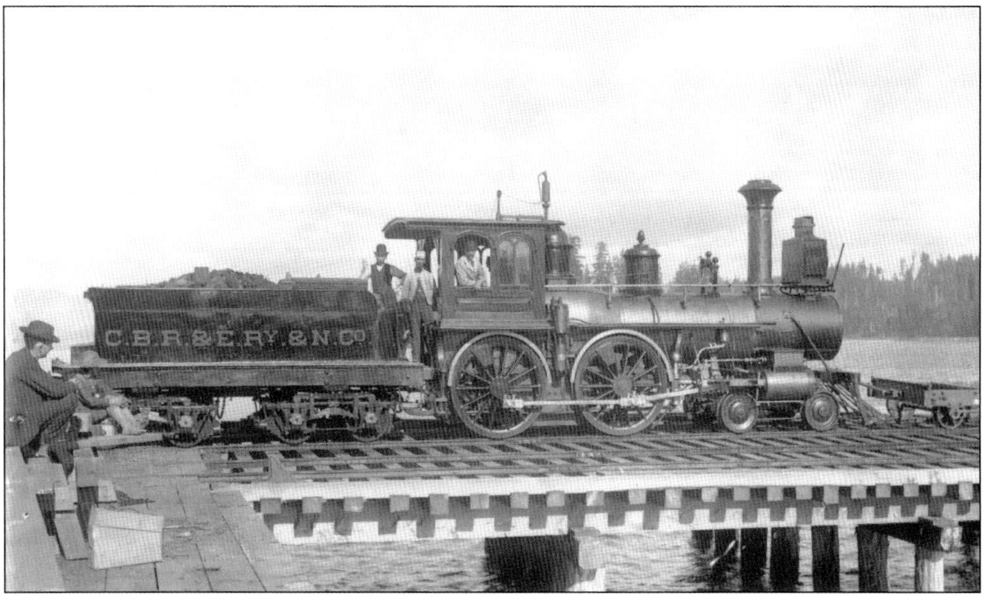

The first local railroad, organized on June 19, 1890, was completed in 1893. The Coos Bay, Roseburg & Eastern Railway and Navigation Company extended 25.81 miles from Marshfield to Myrtle Point. Even though the line was small, it was considered strategically located and was purchased by the Southern Pacific Railroad for $1 million in 1905. (CHMM 959-69.46 a.)

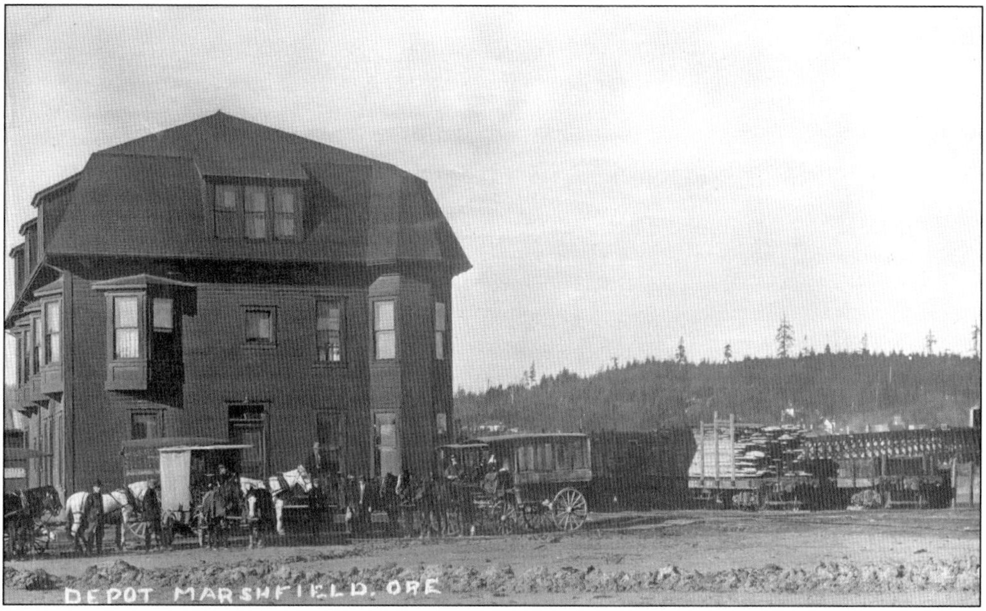

Robert Archibald Graham, an experienced railroad man who built government railroads in South America, built and served as general manager of the Coos Bay, Roseburg & Eastern Railway and Navigation Company line. The railroad depot was located on Front Street at Hall Avenue adjacent to the Coos Bay, Roseburg & Eastern Railway and Navigation Company dock. (CHMM 992-8-1041.)

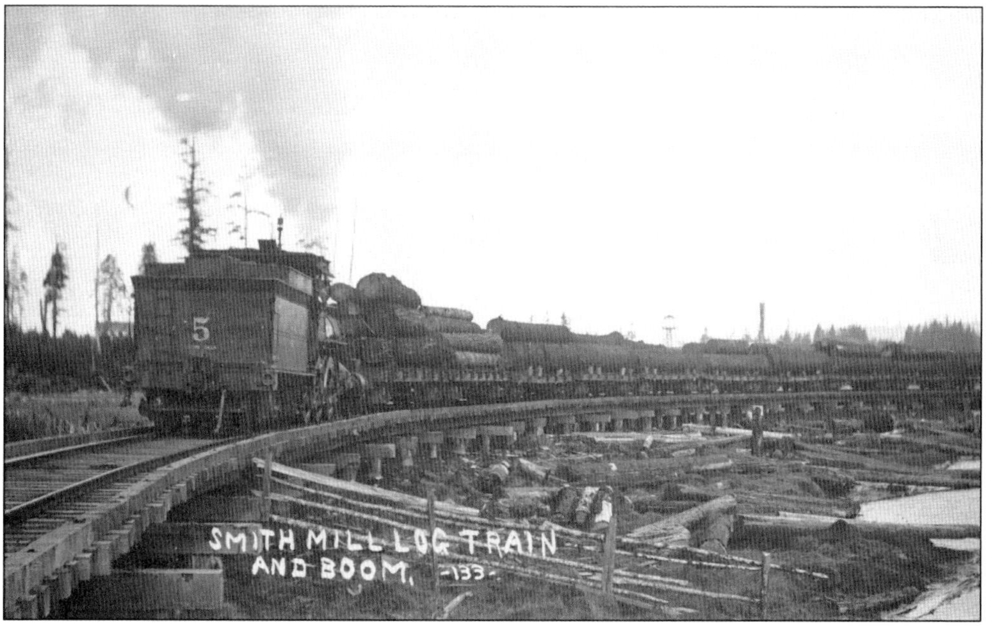

The shortest railroad line in Marshfield's history was the Marshfield City and Suburban Railroad Company. Organized on August 26, 1908, with C.A. Smith serving as president, the line extended one and one-half miles from the C.A. Smith Lumber and Manufacturing Company's mill to Marshfield, Oregon. On April 1, 1911, the company sold to C.A. Smith. (CHMM 992-8-0190.)

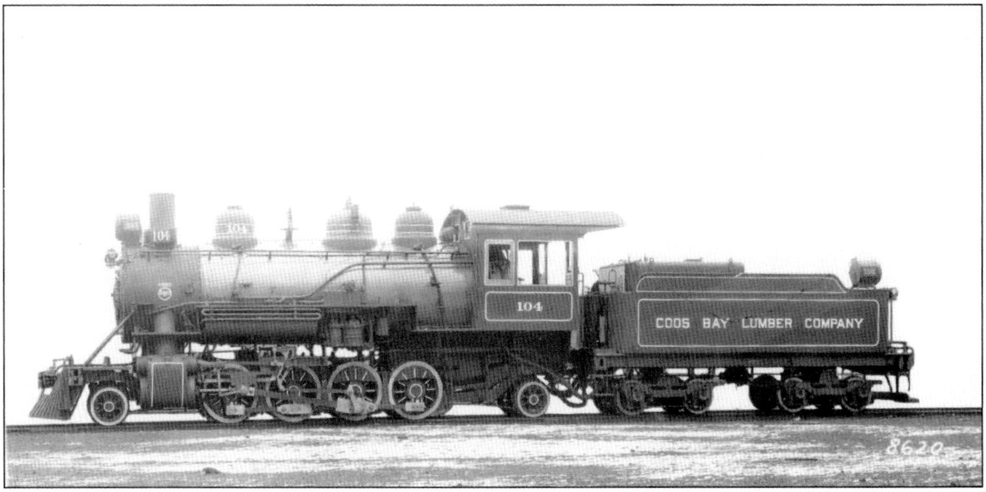

Because the Coos Bay, Roseburg & Eastern Railway and Navigation Company was unable to provide service sufficient for the needs of the Coos Bay Lumber Company, the lumber company established its own line. The steam locomotive No. 104, built in December 1922, was delivered in the spring of 1923. The locomotive was retired in 1954 and was the last steam engine used in logging. (CHMM 006-1.138.)

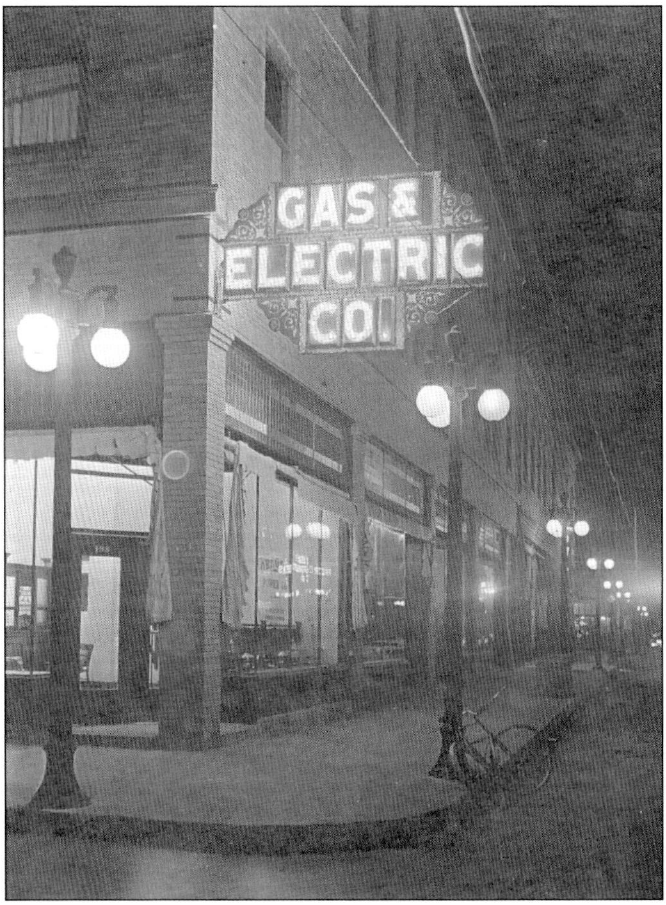

One of the most important features of Marshfield's progressiveness was the success of the Gas & Electric Company, which was built in 1891. The powerhouse was located in west Marshfield near Mill Slough. By 1905, the company provided 700 incandescent and 40 arc lights, 16 of which were all-night streetlights. (CHMM 994-23 a.)

It is unknown when the telephone arrived in Marshfield; however, use of the telephone was first recorded in 1893. Organized in September 1908, the Coos Bay Home Telephone Company provided services not only to Marshfield but also to the other communities. In Marshfield, there were 830 subscribers. (CHMM 987-S1173.)

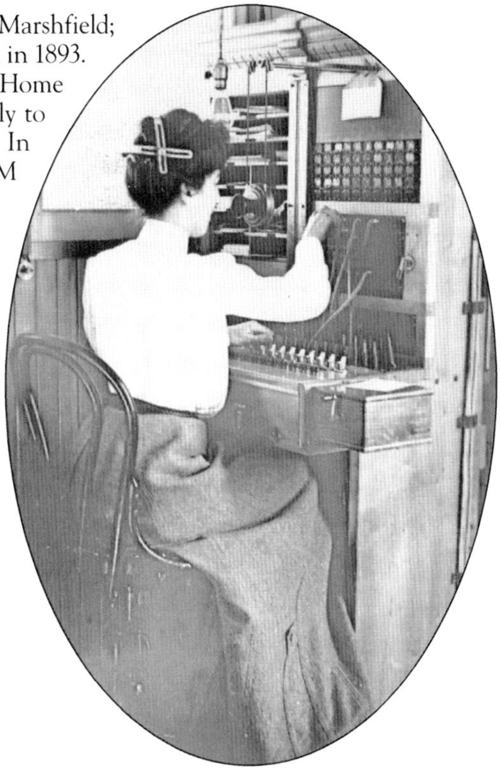

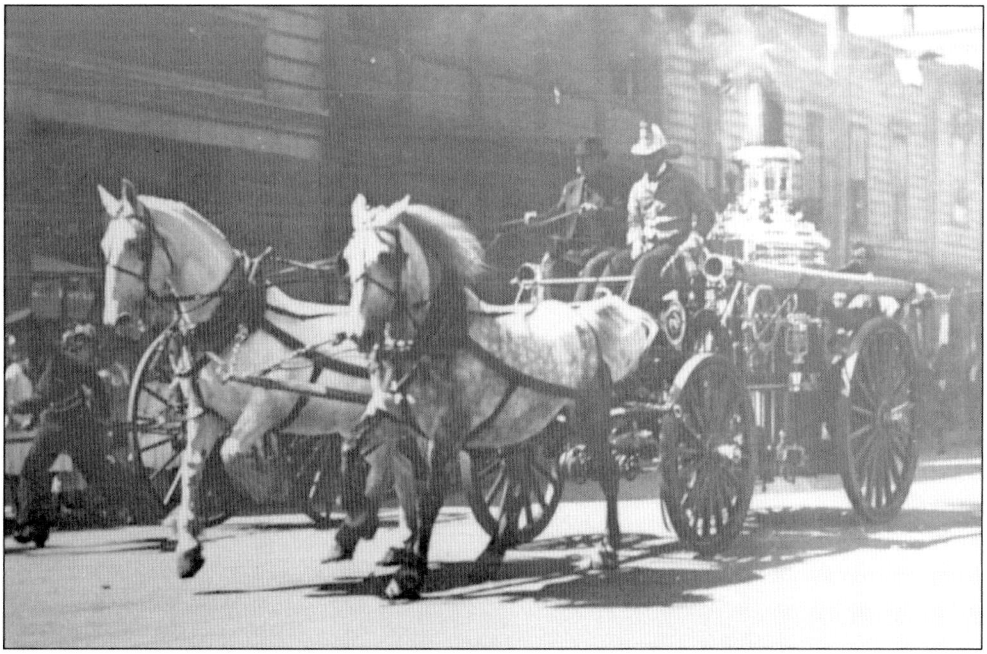

The fire department was always an important part of the city. With buildings of wood construction, the fear of fire always loomed on the horizon. This first piece of fire equipment, named *Jumbo*, was purchased by the city. There were two major fires on Front Street, one in 1919 and the second, more devastating, in 1922. (CHMM 009-16.6327.)

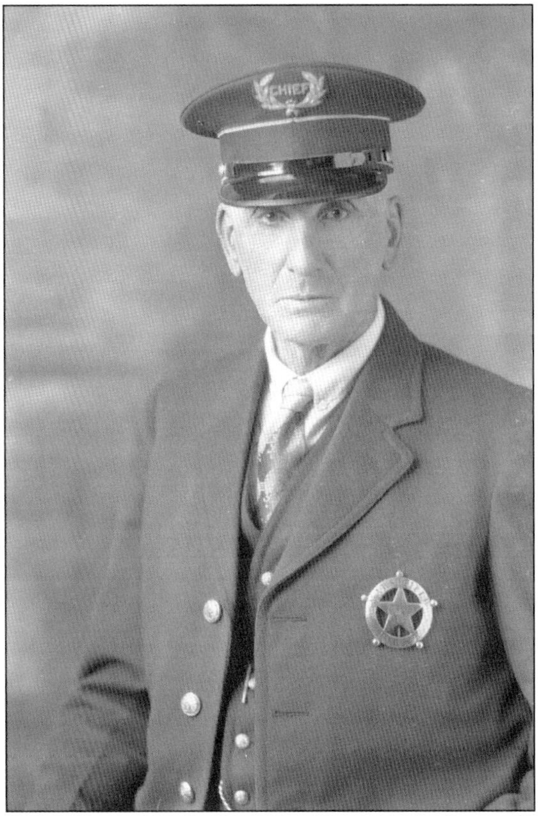

One of the best-known men of early Marshfield was city marshal John W. "Jack" Carter. Having served the city for over 31 years, he was a man who people either loved or hated during his colorful career. To some, Carter was known as "Sneaky Jack" for his ability to appear when least expected. (CHMM 989-S1201.)

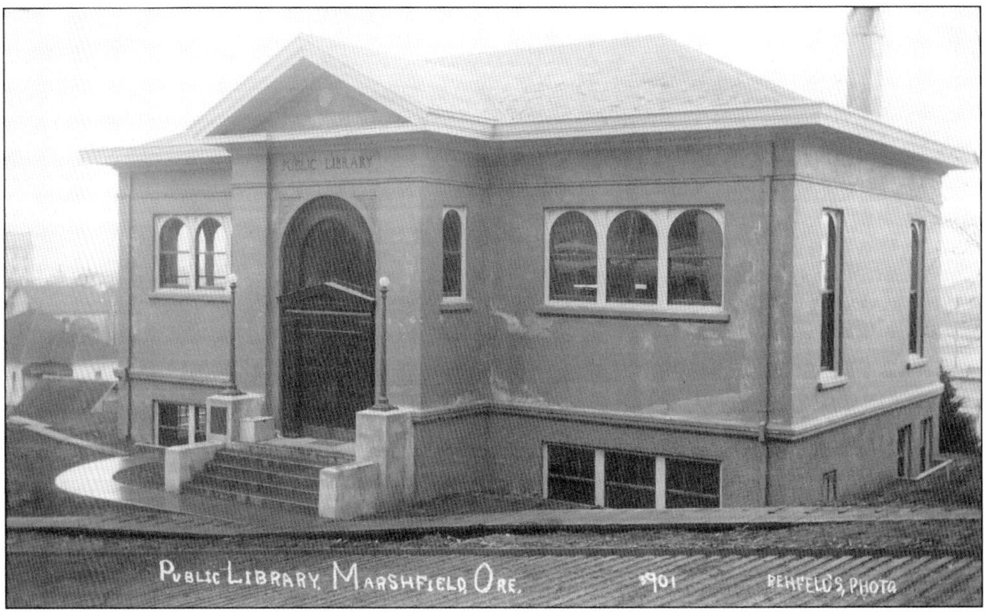

The Marshfield Public Library was established in June 1901 and first opened in the Henry Sengstacken Building. It later moved to rooms 201 and 202 in the Coke Building. In a drive spearheaded by Mrs. Sengstacken, a $12,500 grant was received from the Carnegie Foundation and a dedicated library building was erected in 1914. (CHMM 985-25.40.)

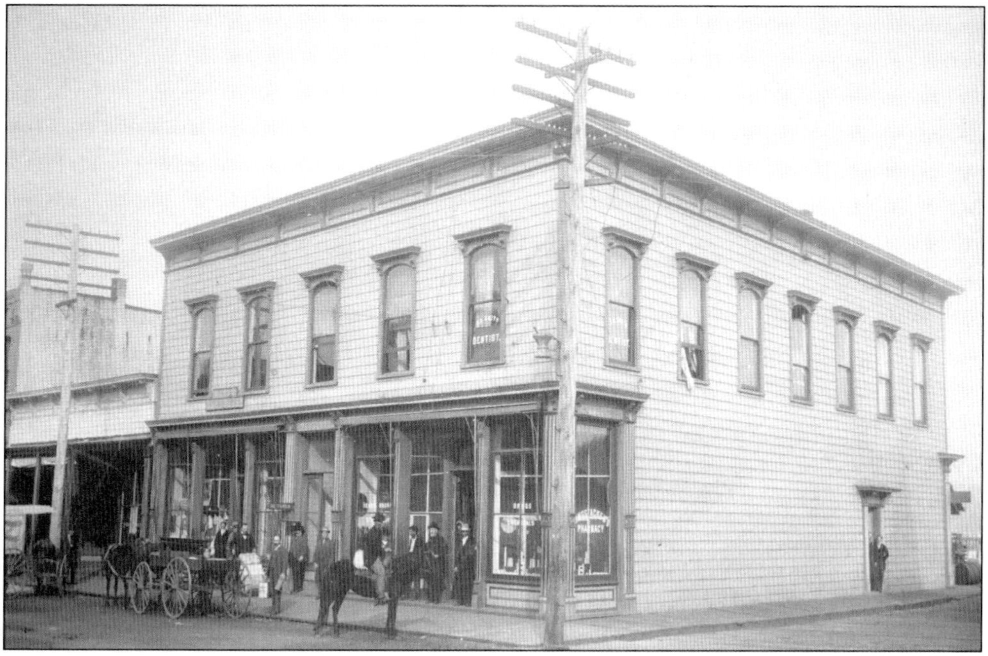

The Sengstacken Pharmacy, located in the Lockhart Building along with Dr. Charles Tower and dentist D.E. Smith, was owned and operated by Henry Sengstacken. Sengstacken, a German immigrant, was one of early Marshfield's premier businessmen. In 1905, he sold his business focusing on real estate and insurance ventures. (CHMM 992-8-1035.)

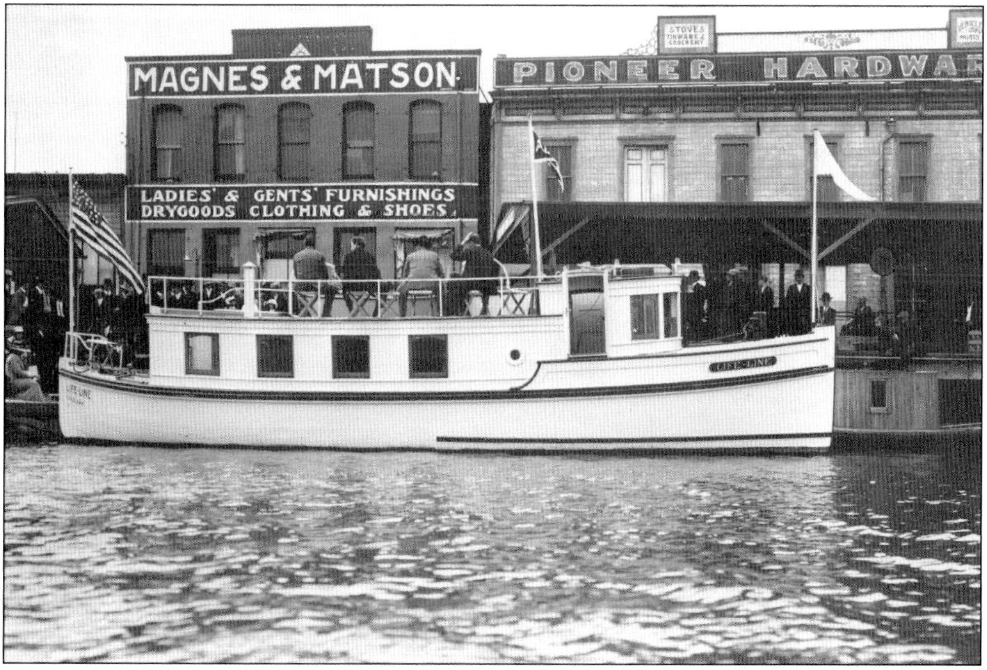

In 1912, Rev. G. Leroy Hall commissioned the first gospel boat to serve inland waters. The *Life Line* was a 40-foot launch that had a chapel that would accommodate 40 to 50 people. The *Life Line* served 40 different meeting places. (CHMM 992-8-2416.)

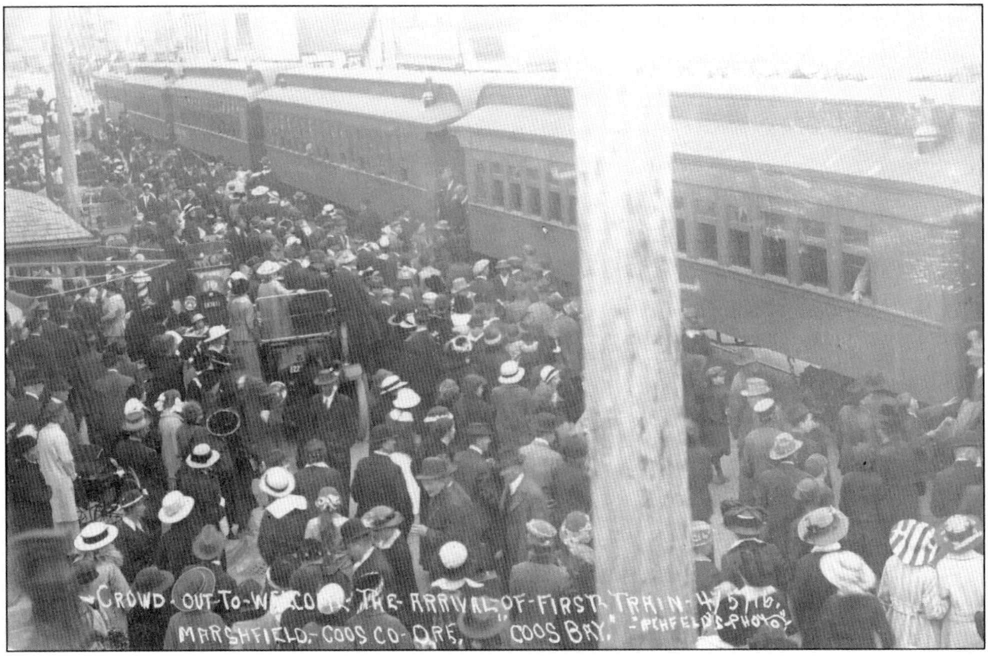

Citizens welcomed the arrival of the Southern Pacific line known as the Willamette Pacific Railroad, which ran from Eugene to Marshfield. When running from Marshfield to Eugene, it was known as train No. 1, and when running from Eugene towards Marshfield, it was known as train No. 2. The line was officially placed in operation on October 1, 1916. (CHMM 960-17.)

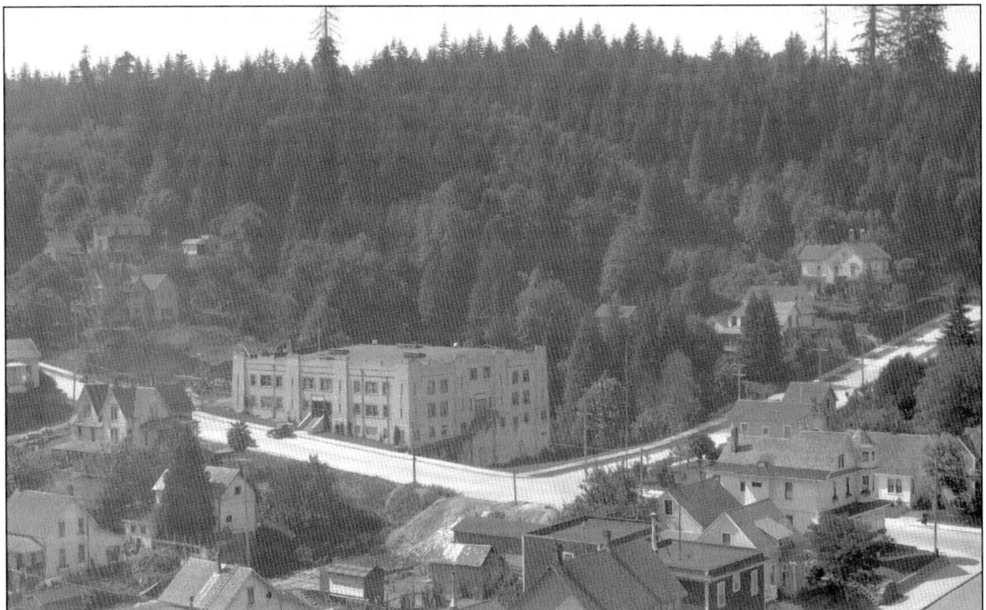

The Marshfield State Armory was built in 1919 and housed the 2nd Company, Oregon Coast Artillery, Oregon National Guard unit, which was organized three years earlier. The building was a multipurpose facility that included a 2,100-seat auditorium. After city hall was destroyed by fire in 1922, the armory served temporarily as city hall. (CHMM 992-8-3390.)

Horse racing was a popular sporting event in the 1910s. Running and trotting races were held at the racetrack in South Marshfield. By 1916, stripped Ford cars were seen racing on the track. For 50¢ admission, one could view the horse and automobile races. (CHMM 007-65.2.)

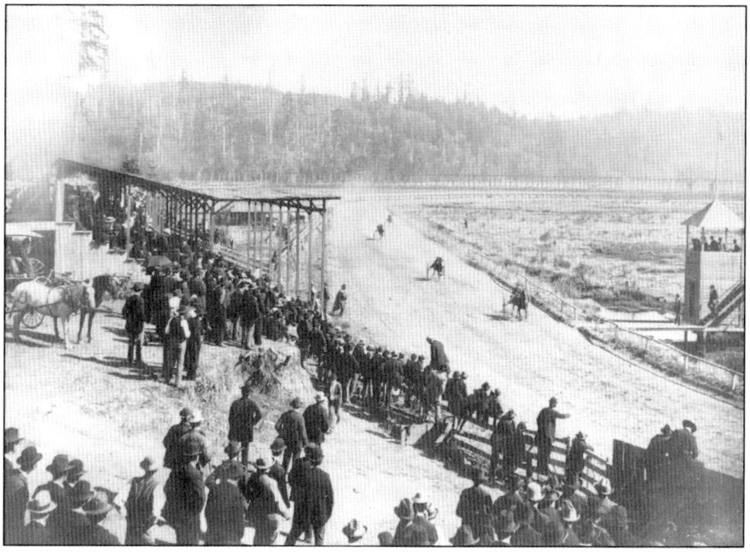

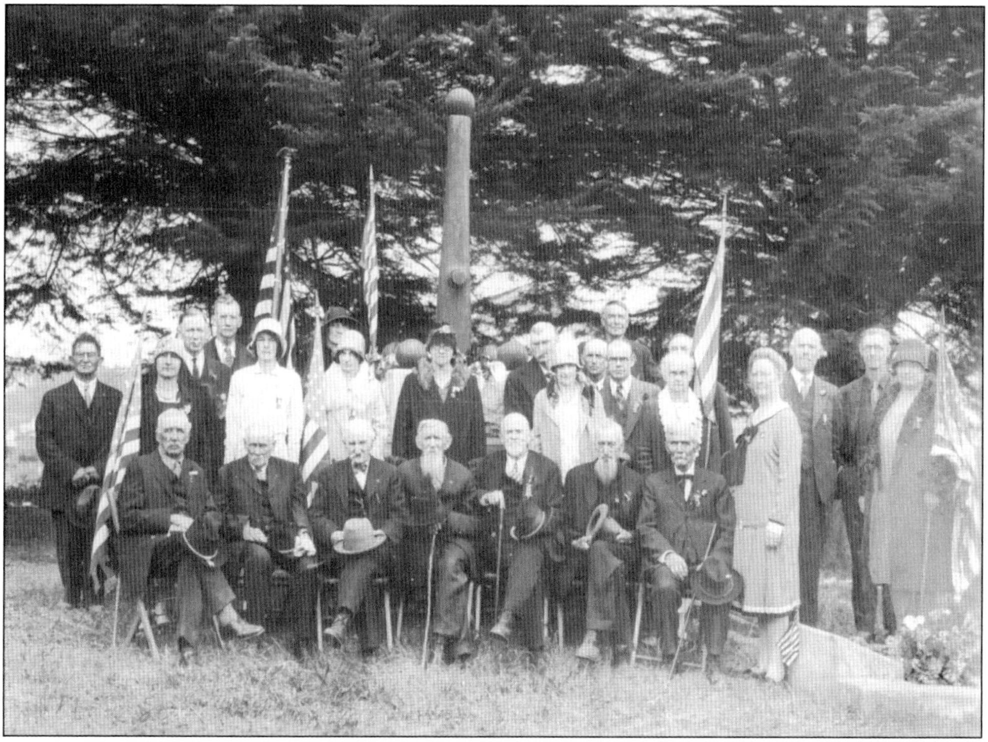

The Pioneer Cemetery was dedicated as the International Order of Odd Fellows Cemetery in 1891. From the late 1880s until 1930, over 2,000 people were buried in the cemetery. During the 1926 Memorial Day celebration at the cemetery, the Coos County members of the Grand Army of the Republic (seated in front) gathered with others around the Soldier-Sailor Monument. (CHMM 988-P135.)

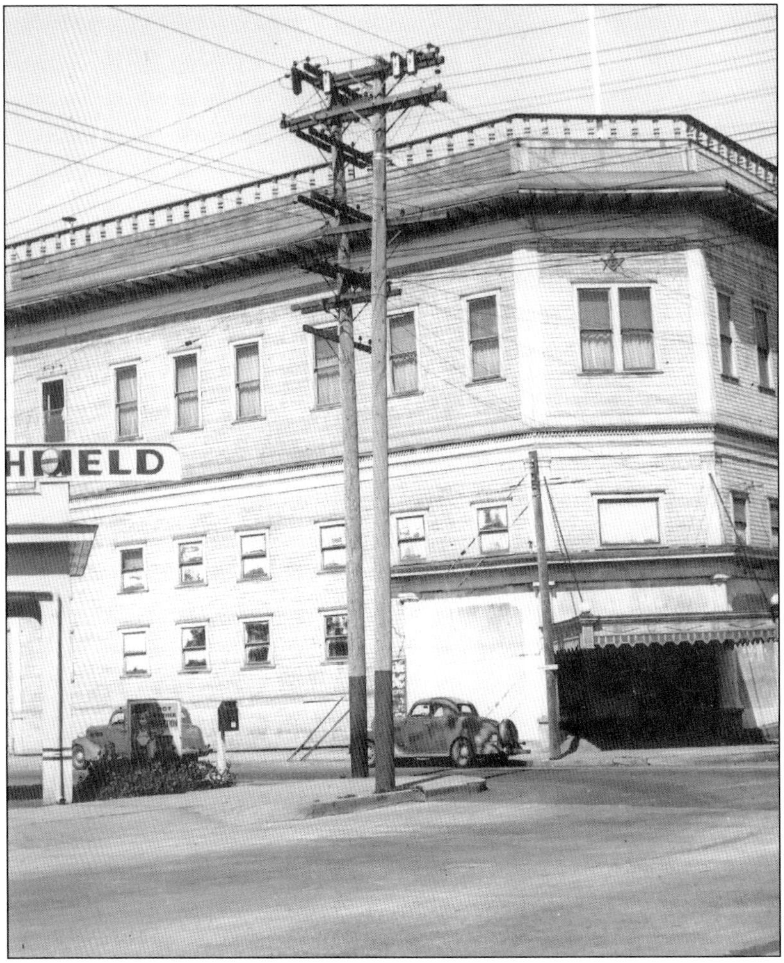

The Masonic Opera House, built in 1899, offered culture in a frontier town. The opera house was also used as a movie theater, opening as such on October 8, 1910. In later years, the opera house would serve as the Blue Mouse Theater and for operation of the Brookmead Dairy. (CHMM 963-83k.)

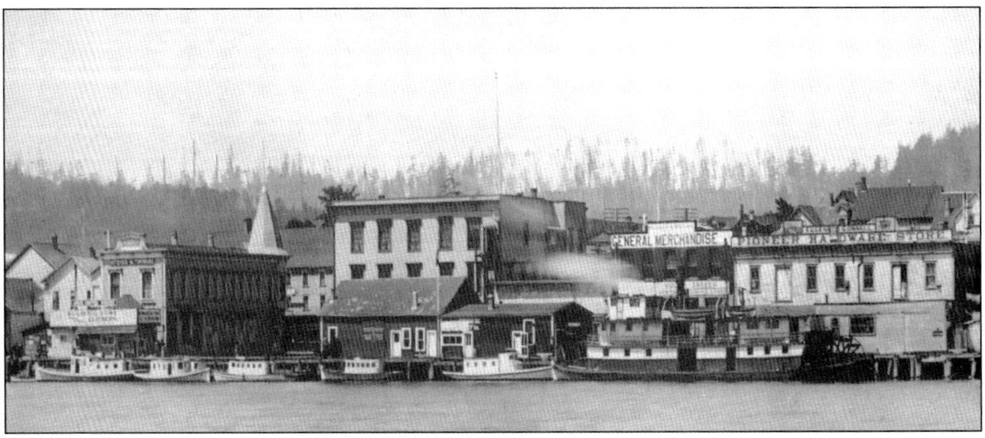

For many years, the Marshfield waterfront bustled with commercial activity. In 1908, many prominent businesses can be seen at Marshfield's commercial district along the waterfront. From left to right, the following businesses are shown: Wooden Mill Store Clothiers, Java Coffee House, Stoves and Tinware, General Merchandise, and the Pioneer Hardware Store. (CHMM 992-8-1119.)

The Chandler Hotel, built in 1909, was the first establishment to break free of the frontier facade. Named after major investor W.S. Chandler, the hotel provided luxurious accommodations for the businessmen with capital to invest. Designed by Chandler's brother, a New York architect, the five-story hotel provided an elevator and telephone service in each room. (CHMM 974-68.7.)

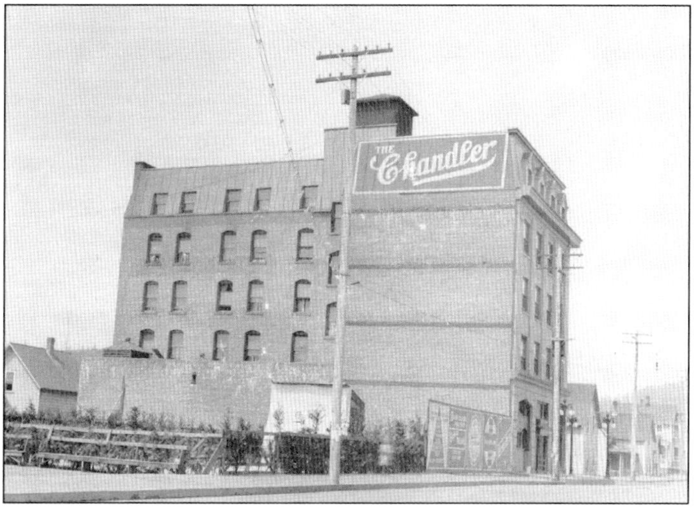

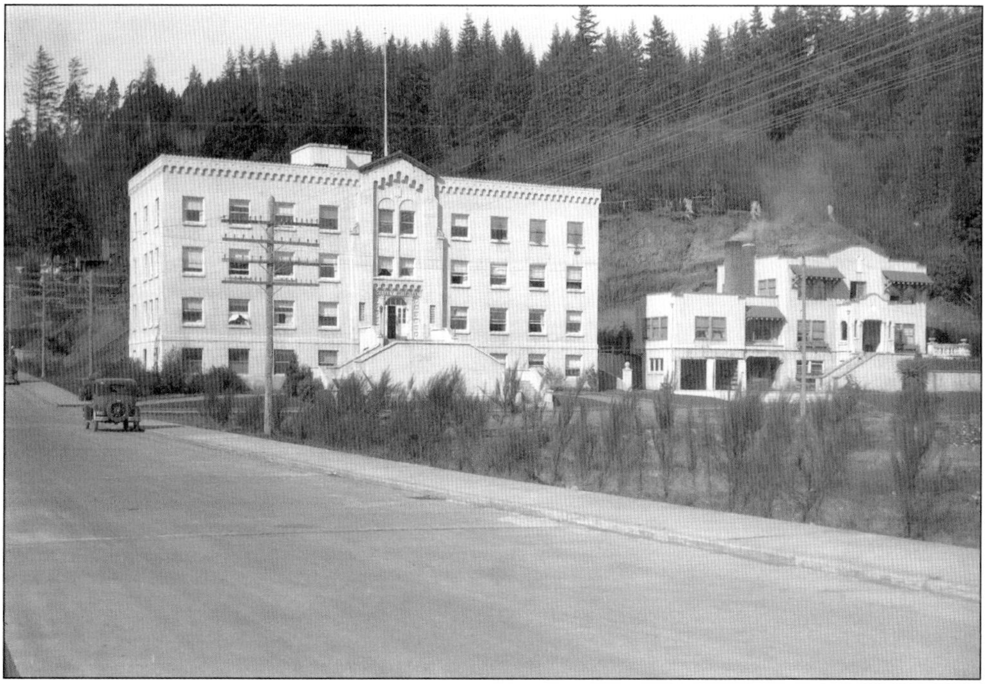

The Wesley Hospital was built in the 1920s. By 1936, the hospital was in serious financial distress. That distress continued until the board of trustees found it impossible to carry on. The hospital was sold to the Catholic Church and renamed the McAuley Hospital. Operated by the Sisters of Mercy, the hospital served the community until 1974. (CHMM 987-S168.)

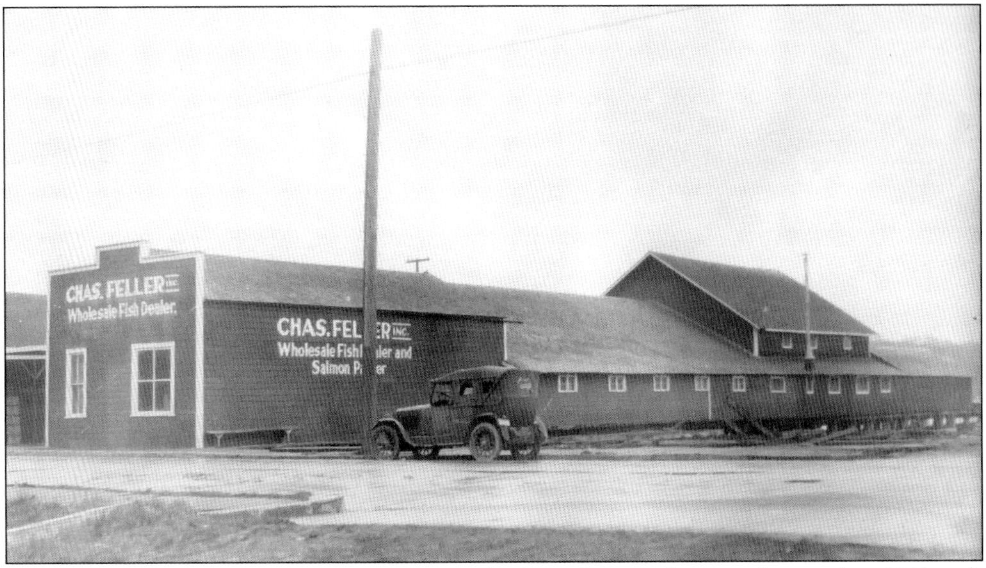

Perhaps the most successful fish dealer was Charles Feller. His business boomed in 1916 with the arrival of the railroad. With the railroad, Feller could easily transport the fish throughout the states in refrigerated cars. The plant was expanded in 1925 with the addition of a large ice storage room. (CHMM 988-43.18.)

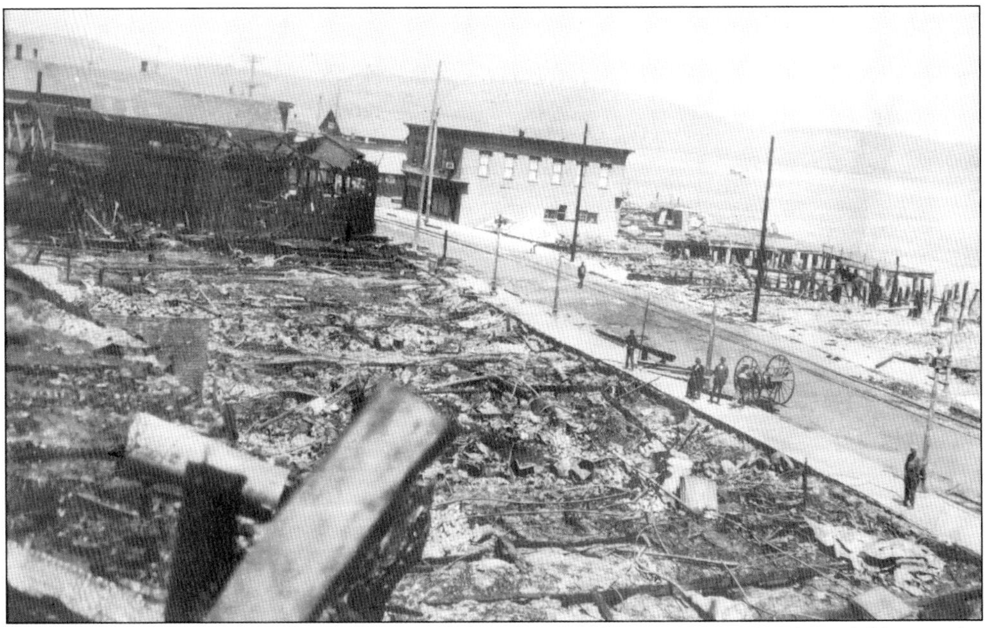

The fire of July 23, 1922, devastated the business district of Front Street. At about 3:30 a.m., the fire started in J. Guildesheim's junk store, and it quickly spread to both sides of the street, wiping out the heart of the business district. City hall, which housed the fire station and jail, also burned to the ground. In total, 24 businesses and four homes were lost in the fire. (CHMM 007-11.245.)

Construction of the Tioga Hotel began in 1929. With the onset of the Great Depression, the owners ran out of money, thus ending the building project. Referred to as a "white elephant," the Tioga remained unfinished until 1946. The hotel touted two restaurants, and the local boosters club, the Coos Bay Pirates, opened a club lounge on the second floor. (CHMM 996-36.40.)

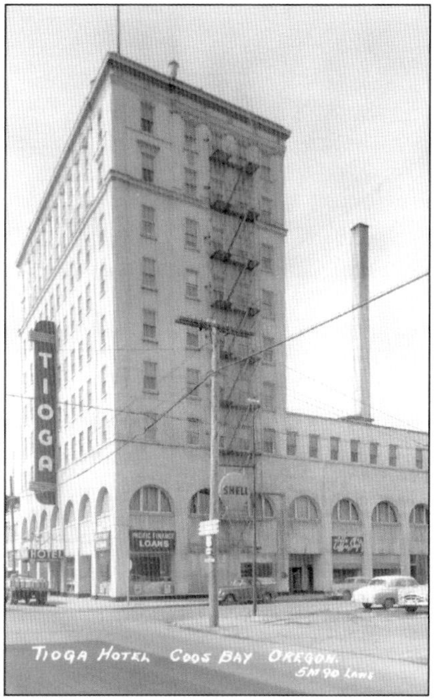

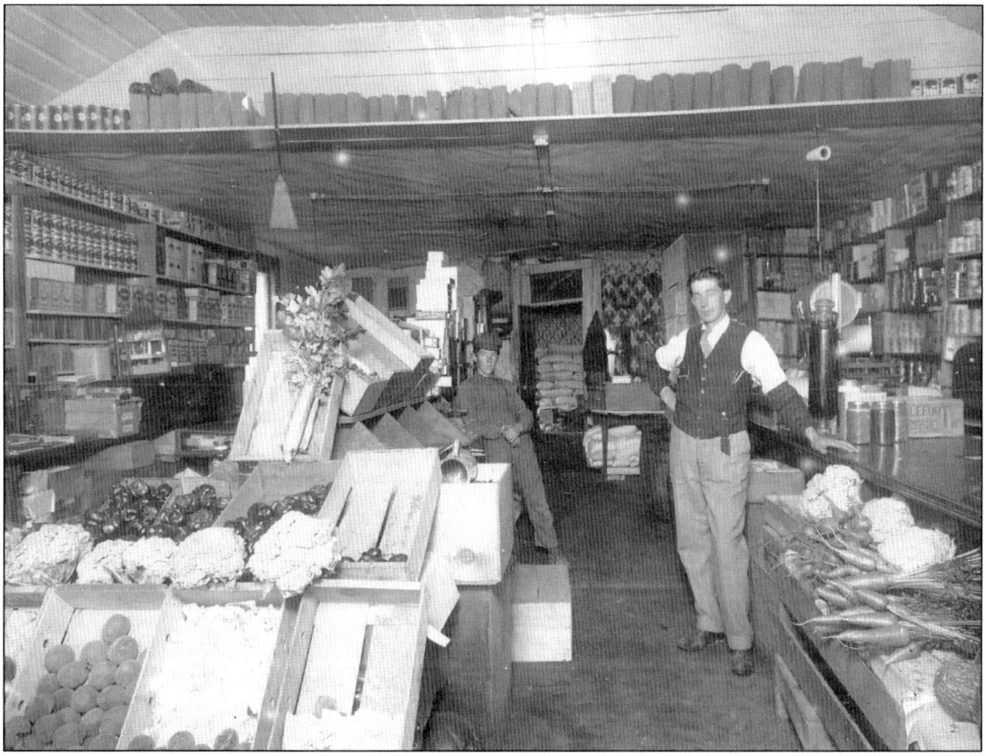

One of the most successful grocery stores in early Marshfield was the one owned and operated by George E. Cook, established in 1907. George Cook operated his store until his death in 1934. Later his son John took over operations and ran the store until the early 1950s. In 1909, a young John E. Cook is pictured leaning against the counter. (CHMM 960-149 a.)

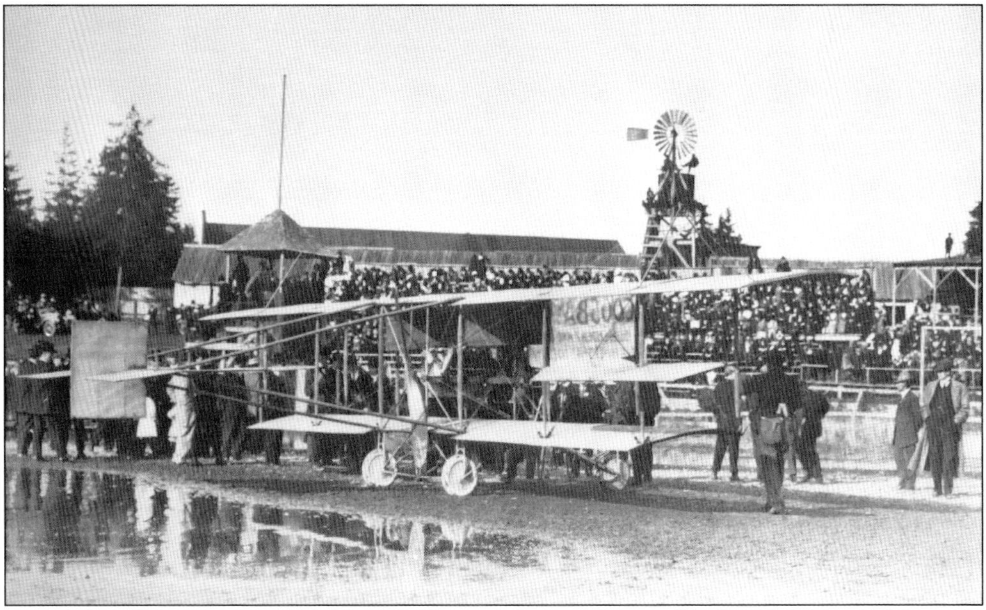

During the week of October 27, 1912, the *Coos Bay Times* hosted pioneer aviator Silas Christofferson at the Marshfield racetrack for five days of exhibition and passenger flights. Christofferson provided the first moonlight-flying exhibition in the Pacific Northwest, hunted ducks from the plane, and used his plane in the rescue of the schooner *Osprey*. (CHMM 992-8-1211.)

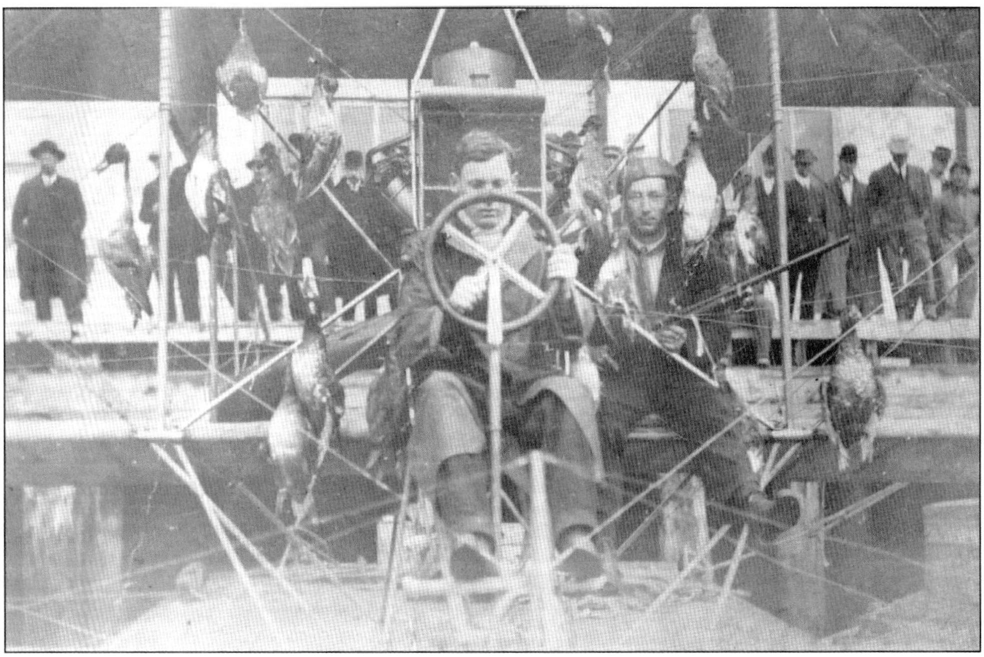

When Silas Christofferson went duck hunting with Cecil Holland, he had to rig his airplane with pontoons. Holland sat on the wing to accomplish his task with a limited view due to the rigging and pilot's location. After shooting into a flock of ducks, the airplane circled around, landed on the water, and retrieved the ducks. Seventeen ducks were bagged in an hour and a half. (CHMM 960-105.)

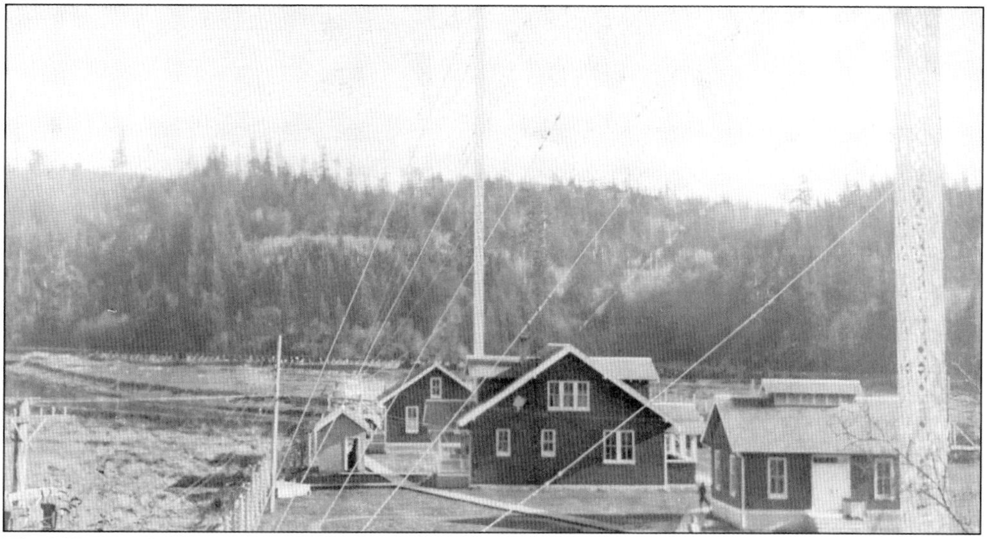

The US Navy Department operated four naval radio stations in the state of Oregon. One of these was located in Englewood. The Englewood Naval Wireless Station was located on four acres of land acquired by deed of gift for use as a radio station on January 3, 1916. (CHMM 980-250.1 a.)

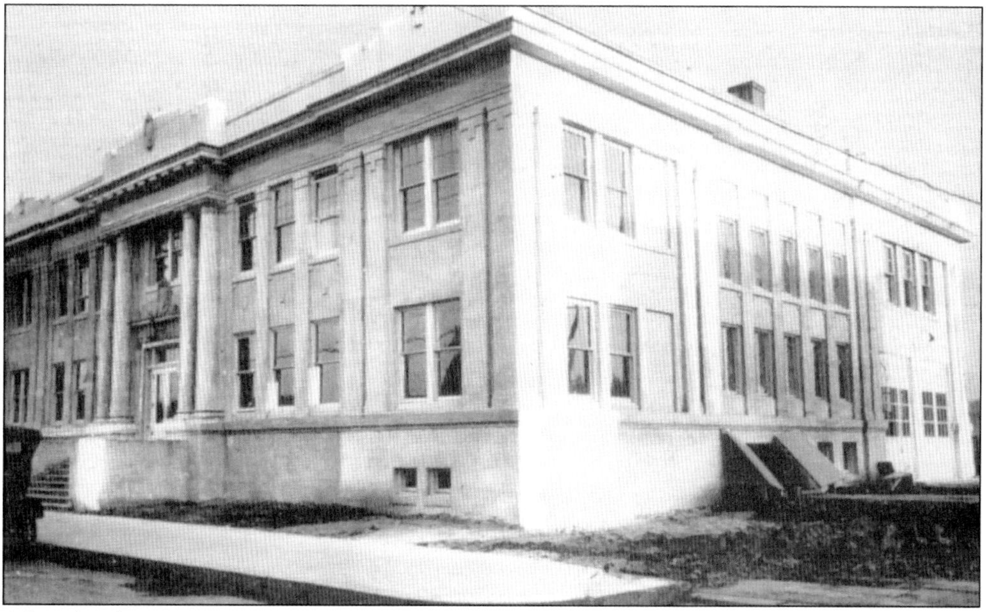

After the devastating fire of 1922, which destroyed city hall, a new modernized city hall was designed by Frank Hummel. Built in 1924, the city hall cost $75,000. The Greek-style building consisted of two stories and a basement, which provided a large council chamber with a balcony, roomy offices for all the city officials, a police station including five jail cells, and large quarters for the fire department. (CHMM 006-44.127.)

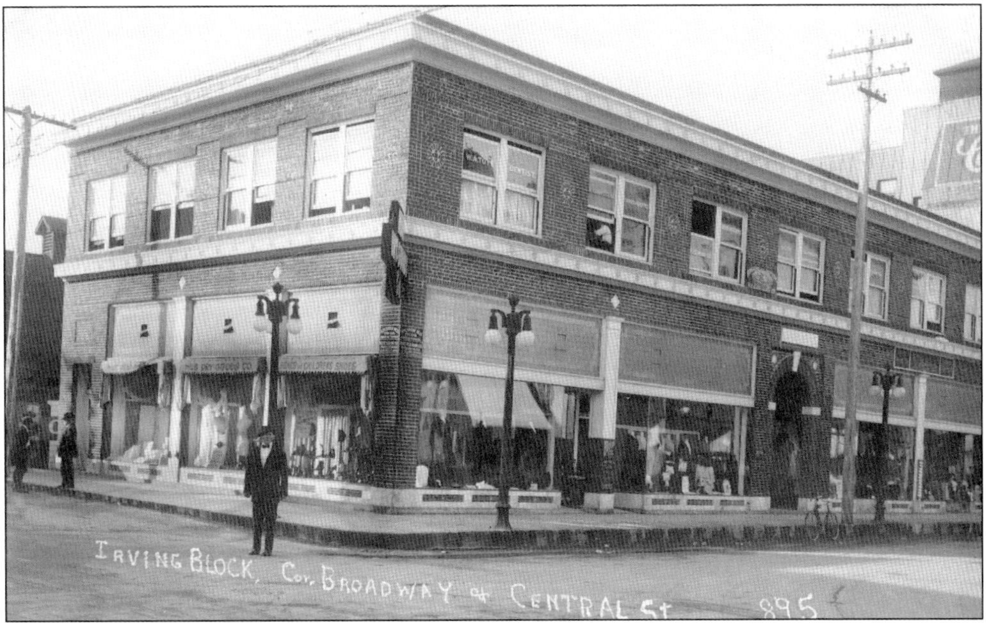

Established in 1911 by Albert S. Kohler, the Hub provided goods for many years. After Kohler's death in 1939, the store was operated by his son Albert H. Kohler, who built the business into a successful three-store complex. The Hub Annex featured bedding, drapes, and fabrics, and the Hub Corner Shop provided women's lingerie. After the death of Albert, the business was sold to the Seattle-based Tri-North Department Store. (CHMM 985-25.47.)

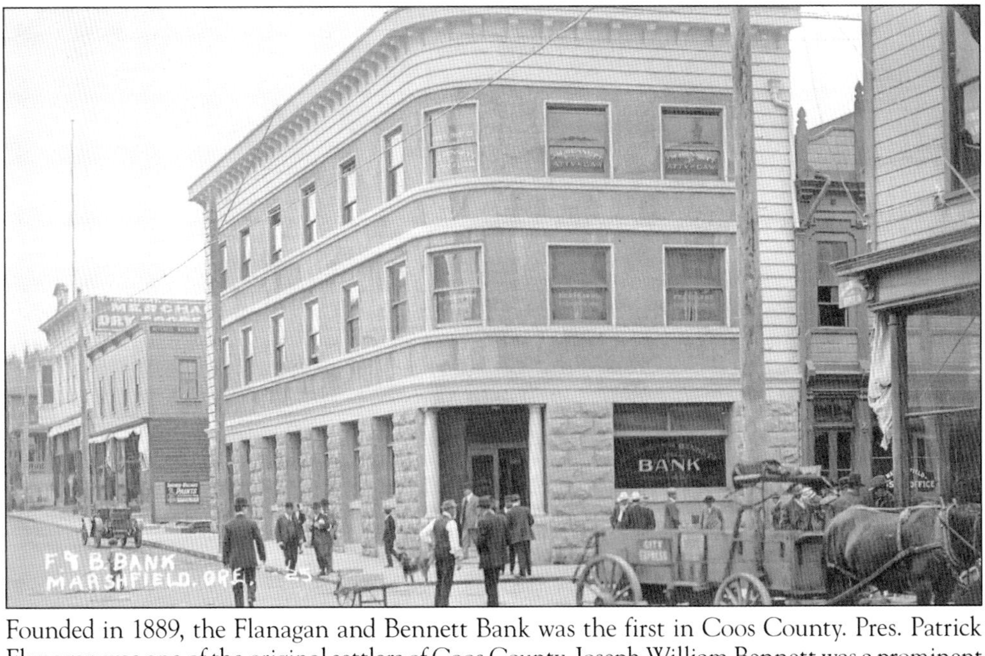

Founded in 1889, the Flanagan and Bennett Bank was the first in Coos County. Pres. Patrick Flanagan was one of the original settlers of Coos County. Joseph William Bennett was a prominent attorney whose law office was located above the bank. The bank was succeeded by the Bank of Southwestern Oregon in 1917. The building was destroyed in the fire of July 23, 1922. (CHMM 985-25.44.)

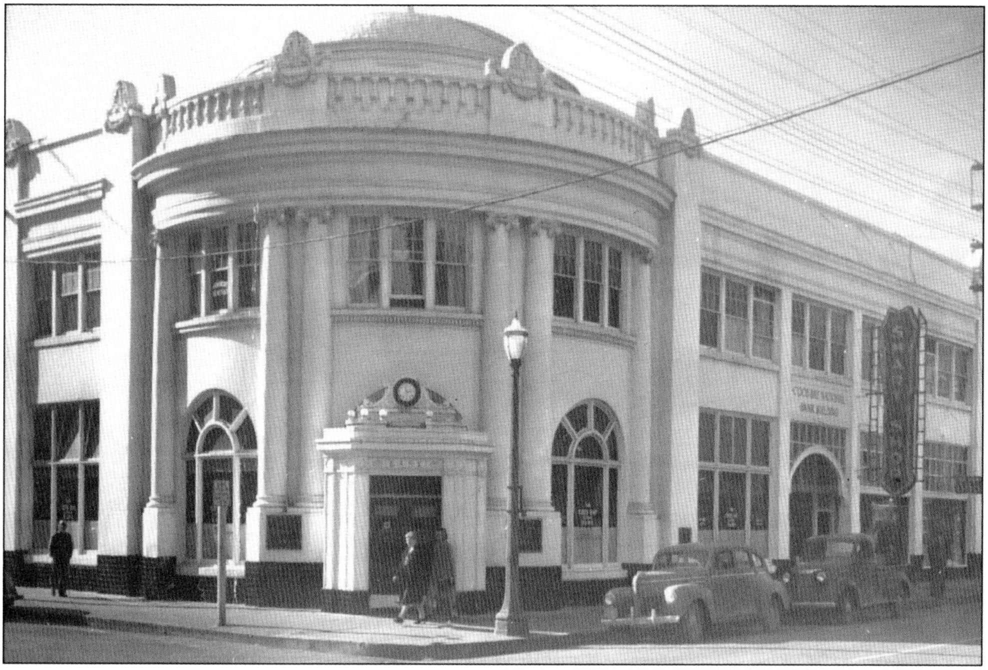

On December 28, 1921, the state-operated bank, Scandinavian-American, converted to a national bank known as the Coos Bay National Bank. The new and architecturally significant bank was erected in 1924. The bank has also been referred to as "Bugge's Bank" for well-known cashier and bank director Reidar Bugge. (CHMM 992-8-1001.)

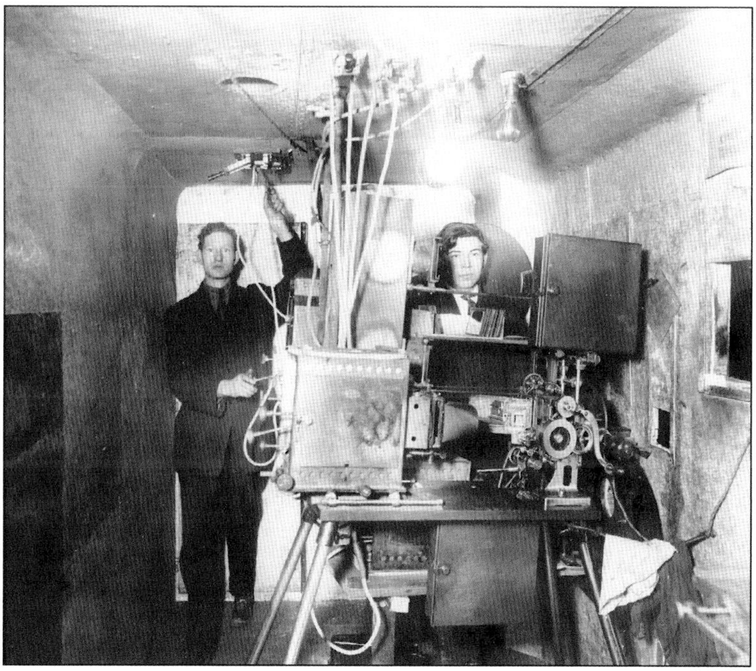

Motion pictures arrived on the scene about 1907. The Royal Theater was the second movie theater in Marshfield. First located on Front Street, the Royal endured two moves, the last of which was to the corner of Third Street and Central Avenue. During the mid- to late 1910s, the Royal was sold to Robert Marsden, who renamed the theater the Noble. (CHMM 990-26.2.)

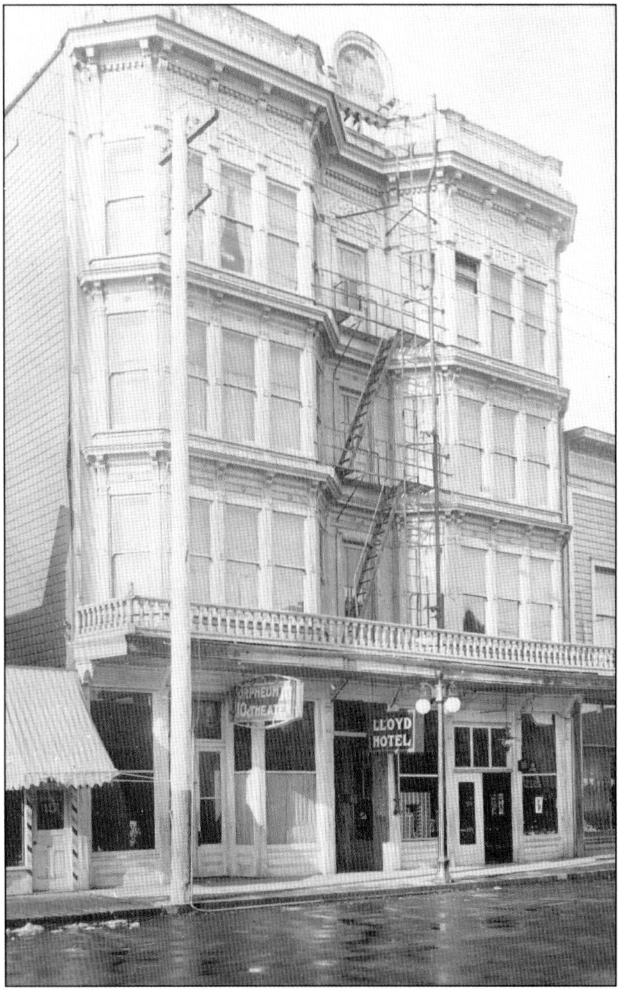

Another early theater was the Orpheum, located next to the Baxter Hotel. Like other theaters of the day, live entertainment was also provided. Events ranged from singing and dancing by the Runeburg Lodge, a Scandinavian group performing folk routines from Europe, to visiting vaudeville troupes. (CHMM 992-8-1015.)

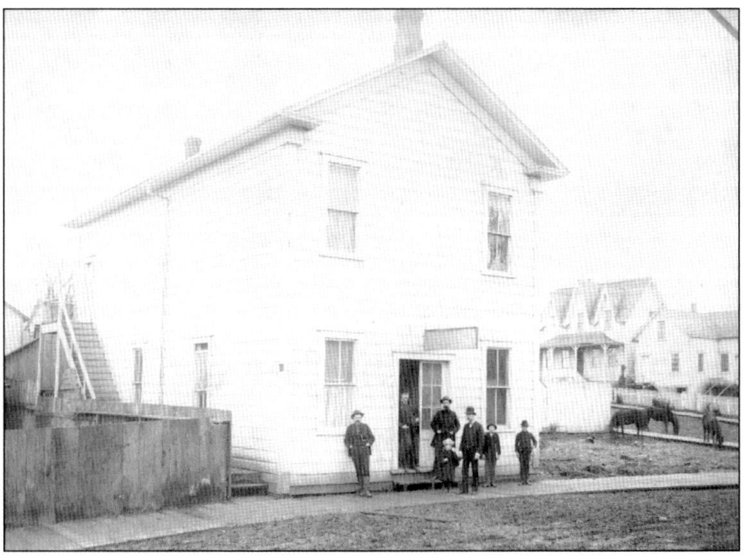

The *Coos Bay News*, purchased in 1875 by Joseph W. Bennett, H.H. Gale, and Jacob M. Siglin, moved from Empire City to Marshfield in 1878. The first Marshfield office was destroyed in the fire of 1922 and was rebuilt. It was the first regularly published newspaper in Coos County. (CHMM 008-31.6.)

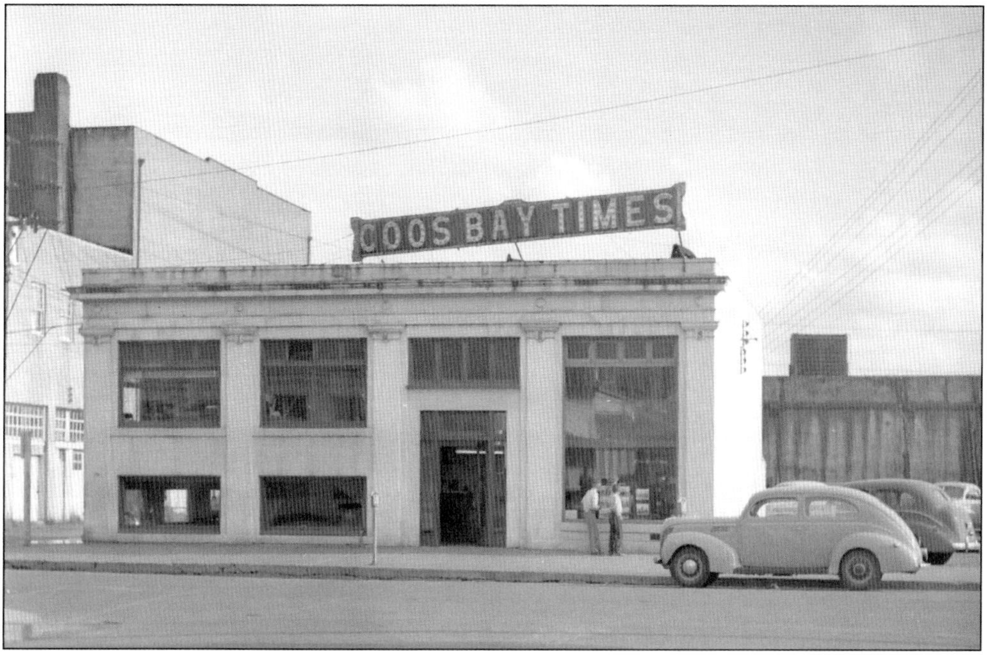

In 1906, the *Coast Mail* newspaper was sold to a group of local businessmen who wanted a stronger community newspaper, and the *Coos Bay Times* was launched. After a year in operation, the *Times* was sold to brothers M.C. and Dan E. Maloney, who operated the paper until 1930. The *Coos Bay Times* became the county's first daily newspaper in 1947. (CHMM 995-1.4068.3.)

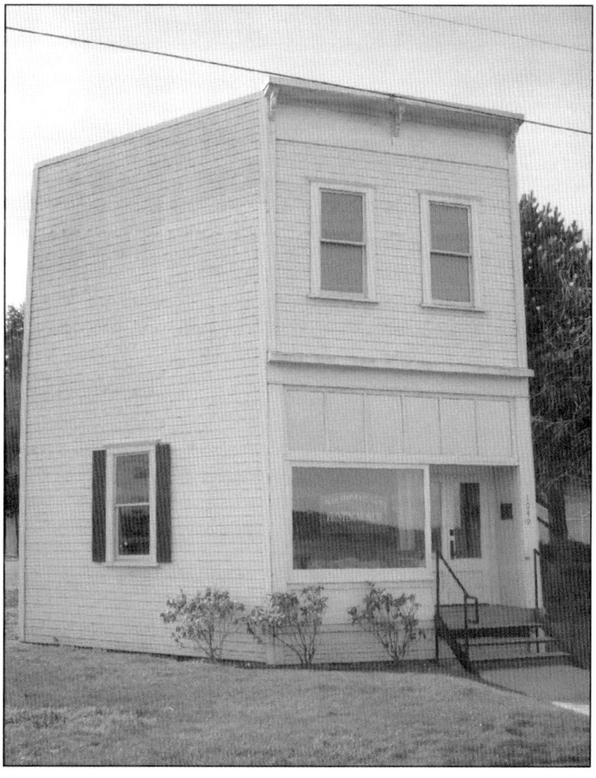

For 53 years, Jesse Luse single-handedly operated the *Marshfield Sun* newspaper. The last issue of the *Sun* was in June 1944, when the presses stopped due to Luse's death. The *Sun* was the last handset newspaper in the Pacific Northwest. The *Sun* building now serves as a museum and is listed in the National Register of Historic Places. (CHMM.)

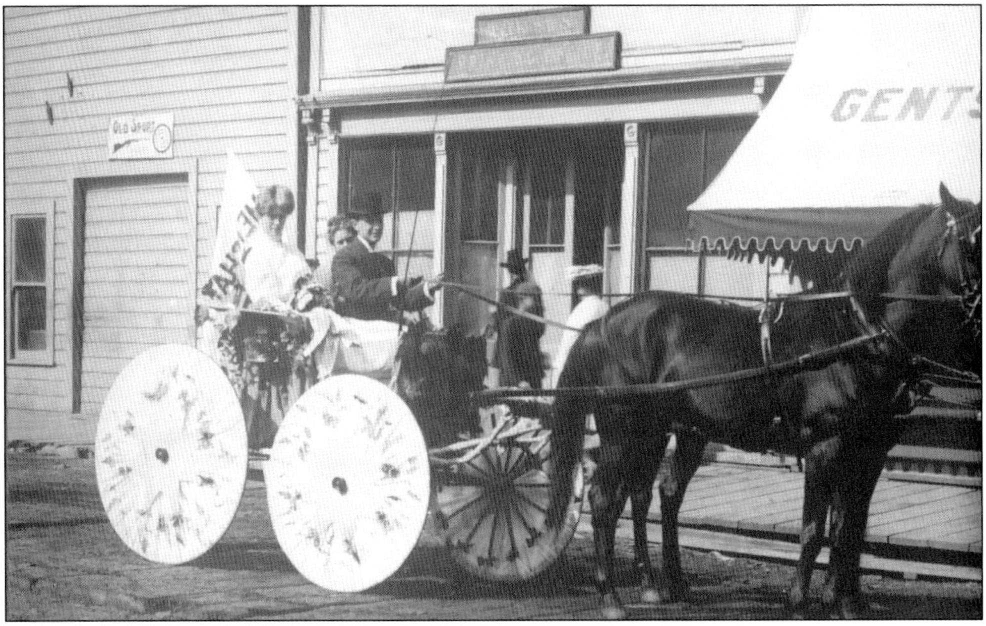

The *Marshfield Sun* newspaper was edited and published by Jesse Allen Luse from 1891 until 1944. For 20 years, the *Marshfield Sun* was located on the second floor of the W.G. Webster building on Front Street. In 1911, Luse moved his newspaper to its present location on North Front Street. At the time of this photograph, the *Marshfield Sun* was located in the Webster building. (CHMM 9992-8-1196.)

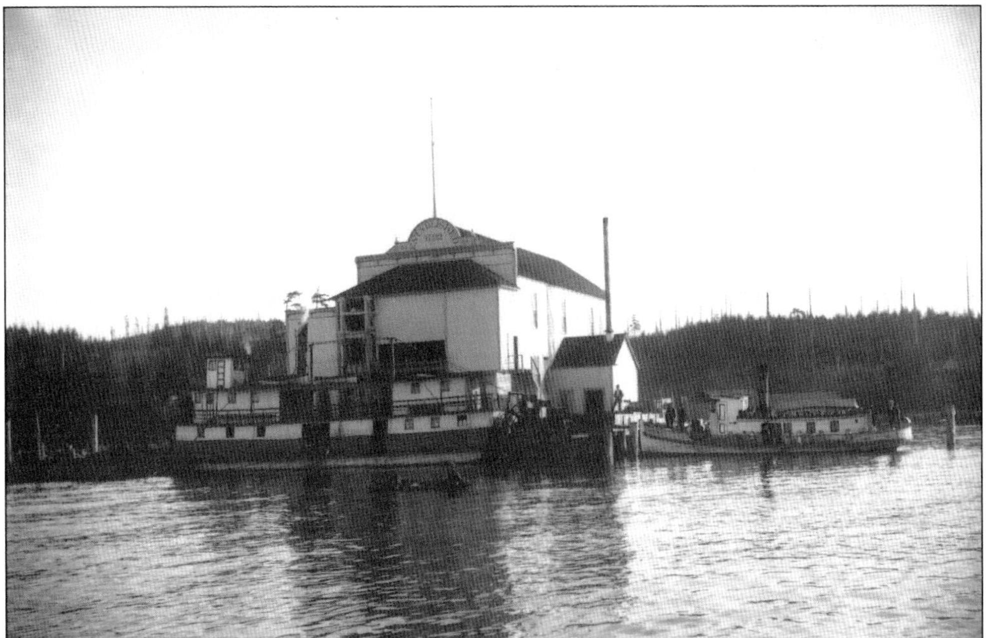

H.E. Bessey organized the Coos Bay Creamery Company in 1892. The Coos Bay Creamery was considered one of the best-equipped enterprises of its kind in this portion of the state. Bessey's success in building the prosperous creamery identified him as one of the enterprising leaders among the businessmen of the area. (CHMM 991-8.1.)

Constructed in 1902, the Coos Bay Ice and Cold Storage Company served as a cold storage and ice-making plant that provided a much-needed service to the fishing community. The machinery of the plant included a 15-ton Vulcan refrigerating machine and a 10-ton ice-making apparatus. On June 25, 1919, the Coos Bay Mutual Creamery took over the building. (CHMM 007-25.290.)

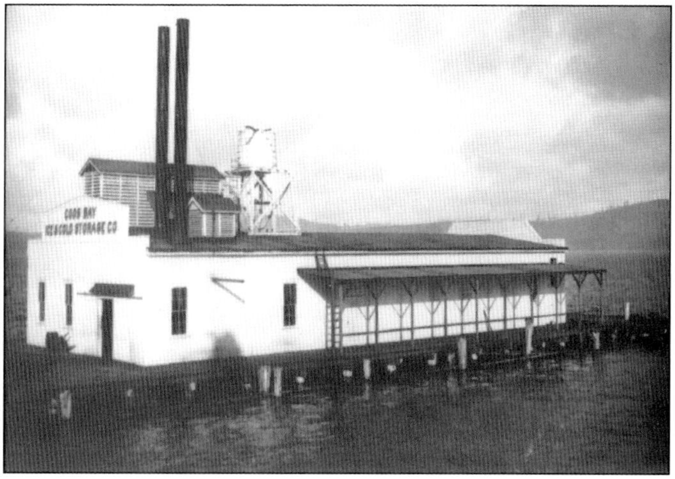

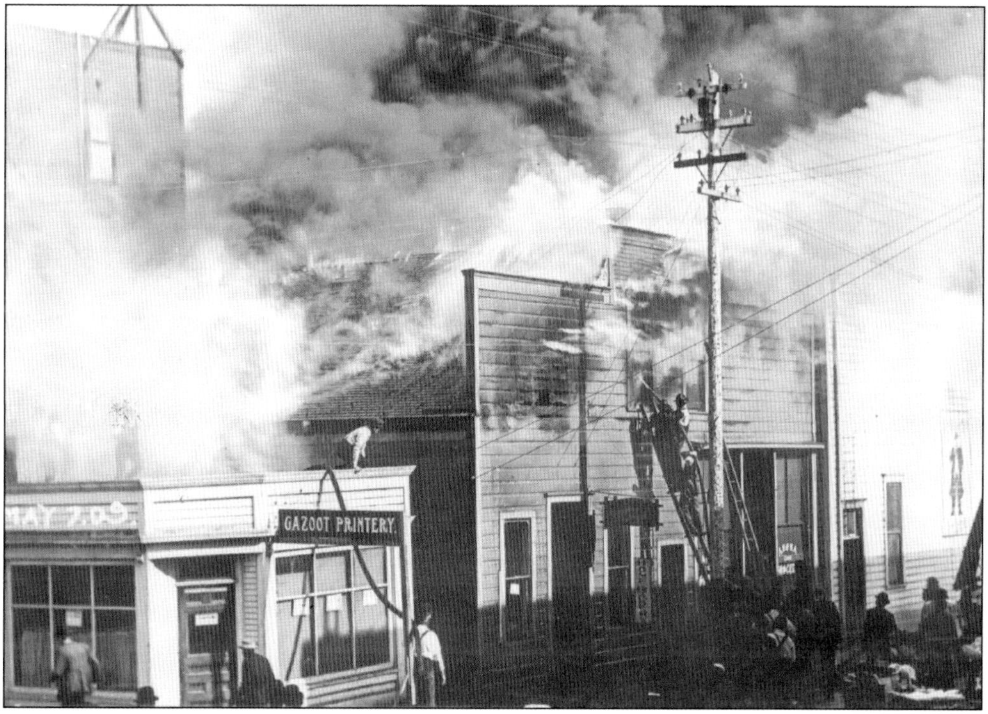

A major fire was diverted on May 7, 1909, when the citizens rallied together to help the fire department extinguish a fire in a building occupied by Mother's Restaurant. In conjunction with the heroic efforts of the firemen and citizens, the spread of the fire was thwarted with the assistance of the dredge *Oregon*. The *Oregon* provided a steady stream of water to help contain the fire. (CHMM 963-83 m.)

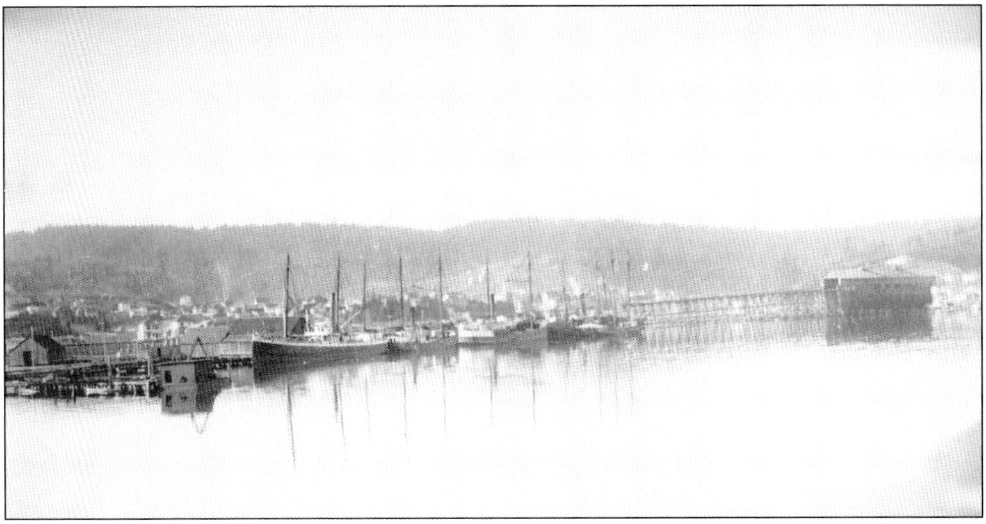

During 1918, the Marshfield waterfront was bustling with activity. Docks, piers, and wharves housed the Port of Coos Bay Dock, the Ocean Dock owned by Reynolds Development Company, the Terminal Dock owned by C.A. Smith Lumber and Manufacturing Company, and the Railroad Dock owned by Southern Pacific Railroad. The oil docks included the Standard Oil Company and the Union Oil Company. (CHMM 009-16.434.)

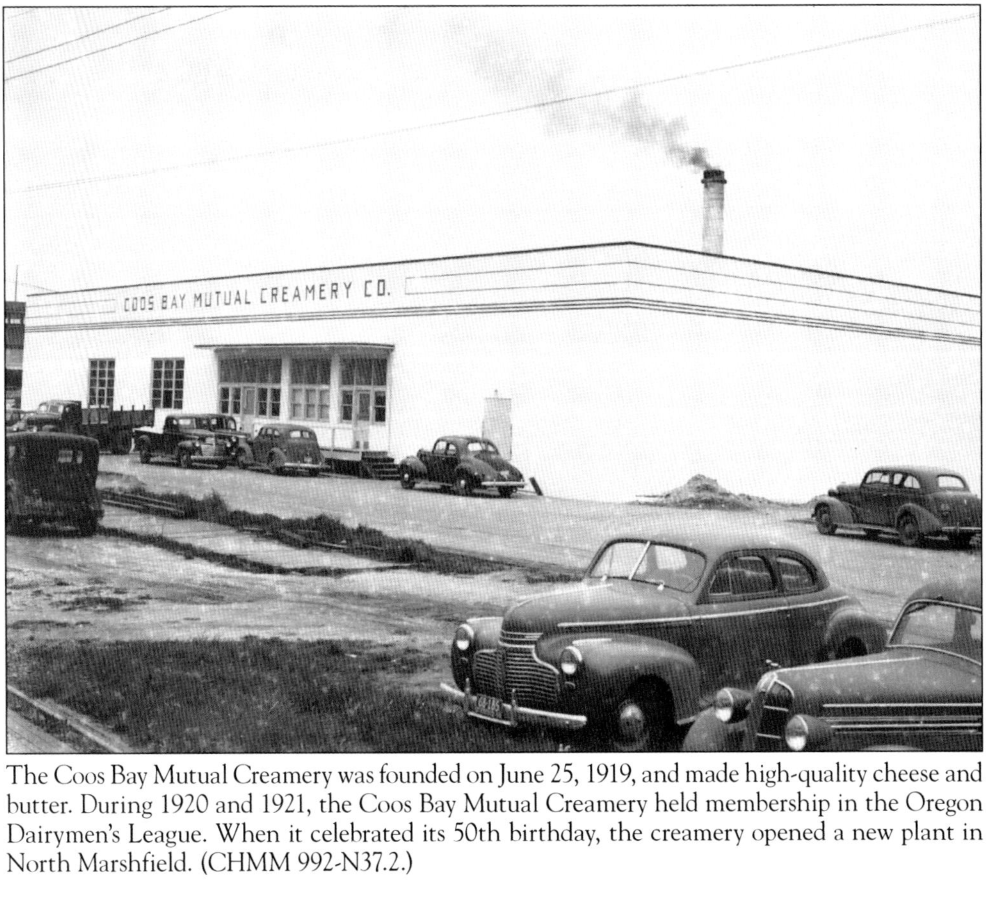

The Coos Bay Mutual Creamery was founded on June 25, 1919, and made high-quality cheese and butter. During 1920 and 1921, the Coos Bay Mutual Creamery held membership in the Oregon Dairymen's League. When it celebrated its 50th birthday, the creamery opened a new plant in North Marshfield. (CHMM 992-N37.2.)

Perhaps the shortest-lived commercial venture for Marshfield was the commercial fishing of pilchards. They were marketed to canneries under the generic name of "sardine." Searching for pilchards off Coos Bay in 1936 spurred development of the commercial fishing. However, by 1939, the Coos Bay catch had declined to an insignificant amount. (CHMM 001-10.5 B.)

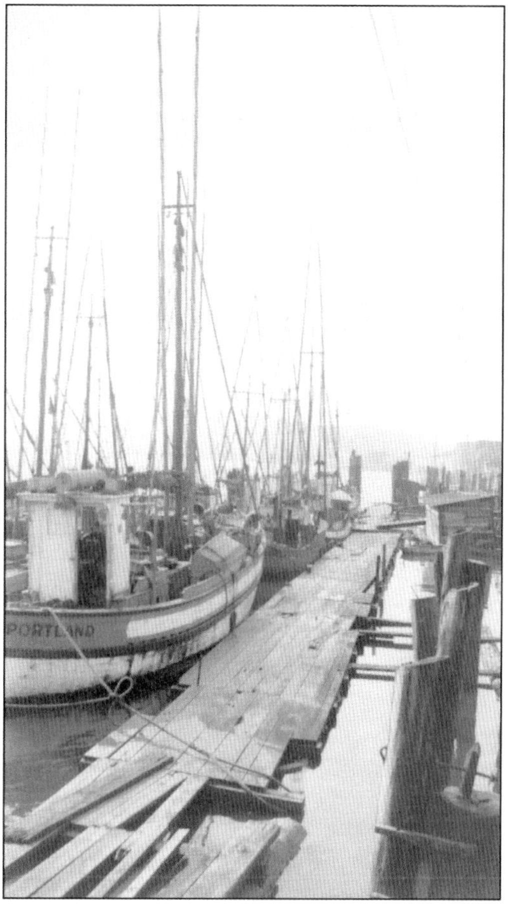

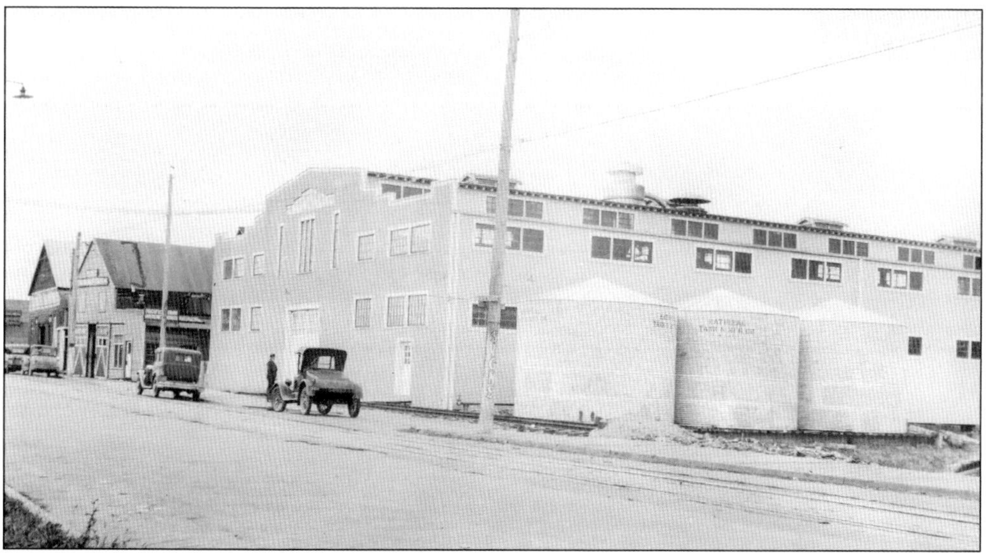

The biggest haul received was 450 tons of pilchards, and it was caught six miles off shore and brought by six purse seiners for processing at the fish plants in North Bend and Marshfield. Around 40 tons of the catch was processed at Cypress Fisheries of Marshfield. (CHMM 994-25.1.)

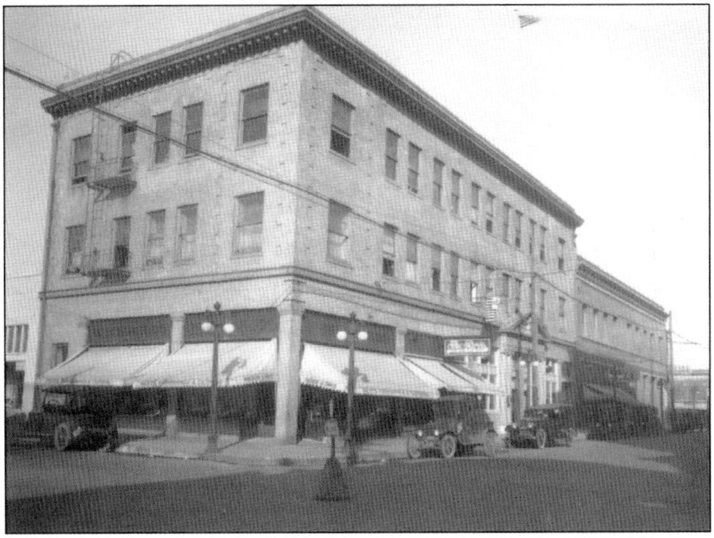

Located in the American Building, the Paris Coat and Suit Shop was another sign of sophistication in Marshfield. Owned and operated by Harry Gittelsohn, the Paris provided the finest-quality modern clothing. Gittelsohn would make an annual buying trip to New York City, where he selected items specially chosen for his favorite customers. (CHMM 992-8-0999.)

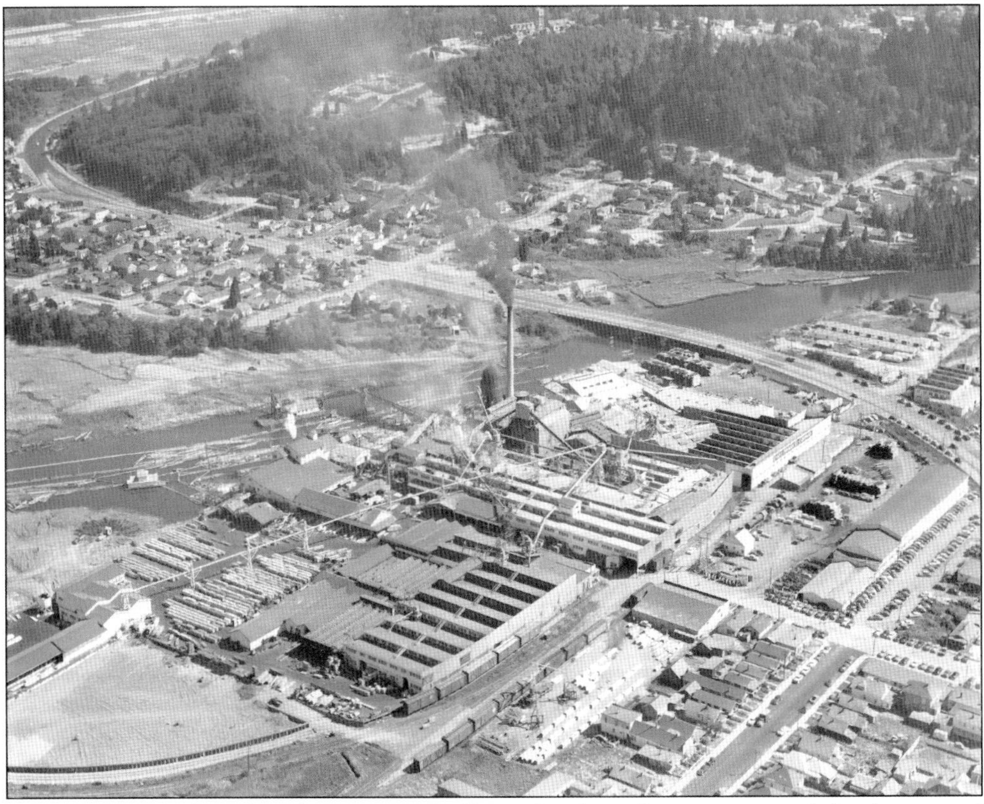

Founded in 1928 by Edward S. Evans, the Evans Products Company provided a diversity of timber-related products until March 1, 1962. During the 1930s and 1940s, the company produced two and one-half million battery separators for domestic and military markets. After World War II, molded furniture and pre-fabricated housing led the product line. Construction of plywood reigned during the post-war housing boom of the 1950s. (CHMM 987-5.24.)

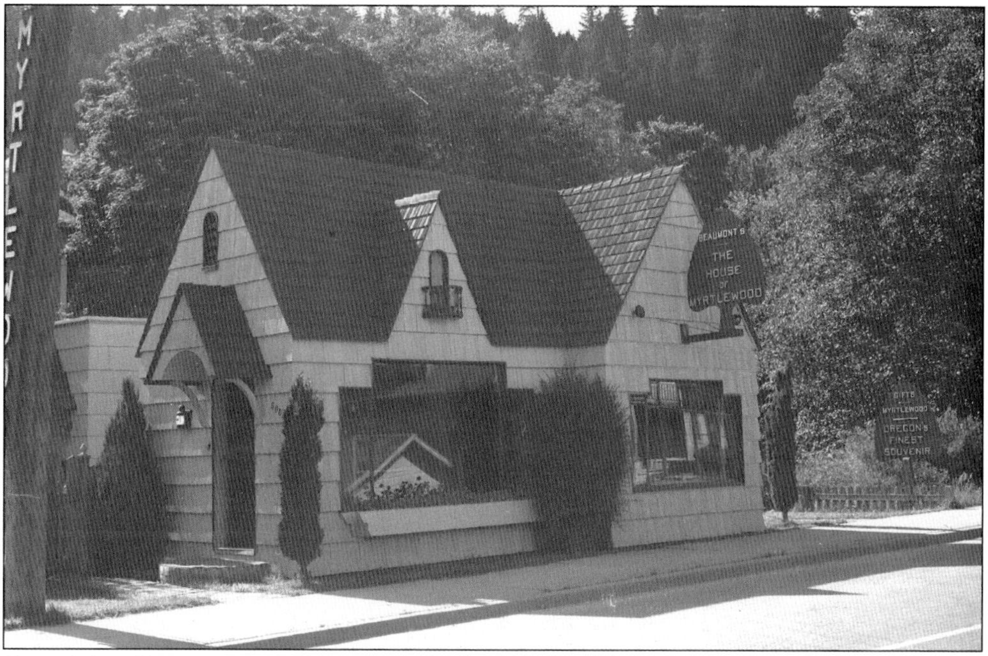

One of the oldest continuously working myrtle wood factories on the Southern Oregon coast is the House of Myrtlewood, which was established in 1929 by William Beaumont. Now known as the Oregon Connection, the House of Myrtlewood is one of the oldest businesses in Coos Bay. In December 2005, the Oregon Connection was sold to the nonprofit organization Star of Hope. (CHMM 995-1.20387.)

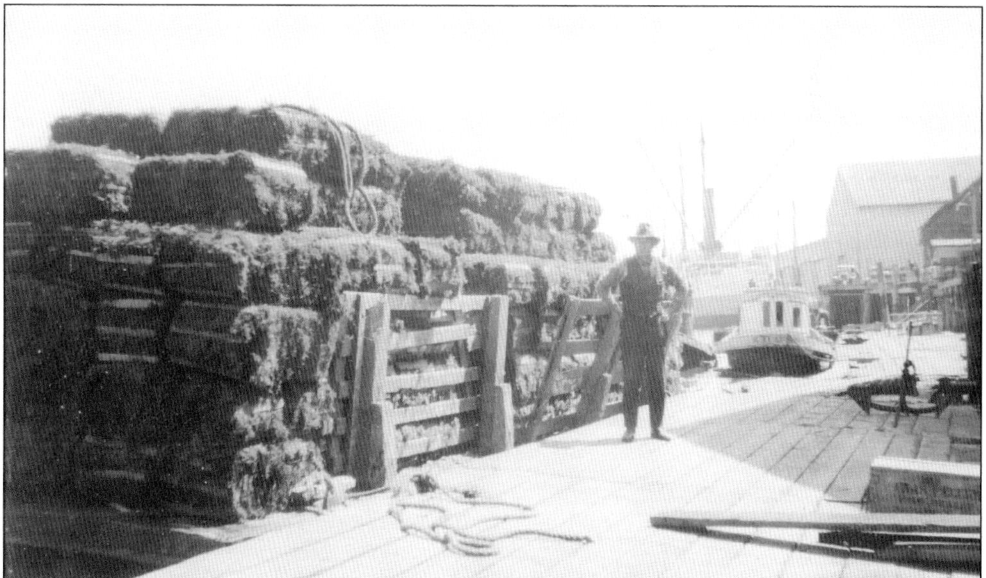

During World War I, one of the most interesting medical discoveries was the value of bog-moss (sphagnum) as a dressing. One of the most unusual business ventures in Marshfield was the exportation of sphagnum moss. Sam Logsdon harvested and baled the moss, which was used for surgical dressings. (CHMM 995-17.11 a.)

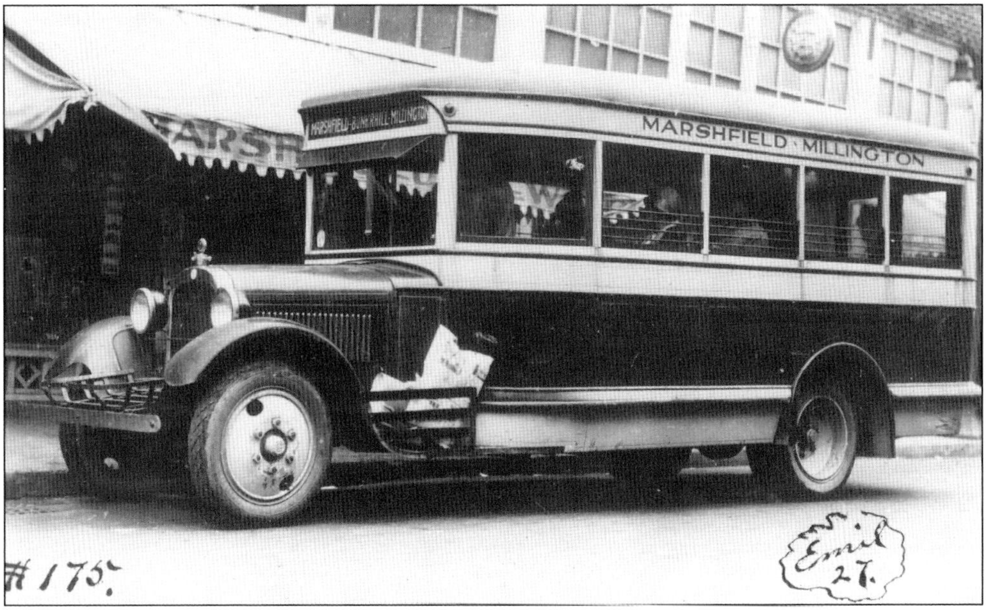

As automobiles became more prevalent, the mode of transportation moved away from the waterways of the bay. Auto stages soon developed, providing transportation to all the points once catered to by the vessels of the bay. The Marshfield, Bunker Hill & Millington Auto Stage served Marshfield and the surrounding area. (CHMM 963-14 d.)

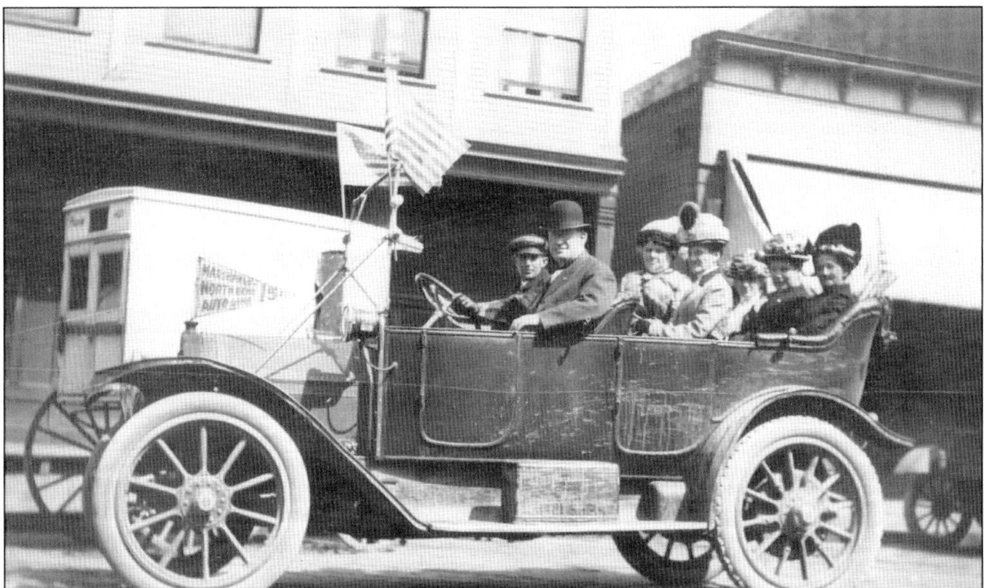

The first auto lines serving Marshfield occurred around 1913. The first two lines established were the Vern Gorst and Charles King Marshfield–North Bend Auto Line, which was headquartered in North Bend and served Marshfield, and Jerry Kinney's Twin City Auto Line, headquartered in Marshfield. (CHMM 995-D231.)

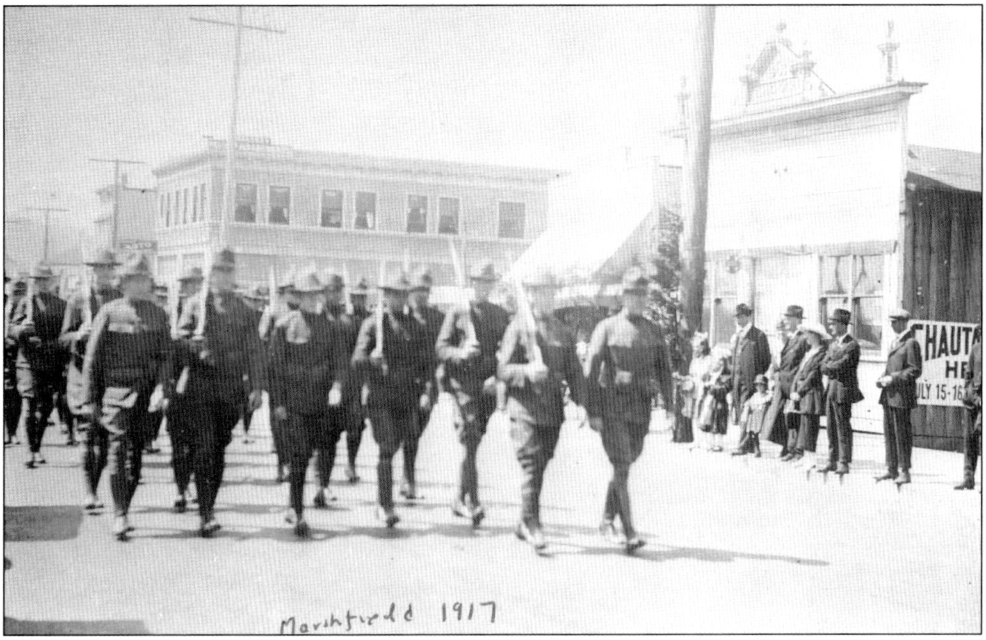

On August 12, 1917, the 11th Company of the Coast Artillery Corps of the Oregon National Guard was organized at Marshfield. Seventy-three men enlisted in the company. The following three officers were in charge of the unit: Capt. F.K. Gettins, 1st Lt. F.W. Smith, and 2nd Lt. J.H. Mills. The company marches on Front Street above. (CHMM 992-8-1158.)

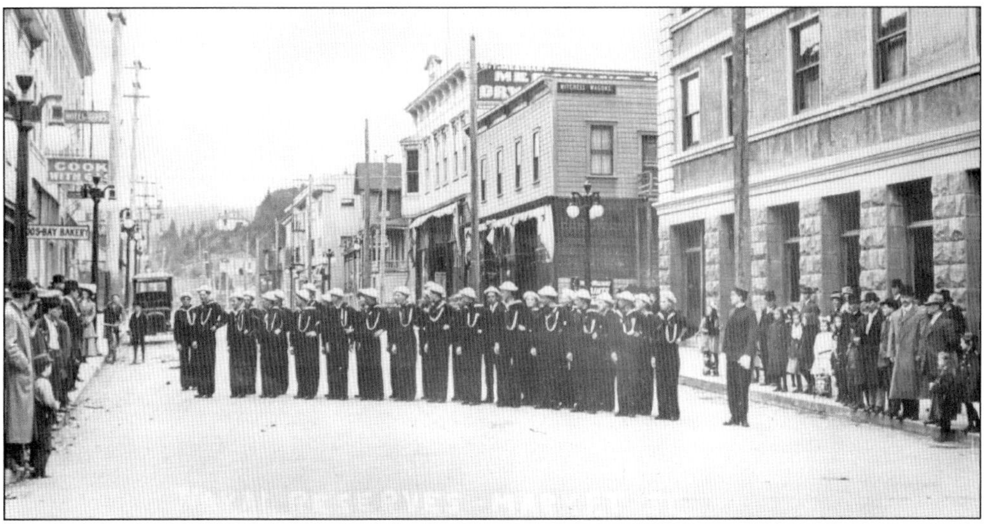

Dedication to military service was not limited to the National Guard. Men from Marshfield also enlisted with the 3rd Division of the Naval Militia of Oregon. In 1912, Lt. Comdr. Edwin E. Strawn was in command of the Marshfield unit. Pictured is the unit some time between 1917 and 1919. (CHMM 963-831.)

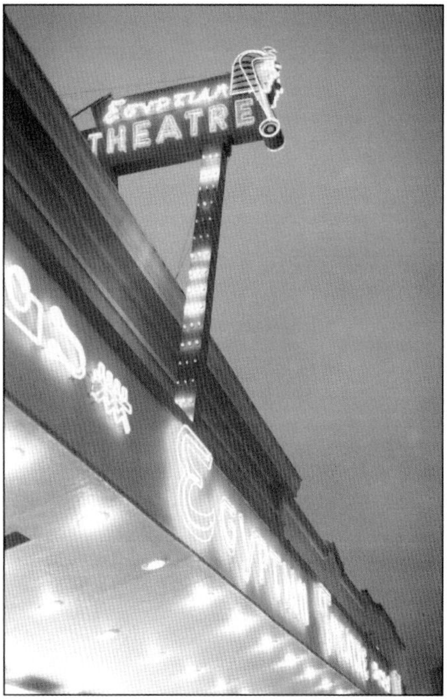

Originally called the Motor Inn Auto Garage, this building was constructed by Harry C. Noble in 1922. The building was remodeled into the Egyptian Theatre in 1925 by the Coos Bay Amusement Company. Portland architect Lee Arden Thomas was retained to create a 1,240-seat silent movie and vaudeville house designed with a pharaonic motif. The centerpiece of the new theater was a state-of-the-art Wurlitzer Theater Organ. The Egyptian Theater opened on November 19, 1925. (Benjamin Brayfield.)

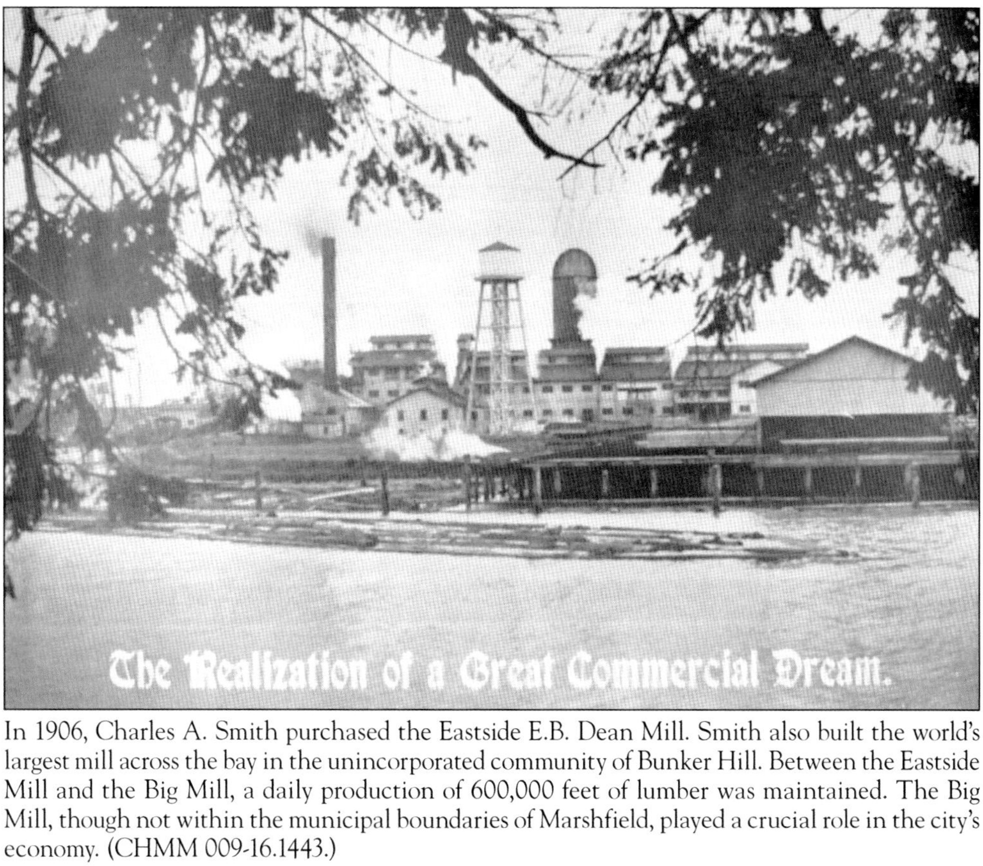

In 1906, Charles A. Smith purchased the Eastside E.B. Dean Mill. Smith also built the world's largest mill across the bay in the unincorporated community of Bunker Hill. Between the Eastside Mill and the Big Mill, a daily production of 600,000 feet of lumber was maintained. The Big Mill, though not within the municipal boundaries of Marshfield, played a crucial role in the city's economy. (CHMM 009-16.1443.)

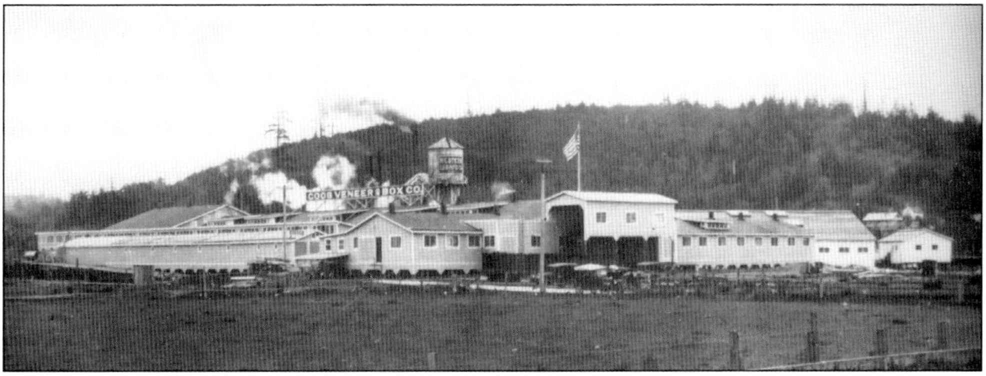

Organized on March 15, 1920, by Benjamin Ostlind, the Coos Veneer and Box Company was owned by local shareholders. By 1923, there were 275 employees, 160 of whom were women. The plant doubled its production in 1922 using 30,000 feet of cedar logs to create enough battery separators for 10,000 automobiles. In 1948, the plant was remodeled for plywood production. (CHMM 007-25.268.)

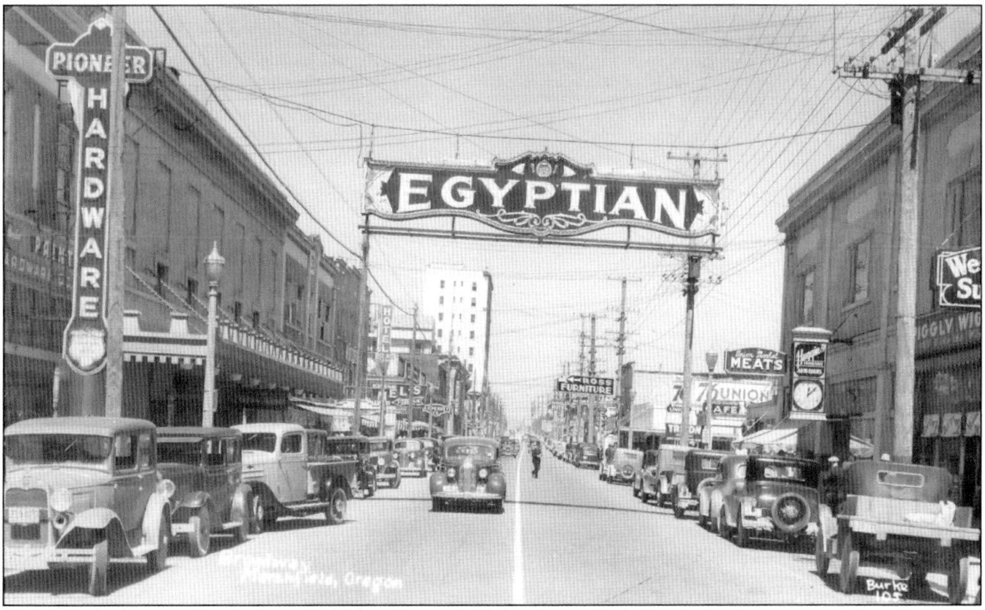

By the 1920s, downtown Marshfield took on a whole new look. Broadway became the primary street of the business district. Wood streets gave way to asphalt surfacing, thus providing a safer traveling environment for the automobiles. An era of land travel emerged, competing with the waterfront activities. (CHMM 997-D18.)

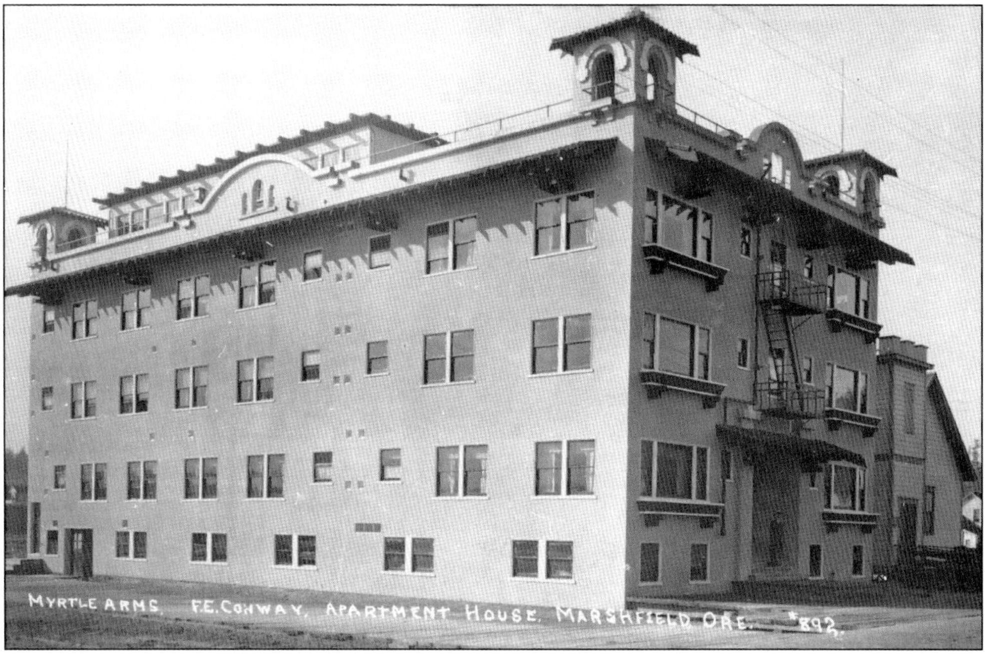

The Myrtle Arms Apartments building has one of the more unique architectural styles of the city. Combining Mission and Pueblo styles in its architecture, it was one of the first large apartment buildings in the city. In a naming contest, some 500 contestants submitted names from as far away as Paris, France. North Bend's F.H. Brigham's submission was selected. (CHMM N797.)

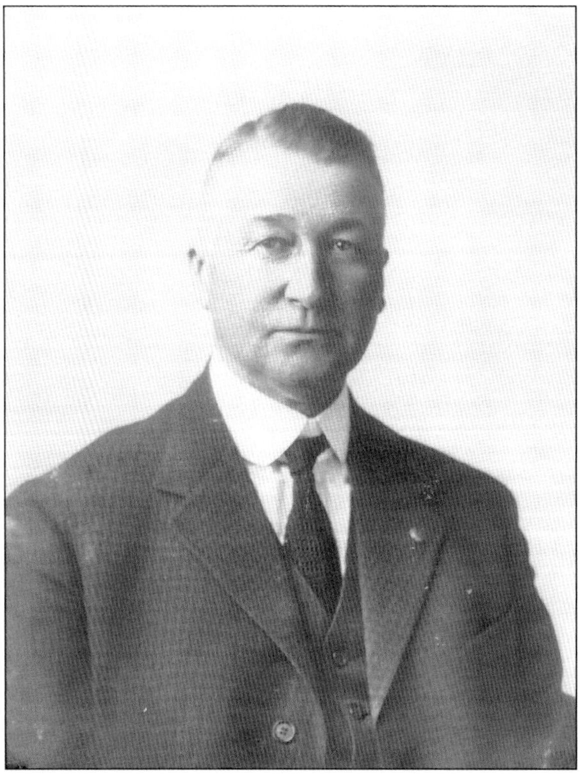

On January 4, 1928, the parks commission was established, and Dr. Everett Mingus served as the first president. After a four-year fundraising campaign at the Paul Bunyan Birthday celebrations, a park was created by 1934 and was known as Paul Bunyan Park. In 1937, Dr. Mingus died. Honoring the man who spearheaded all development, the park was renamed Mingus Park in 1940. (CHMM 978-1.39.)

Four

The Eastside Years

Like Coos Bay, Eastside was a blending of communities. The first settlement of present-day Eastside occurred in 1868 or 1869. The land was sought due to its low price and lack of building regulations. In 1874, Donald McKay, assisted by others, platted the new town of East Marshfield. By September 1891, the US Postal Service established a post office there.

The area was a logical choice, since the town was situated on the east side of the bay across from Marshfield. Eastside originally consisted of three different plats: Bay City, located in the southwestern portion of town; East Marshfield; and Eastside, which was located east of East Marshfield. Additionally, there were two well-known areas: Timmerman's Point and Aaronville. Timmerman's Point became an ending point of the Coos Bay Wagon Road when the road was extended from Sumner to Eastside. Prior to the arrival of the road, the area was only accessible by water. Timmerman's Point was also the location of the ferry dock. Aaronville, associated with the Lobree Mill, was located in Bay City and was named after Lobree's son Aaron.

On November 25, 1907, there was a meeting at the schoolhouse to discuss and draw up a petition for the incorporation of Eastside, East Marshfield, and Bay City. The City of Eastside was incorporated on February 8, 1908, and the city officers were sworn in on March 31, 1908, with Charles E. Jordan serving as the first mayor. The new City of Eastside had a population of 252 and covered an area of 900 acres. City hall was not built until 1912.

In October 1914, there was a vote to annex Cooston with Eastside. Even though approved, Cooston remained a part of Eastside for only two years. On May 1, 1917, a special election was held that once again separated the two communities.

In 1956, a new city hall, which included the fire and police departments, was built. After the merger with Coos Bay, city hall became a fire station.

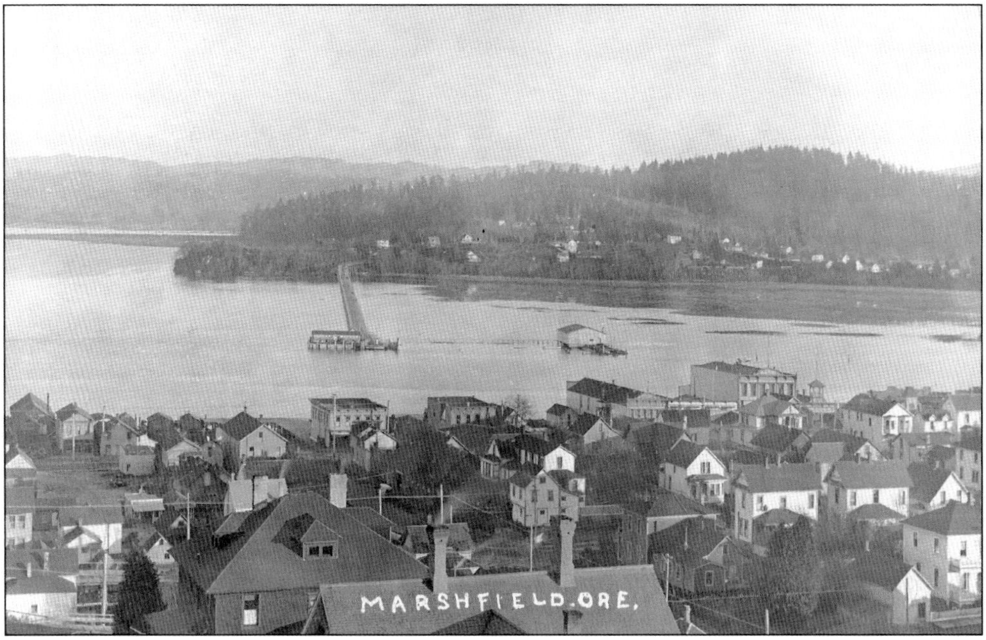

Early on there were only two entrances into Eastside. First was the old wagon road running from Sumner and ending at Timmerman's Point at the base of the city. From the point, the second mode of transportation was available: a ferry to Marshfield. The ferry ran every hour on the half-hour, with the last ferry of the day departing at 6:30 p.m. (CHMM 970-69 b.)

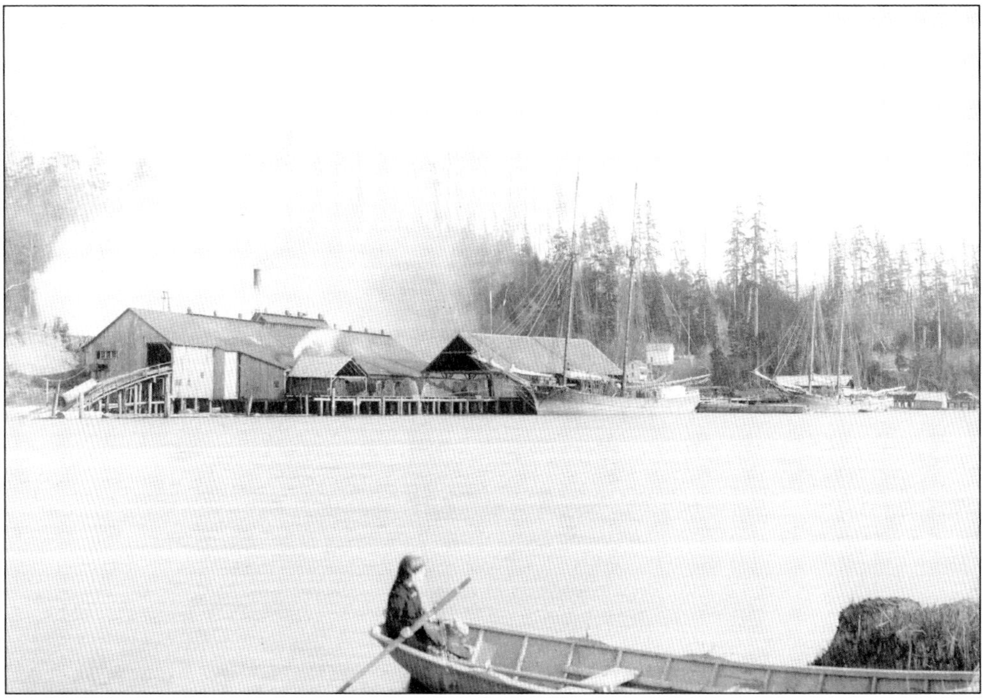

It is not known when A. Lobree built his mill at Bay City. In 1880, the mill produced about 15,000 feet of lumber per day. The site became known as Aaronville, named after Lobree's son Aaron. In 1885, the mill was sold to the E.B. Dean Company. (CHMM 961-139.)

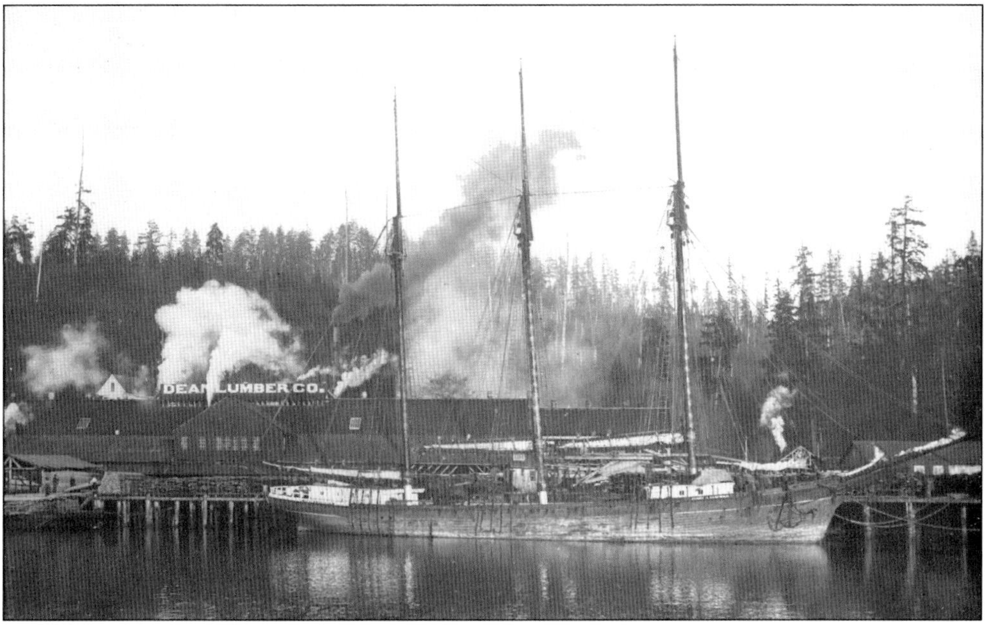

In 1885, the E.B. Dean Mill moved to East Marshfield after purchasing the Lobree Mill. At the time, it was the largest sawmill in Oregon. As it succeeded, the company expanded to include a steam-powered facility, which initially produced a daily output of 50,000 board feet. The Dean Company included a general store. (CHMM 992-8-1233.)

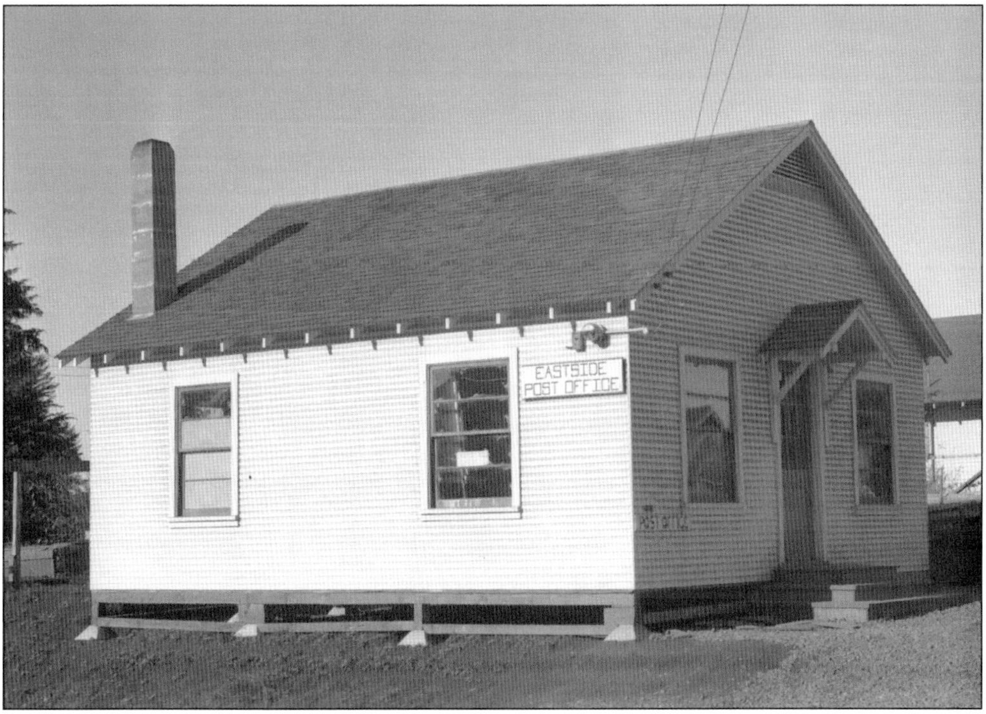

The first Eastside post office was established in September 1891 as East Marshfield. On February 8, 1908, the City of Eastside was incorporated, and the post office name was subsequently changed to Eastside. (CHMM 986-N601.)

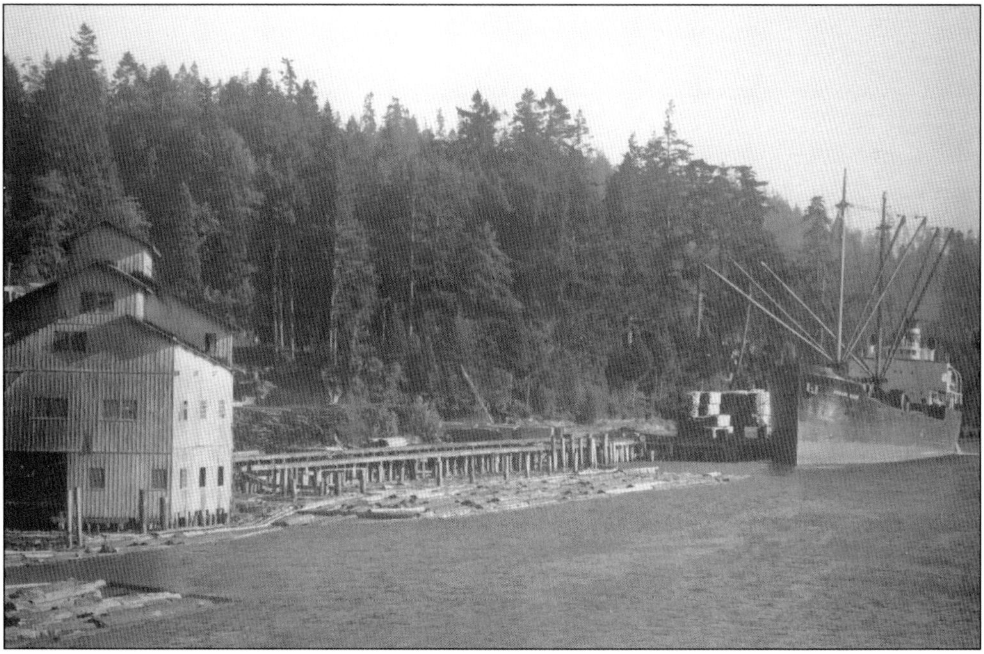

The Bay City Sawmill was a small mill owned by Bill McKenna. The mill would often sell whole logs or cant logs (logs that were roughly slabbed into huge beams) to Japan. In the spring of 1949, the McKenna plant operated as a division of the Coos Head Timber Company. (CHMM 992-8-3082.)

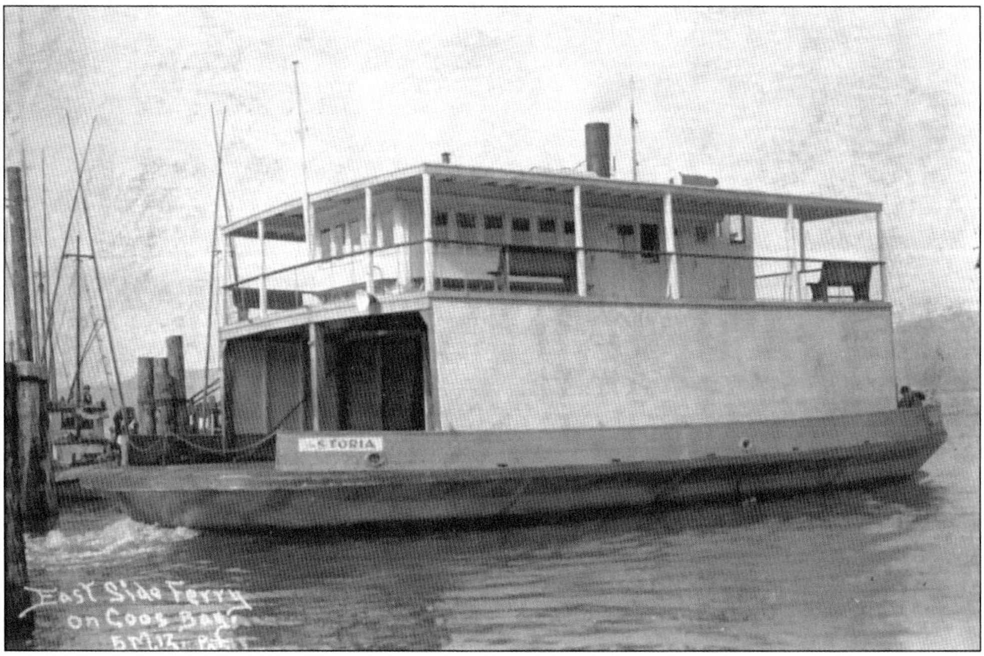

The *Astoria* was the last vessel to serve as the Marshfield-Eastside ferry. The privately owned ferry was in operation until 1932. After the opening of the Isthmus Bridge, which connected the east side with the west side of the bay by land, the need for ferry service was eliminated. (CHMM 009-8-2454.)

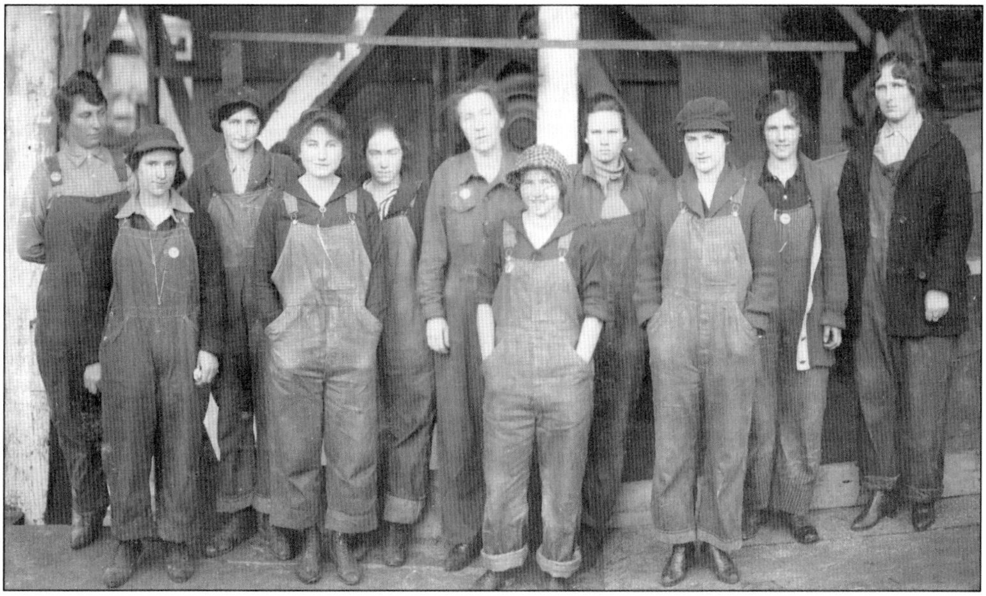

The workforce in the lumber business was not limited to men. Women played an important role at the local mills. In 1915, these women were the first veneer workers at the Eastside Mill. (CHMM 007-11.4690.)

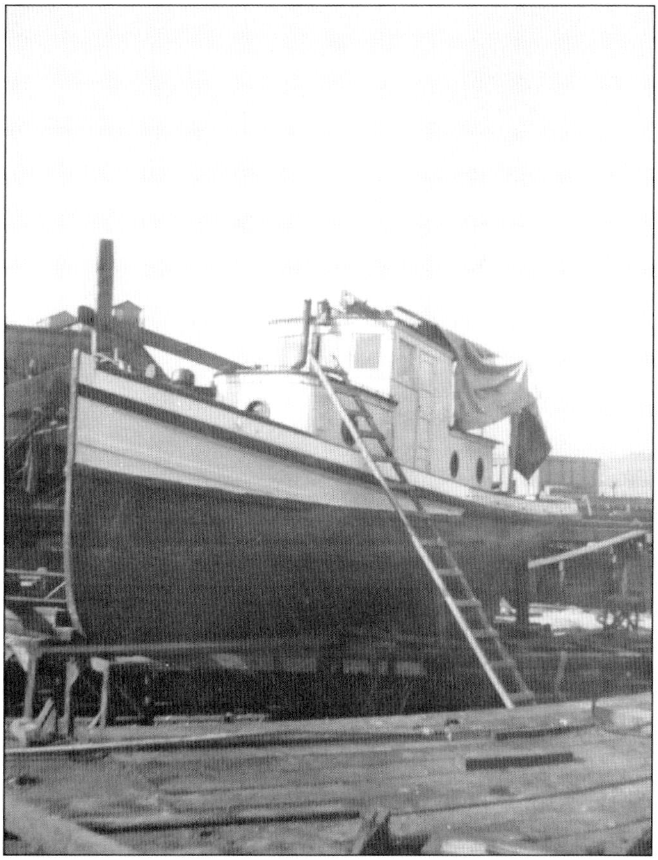

In 1921, the tug *Coos King* transported the film crew up and down the inlet for the making of the silent movie *Kindred of the Dust*. Directed by Raoul Walsh, the film starred his wife, Miriam Cooper. The movie was released for viewing on February 27, 1922. (CHMM 009-16.9232.)

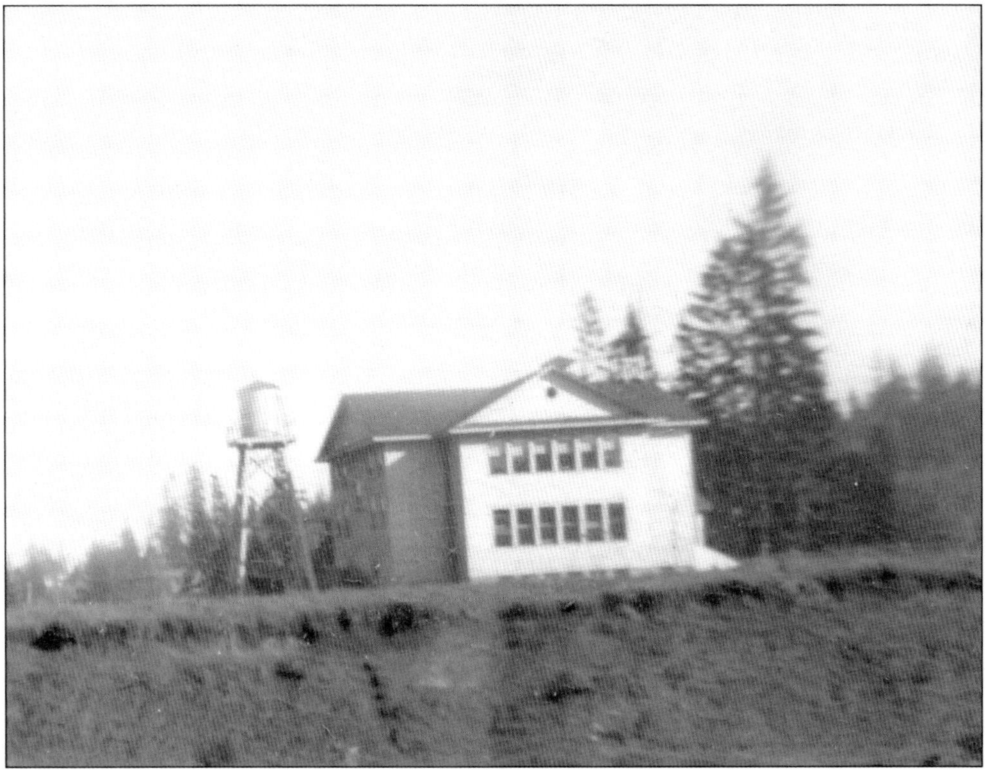

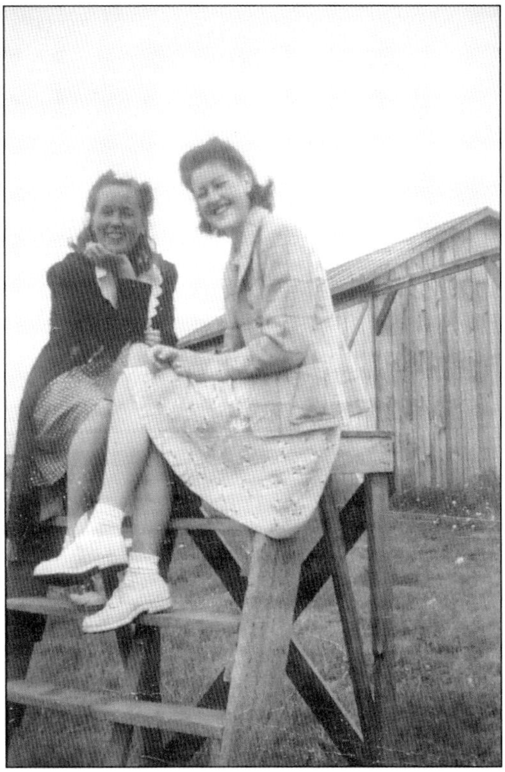

Built in the 1920s, the Eastside Grammar School was the educational and social hub for local children. The building was two stories with one room on each floor. Two classes were held in each room. The school also served as the city hall and was used by the fire department. The school remained in operation until the 1950s, when it was burned down by the fire department. (Besse Guthrie.)

Bernice Nelson and Besse Guthrie (right) sit before the Eastside Airport hangar. The Eastside Airport was built in the early 1940s and was in strong competition with North Bend to serve as a military site. Losing the battle with North Bend, the airport remained small and was used for cargo transport. Stunt pilots would use the strip to provide entertainment to the locals. (Besse Guthrie.)

Located behind Betty and Barbara Ostberg is the Eastside Dance Hall. Operated from the 1930s to the early 1940s, the dance hall provided the social entertainment on Saturday nights. Described as wild and woolly, the dance hall was the place to be. (Besse Guthrie.)

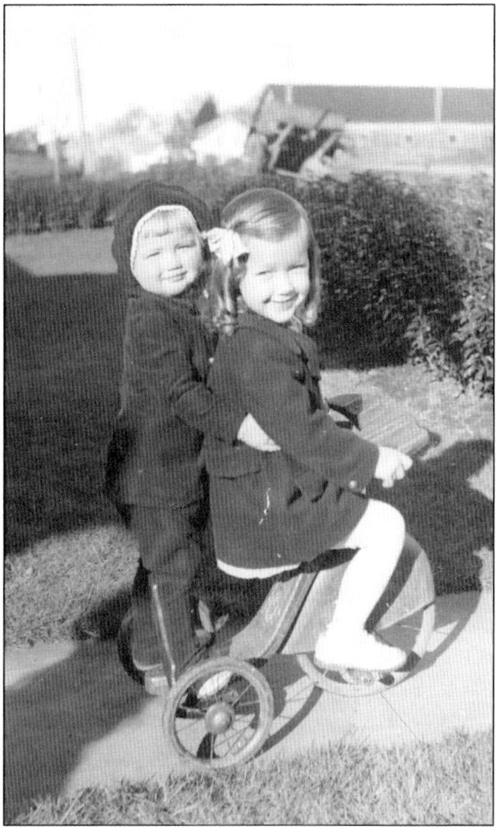

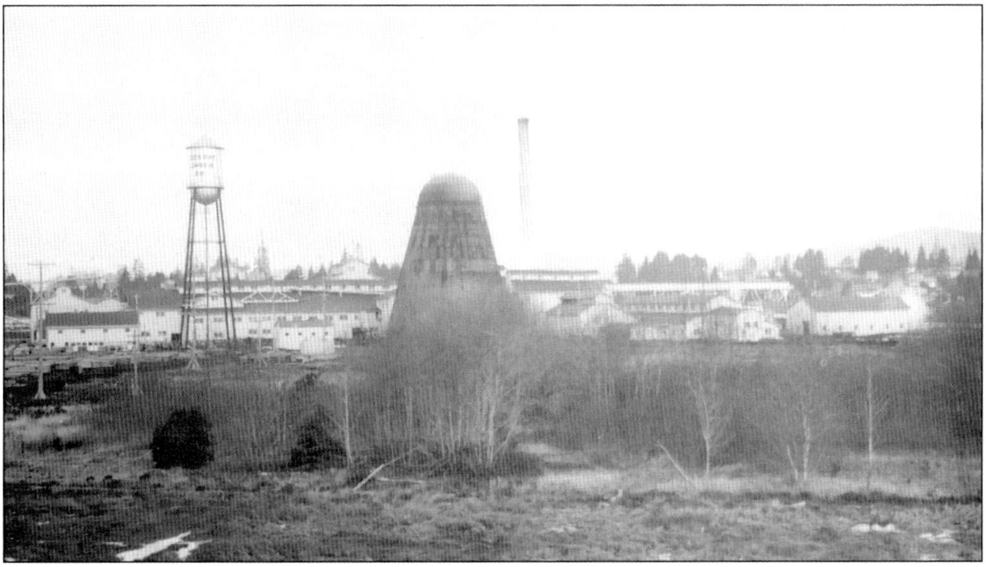

The Coos Bay Lumber Company plant at Bay Point was damaged in a fire the morning of May 26, 1920. Backfire from a truck engine used in the yards is supposed to have ignited a pile of sawdust, and this smoldered until it set fire to nearby lumber piles. Three million feet of lumber, 25 flat cars, an electric tramway, and a $50,000 loading derrick were destroyed by the flames. (CHMM 009-16.1469.)

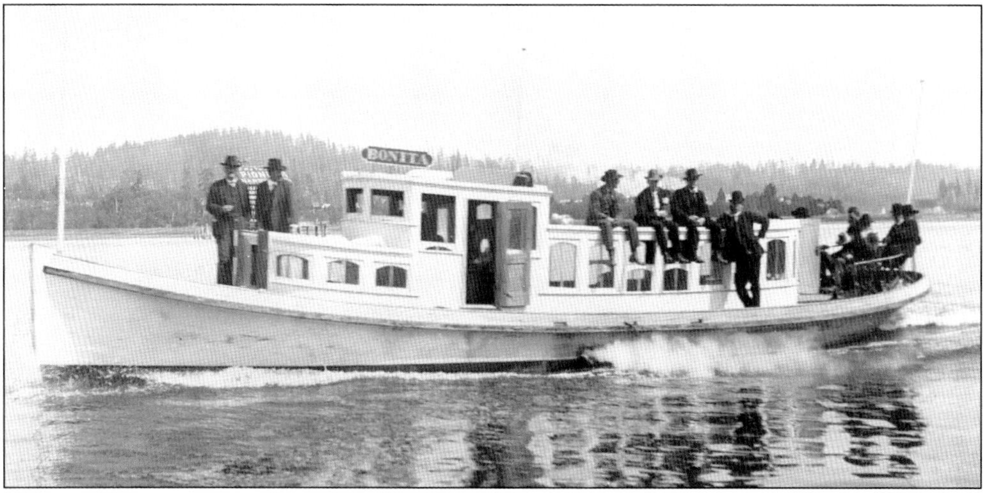

The last week in July 1907, a 25-mile motorboat race was held on the bay from Marshfield to Charleston and back. The two competitors were *Bonita* and *Express*, between which there had been great a rivalry. About 75 percent of the local populace turned out to cheer their respective favorites. With a comfortable lead, the *Bonita* won the race. (CHMM 992-8-2395.)

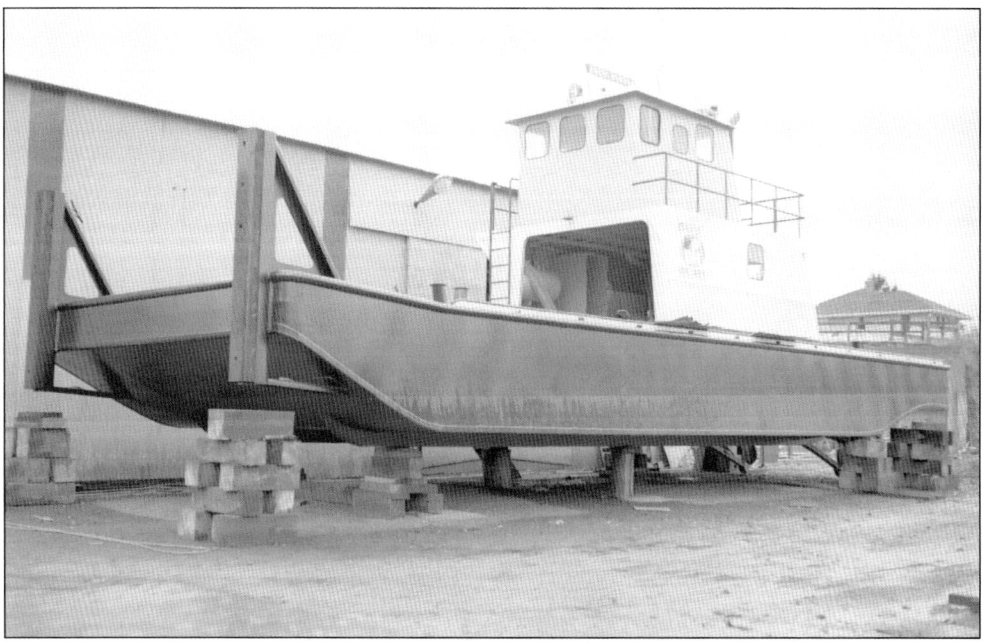

In 1955, Fred Nelson received a patent for a small, highly maneuverable steel vessel named a "Log Bronc" he designed for moving and sorting logs in log booms and rafts. Nelson built a shop at the foot of Whitty Street. The first Log Bronc built was the *Robert M. Ingram*. The Log Bronc is the only vessel of its type built in the United States. (CHMM 009-16.1114.)

Five

SHIPBUILDING

Shipbuilding was an important component of Coos Bay commerce. The first to partake of the industry in modern-day Coos Bay was Henry Heaton Luse in Empire City. Closely tied to sawmills, Luse built his shipyard in 1866. However, it was two years before he completed construction of his first vessel, the steamer *Alpha*. Seven more vessels would be built at the Luse shipyard.

The first vessel reported to be built in Marshfield was the steam-powered tug *Escort*, which was built at the shipyard of John Pershbaker. Pershbaker operated his shipyard until 1873, at which time he sold it to the firm of Dean, Wilcox & Merchant. By 1884, it was under operation as E.B. Dean and Company. E.B. Dean and Company operated its shipyard in Marshfield until 1885, after which it moved to East Marshfield. In 1882, the shipyard employed 25 men, and the adjoining sawmill cut 1 million feet of lumber per month.

By 1878, Coos Bay (Empire, Marshfield, and North Bend) had established a reputation for the principal shipyards in Oregon. About 40 vessels of all classes were constructed on the bay by that date. The vessels built on the bay had a reputation for quality due to the strength, durability, and buoyancy of the local timber. The quantity of timber on the bay was practically inexhaustible and easily accessible, and it was considered to be of a superior character for shipbuilding. The vessels constructed here were rated "A-1." It was also established that the cost of shipbuilding was a small percent less than at eastern shipyards for vessels of the same class and capacity.

By 1900, thirty-seven vessels were built in Marshfield alone. As the population increased, so did the demand for vessels on the bay. A transition from steam and sailing vessels to gasoline launches emerged to meet the demands of the growing commerce on the bay. Gasoline launches were smaller and cost-efficient, making them the ideal mode of transportation. By 1930, seventy-four more vessels were built in Marshfield.

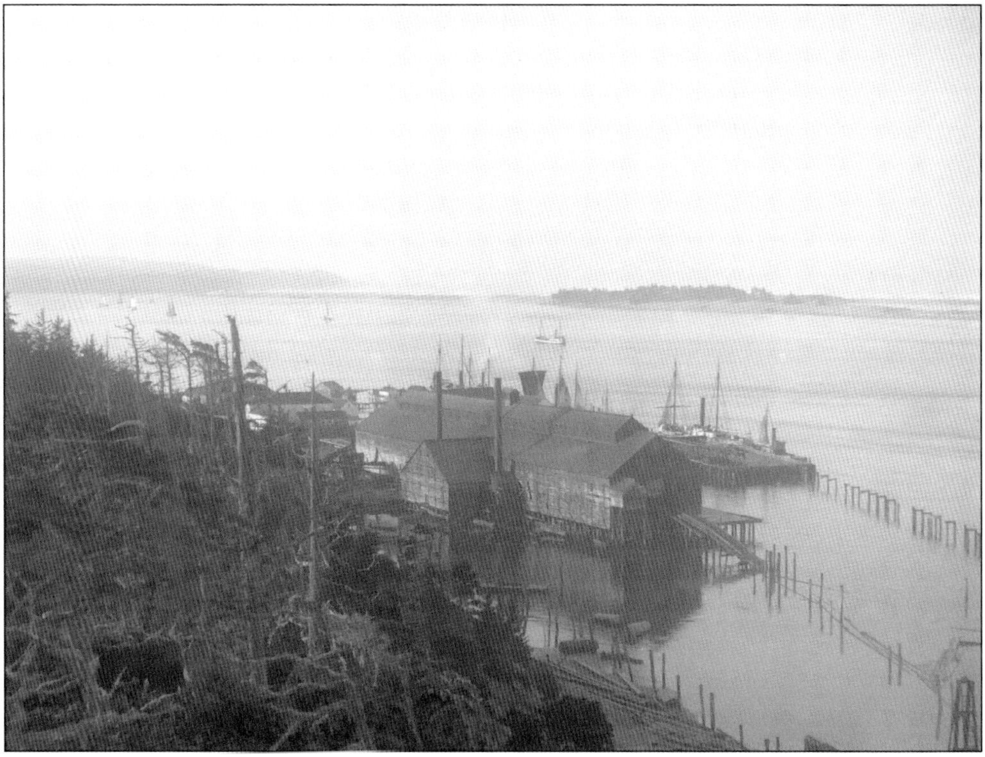

Pennsylvania-born Henry Heaton Luse was the first to build a sawmill in Empire City in 1854. Luse expanded his enterprises, building a shipyard 10 years later and also building a general store. In November 1883, Luse sold his holdings to the Southern Oregon Improvement Company. The Southern Oregon Improvement Company remained in operation until 1893. (CHMM 992-8-0760.)

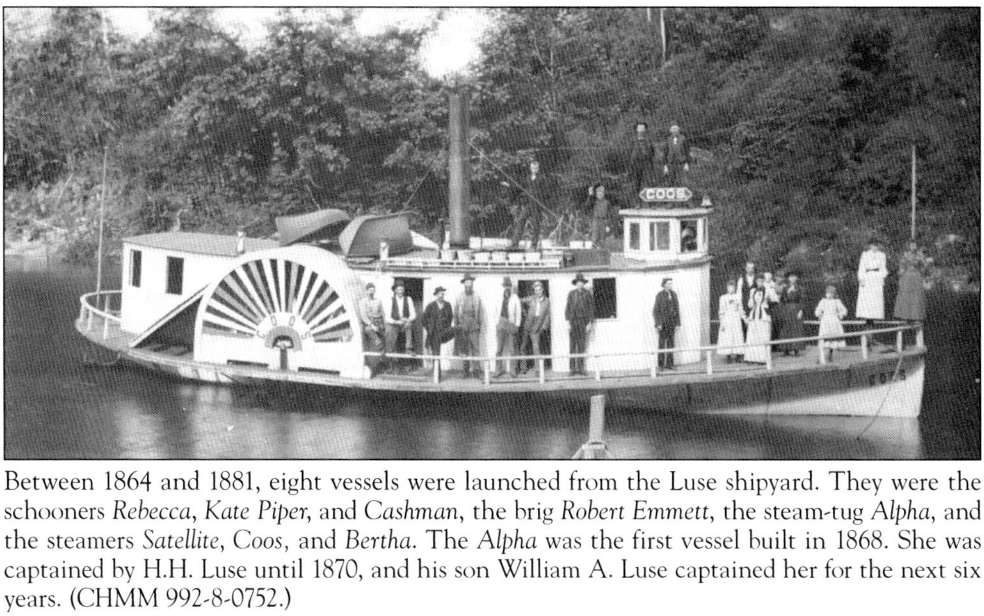

Between 1864 and 1881, eight vessels were launched from the Luse shipyard. They were the schooners *Rebecca*, *Kate Piper*, and *Cashman*, the brig *Robert Emmett*, the steam-tug *Alpha*, and the steamers *Satellite*, *Coos*, and *Bertha*. The *Alpha* was the first vessel built in 1868. She was captained by H.H. Luse until 1870, and his son William A. Luse captained her for the next six years. (CHMM 992-8-0752.)

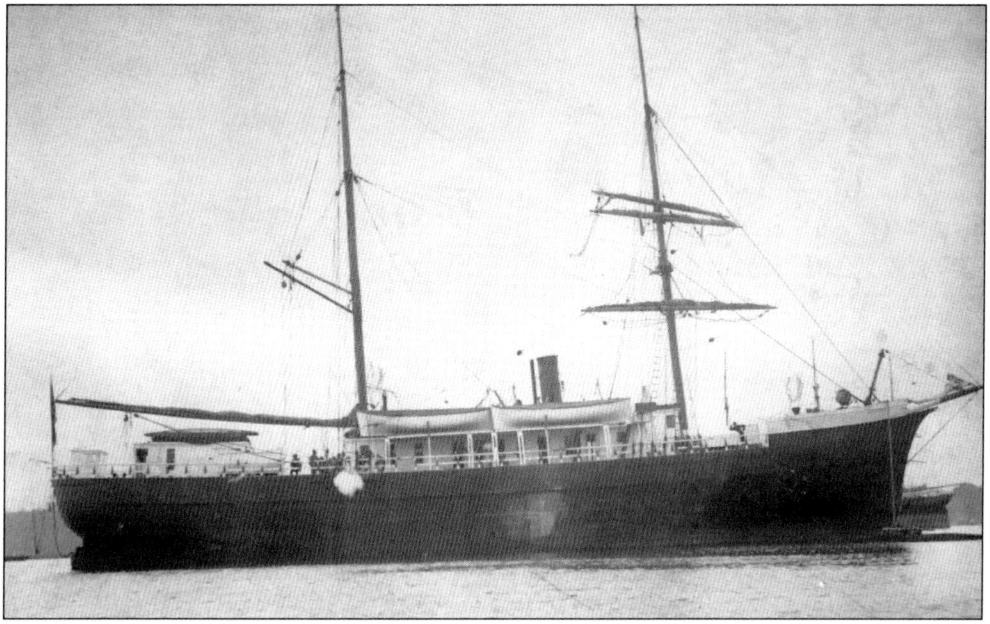

R.C. Cordes constructed the steamer *Bertha* at the H.H. Luse shipyard at Empire City and operated her for many years. The vessels built at Empire City were smaller than the North Bend vessels, having been designed for use on the bay. (CHMM 009-16.4455.)

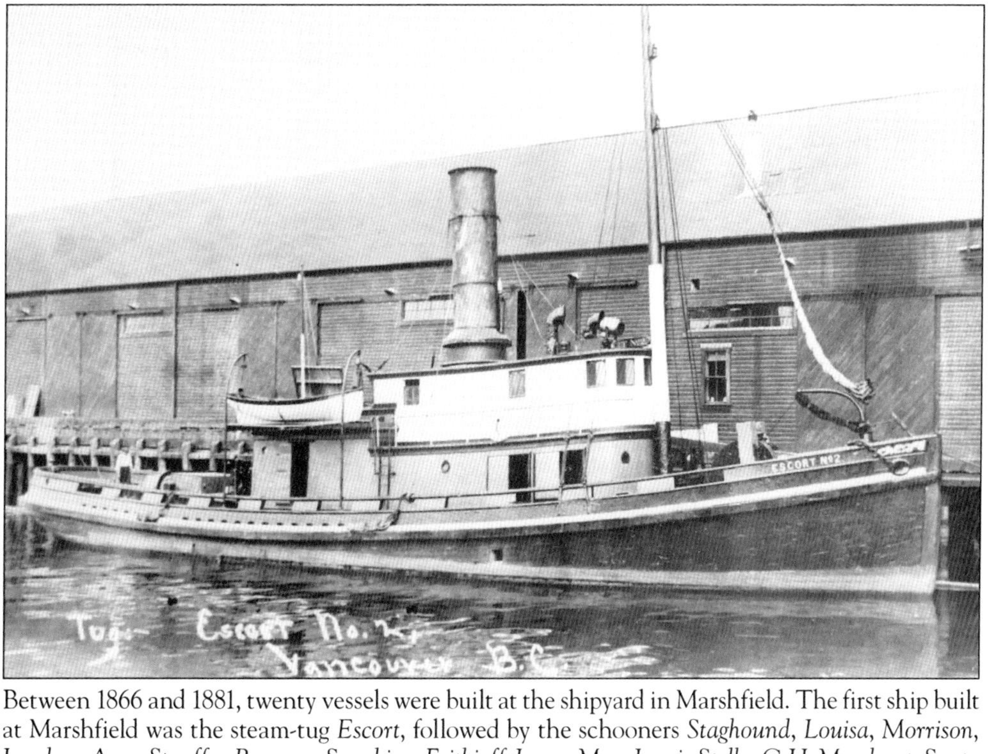

Between 1866 and 1881, twenty vessels were built at the shipyard in Marshfield. The first ship built at Marshfield was the steam-tug *Escort*, followed by the schooners *Staghound*, *Louisa*, *Morrison*, *Ivanhoe*, *Anne Stauffer*, *Panama*, *Sunshine*, *Frithioff*, *Laura May*, *Jennie Stella*, *C.H. Merchant*, *Santa Rosas*, *George C. Perkins*, and *J.G. North Dakota*, the barkentine *Amelia*, the steamers *Messenger* and *Wasp*, and the tug *Escort No. 2*. The name of the 20th is unknown. (CHMM 009-16.194.)

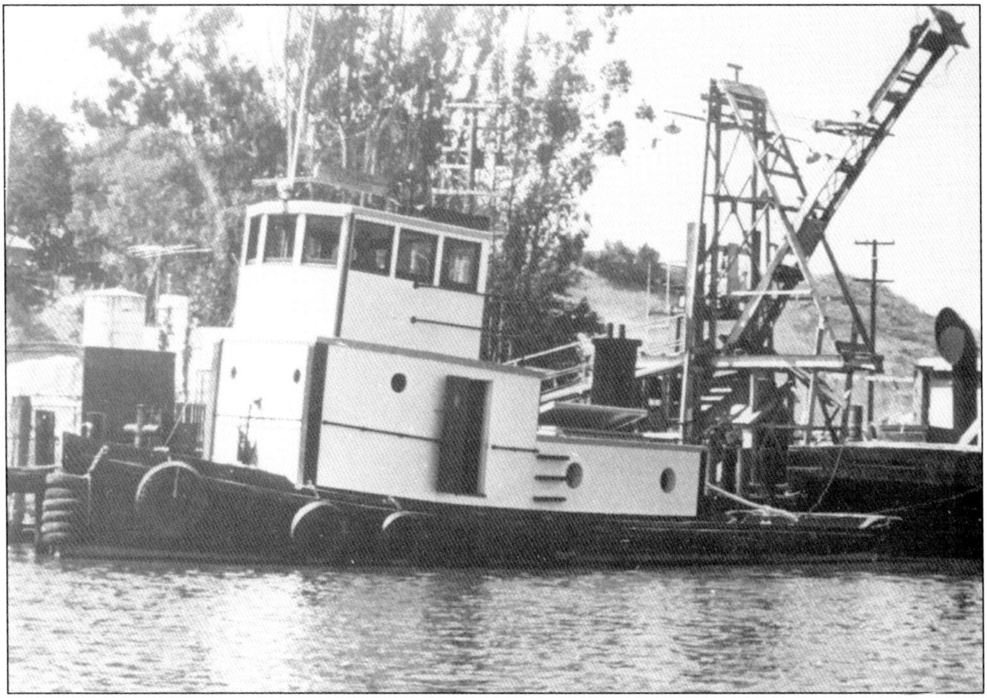

The *Escort*, completed at Marshfield in 1869, was reportedly the first vessel built in Marshfield. She was built by John H. Howlett and Capt. James Magee from a model by John Pershbaker, who was one of her owners. The *Escort* went to San Francisco under sail, was supplied with engines there by John Lockhead, and made her trial trip on February 16, 1870. (CHMM 009-16.1323.)

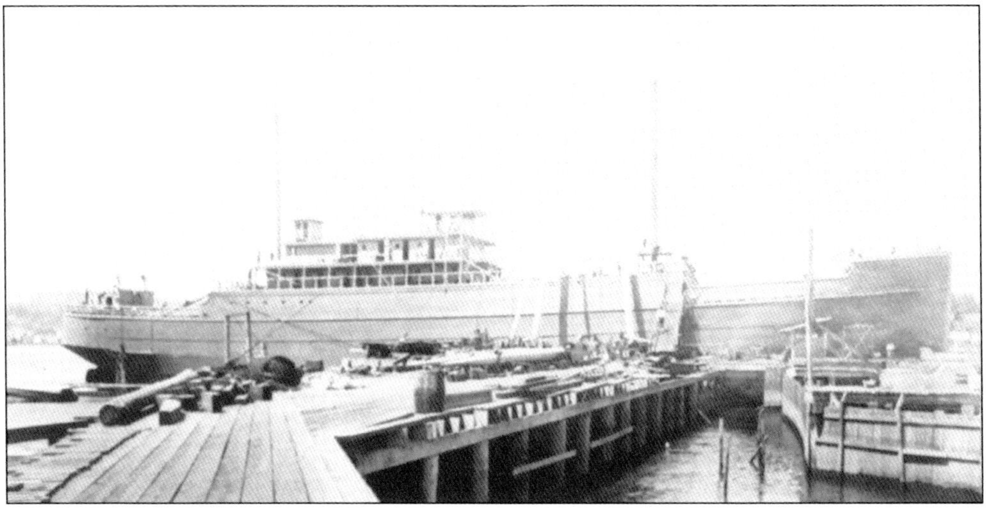

Coos Bay Shipbuilding Company was established in May 1917. The head office and plant were located in Marshfield. The area of plant encompassed 12.5 acres. The number of building slips totaled four. The number of employees under normal working conditions totaled 300. The *Marshfield* was fitted out on March 24, 1918. (CHMM 009-16.1772.)

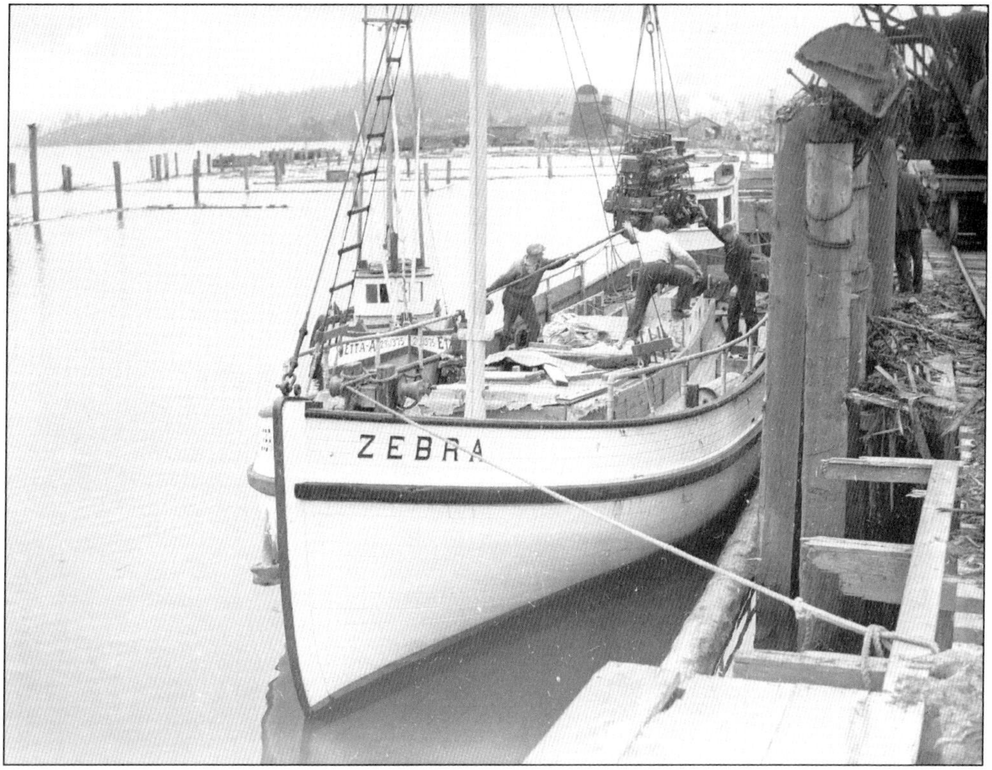

The last shipbuilder in Empire was John Swing. Considered an eccentric, Swing began shipbuilding in 1903 with the gas launch *Fish* and continued until 1948 with the completion of the *Koos No. 4*. The *Zebra* was built in 1921 to run the bar at Gold Beach. (CHMM 009-16.748.)

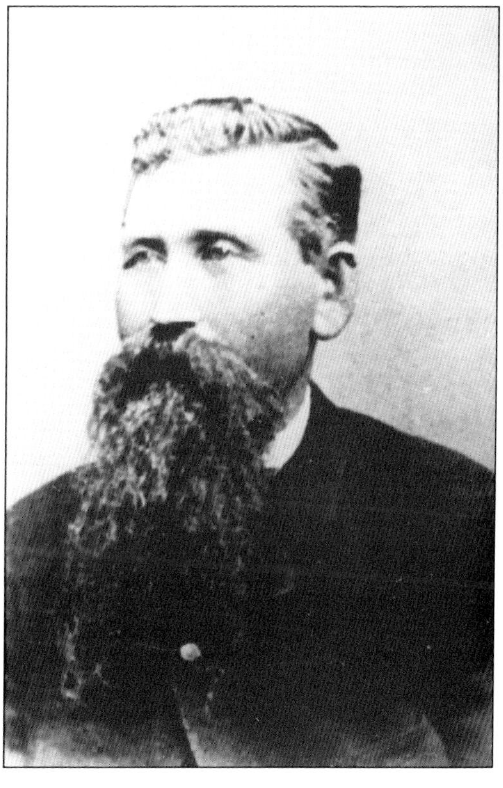

Hans R. Reed, born in Norway in 1840, came to California in 1859. After his arrival, he was employed as a draftsman in North's Ship Yard in San Francisco. He subsequently went to Washington and, in partnership with his brother, built a number of vessels at Port Madison. In 1869, he moved to Marshfield, where he built a number of vessels over the next 13 years. (CHMM 009-16.195.)

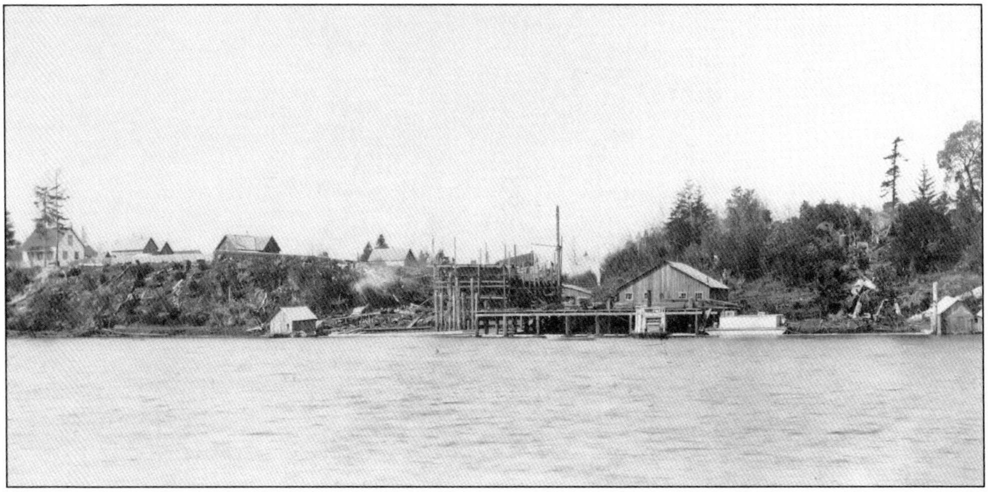

Reed left for Washington State, but he returned to Marshfield in 1874 and established his own shipyard. From 1872 to 1886, Reed built 14 vessels at Marshfield. There Reed built the steamers *Coos Bay* and *Antelope*, the schooners *Panonia, Laura May, Jennie Stella*, *C.H. Merchant*, *Glen*, *John G. North*, *Dakota*, *Viking*, and *Jennie Maud*, and the barkentines *George C. Perkins* and C.C. *Funk*. (CHMM 989-P131.)

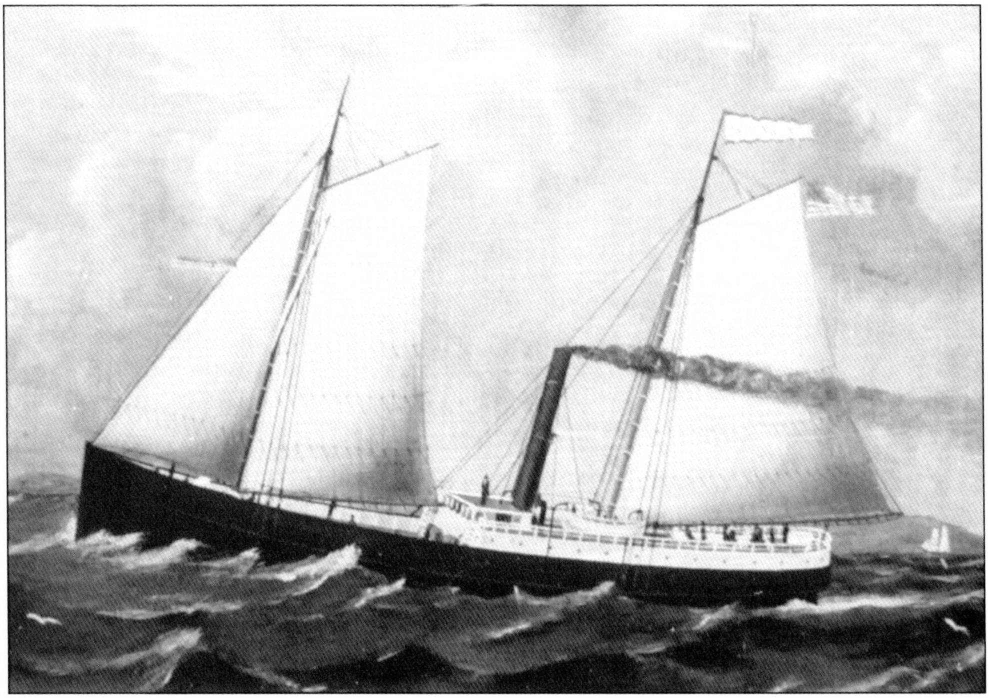

The steamer *Eastport* was built at Marshfield in 1869 by Hans Reed for Howard and Pool of San Francisco, who put her in the coal trade between Coos Bay and California. She had excellent passenger accommodations and carried about 450 tons of coal per trip. The *Eastport* also provided passenger service between Empire City and San Francisco. (CHMM 009-16.1228.)

On June 23, 1949, Mrs. Hans Adolphson of Engelwood christened the tug *Kate* with the traditional champagne bottle. The *Kate* was built by the Elfving Boat Builders in Coos Bay and was designed by Hans Adolphson. The *Kate* was delivered to her new owners the Siuslaw Forest Products Company of Florence, Oregon. (CHMM 995-1.6716.1)

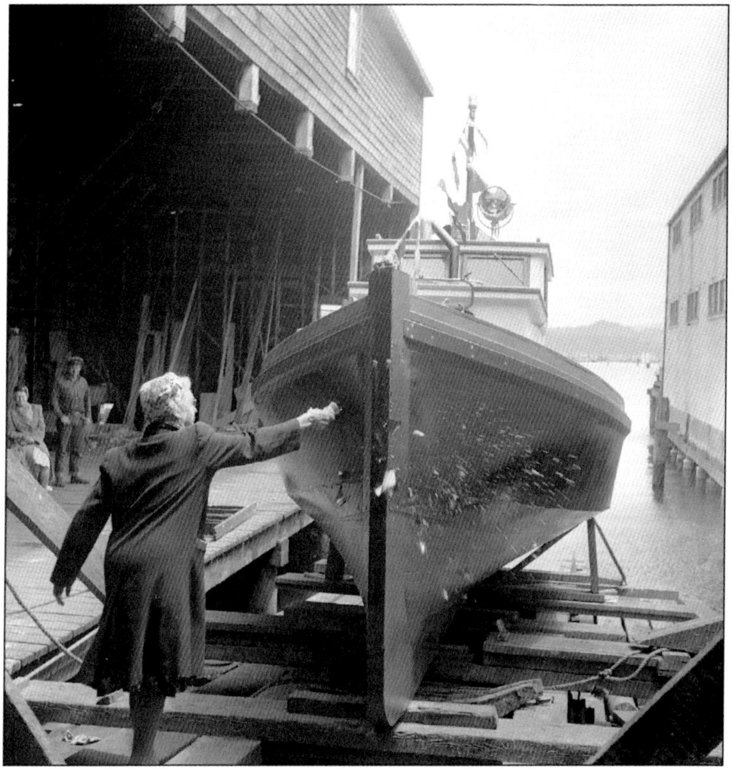

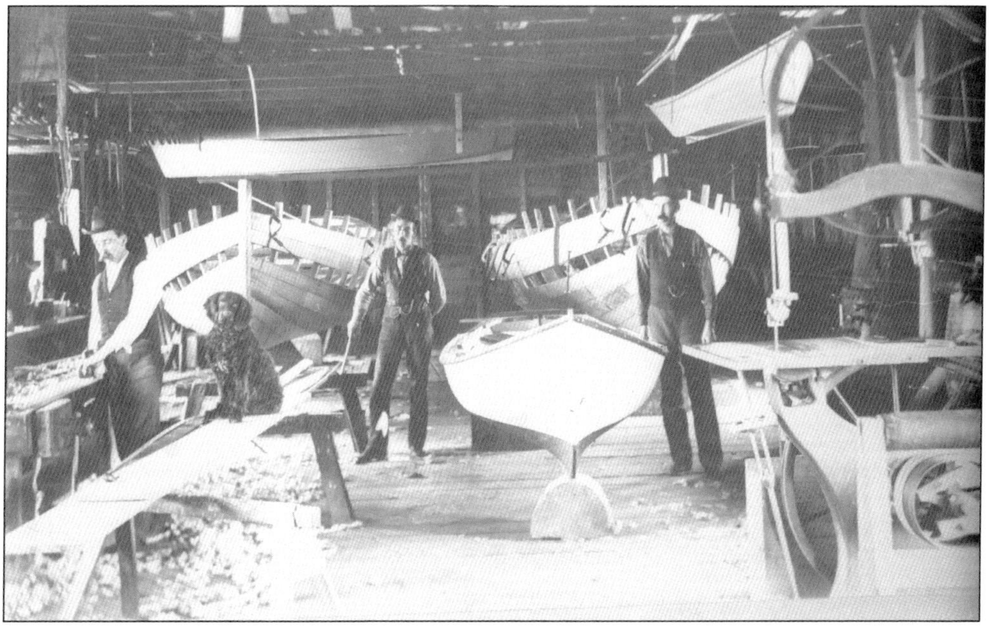

Brothers William and Parker Holland owned and operated Holland Brothers Boat Building Company on Front Street, where they built smaller river and bay boats that kept the bay humming with activity. Frank Lowe stands with brothers William Holland and Parker Holland. (CHMM 009-16.614.)

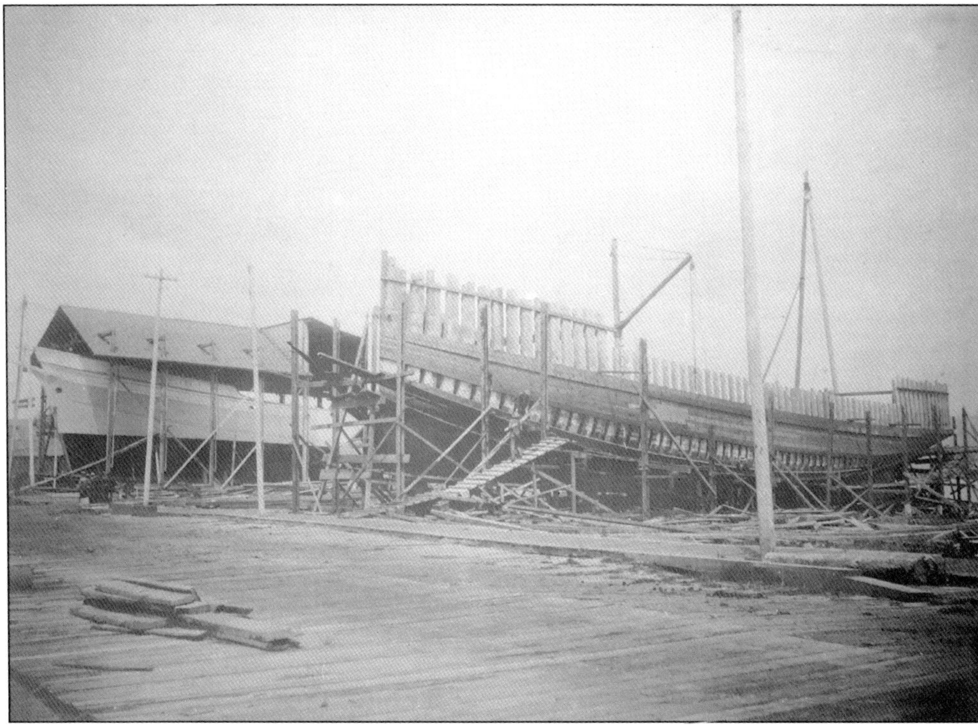

Master shipbuilder Emil Heuckendorff established his shipyard, known as the Pacific Shipbuilding Company, in Marshfield. In 1900, he built the three-masted schooner *Forest Home*. He also constructed the schooner *David Evans*. The steam schooner *Marshfield* (background) and the of the schooner *James Bennett* (foreground) were built in 1901. In total, eight vessels were built at Heuckendorff's shipyard. (CHMM 992-8-2565.)

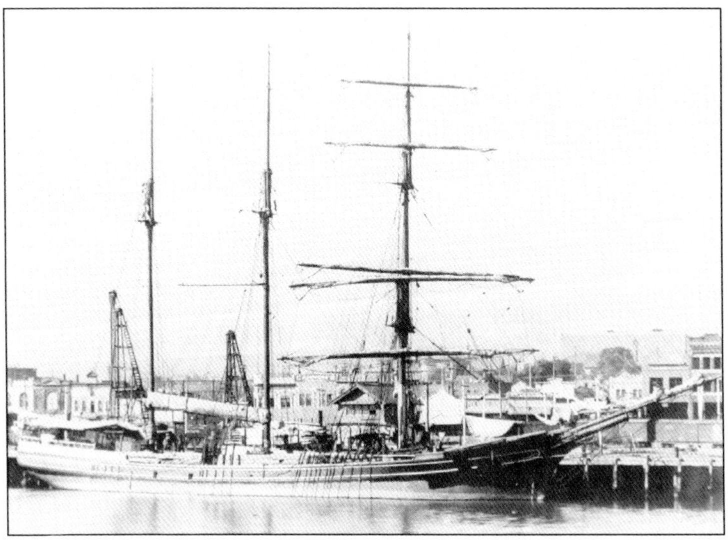

The first vessel Emil Heuckendorff built was the three-masted barkentine *Joseph L. Eviston*. Launched on January 20, 1900, she was towed to sea for the first time on March 30, 1900. The *Joseph L. Eviston* was managed by Captain Ackerman and had a hauling capacity of 900,000 feet of lumber. (CHMM 009-16.929.)

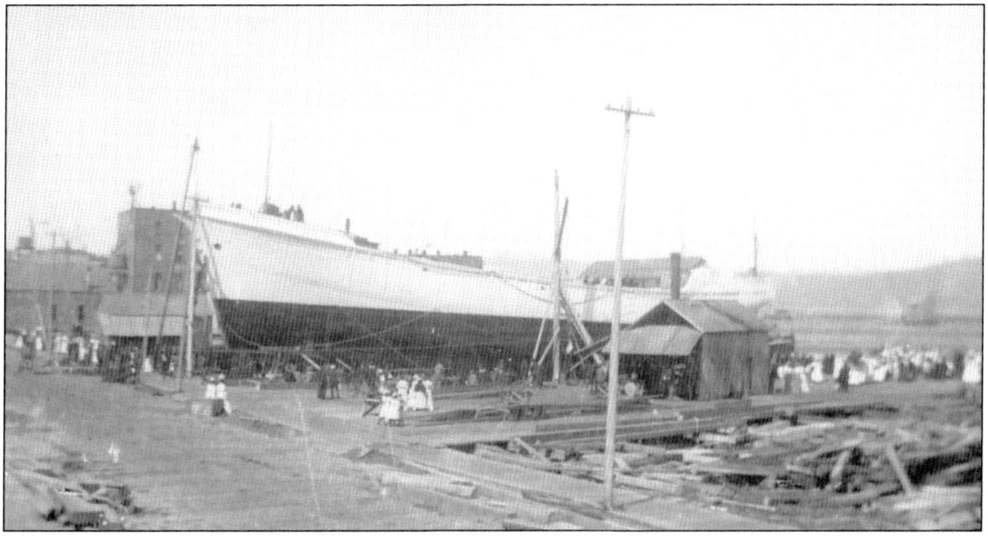

The *Forest Home* was built by Emil Heuckendorff for Swaynt Hoyt and later purchased by C.A. Hooper of the Washington-based McCormick Lumber Company. The vessel was engaged in carrying lumber from Puget Sound to San Francisco. The *Forest Home* was later sold to New Zealand owners and renamed the *Holmwood*. (CHMM 963-35F.)

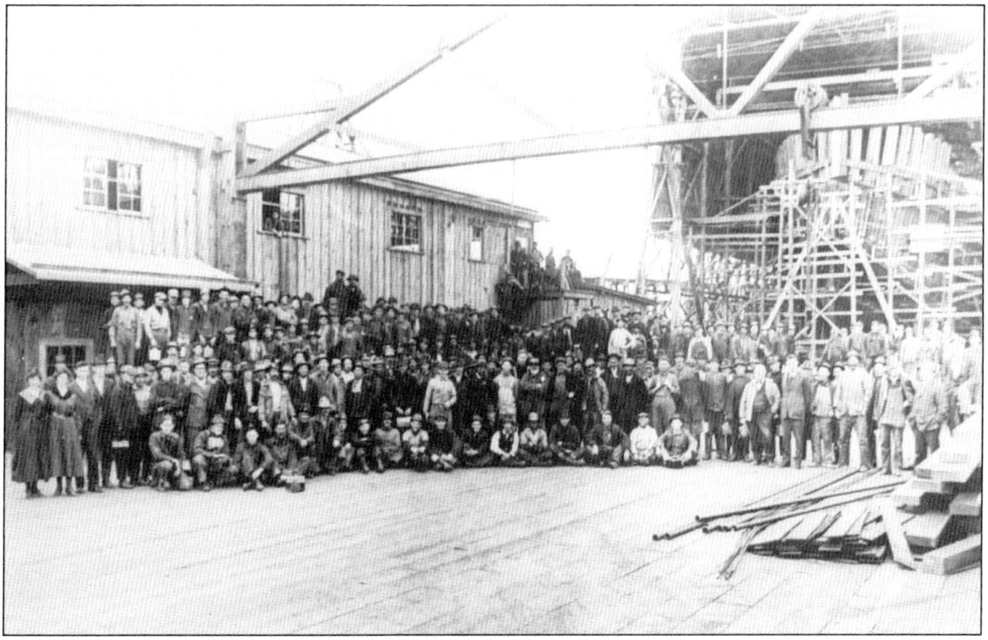

With local success in building warships for World War I, Marshfield businessmen organized the Coos Bay Shipbuilding Company. By December 1918, the company was contracted to build four ships. By the end of World War I, three Hough-type ships and one Ferris-type vessel were completed, with several others still under construction. (CHMM 009-16.1779.)

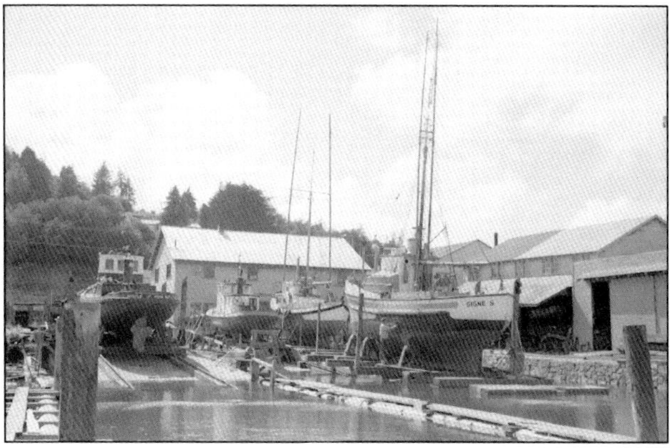

Brothers James R. and John W. Hillstrom owned and operated Hillstrom Shipbuilding Company in 1914. During World War II, the company was awarded a contract for the construction of three wooden rescue boats for the Army Air Corps. The Hillstrom Shipbuilding Company was one of the longest surviving shipbuilding companies on the bay, lasting until 1979. (CHMM 009-16.272d.)

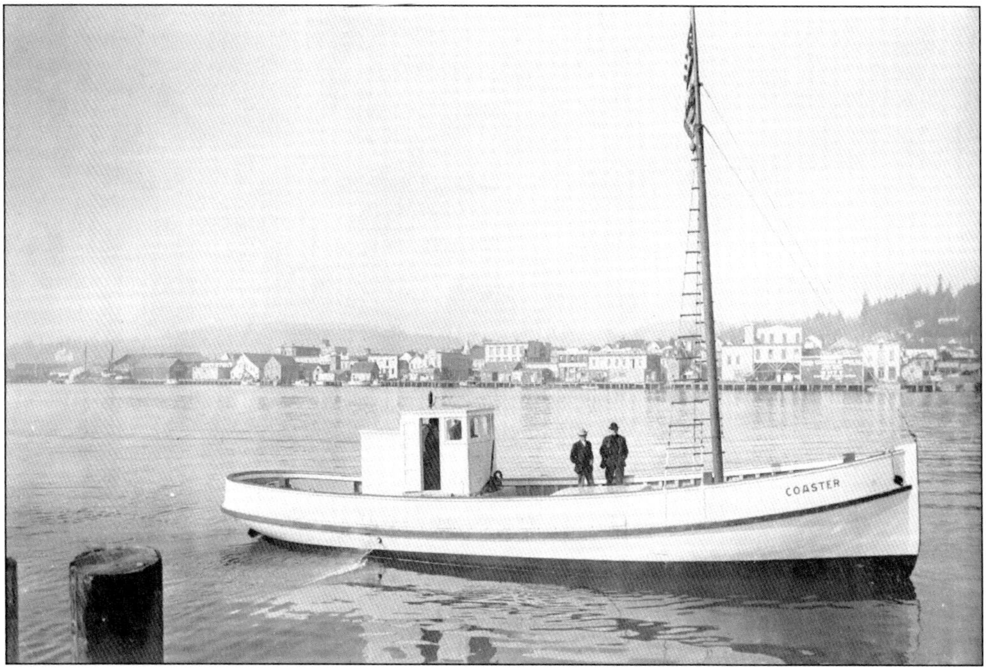

Max Timmerman built the *Coaster*, a gasoline schooner that was launched on September 7, 1910, for Peter Olson. At the age of three, Virginia Coke, daughter of Judge J.S. Coke, was the youngest person to christen a vessel on the coast. Olsen ran the *Coaster* out of Coos Bay to Port Orford and the Rogue River. On August 22, 1925, the *Coaster* burned at Pigeon Point, California. (CHMM 009-16.249.)

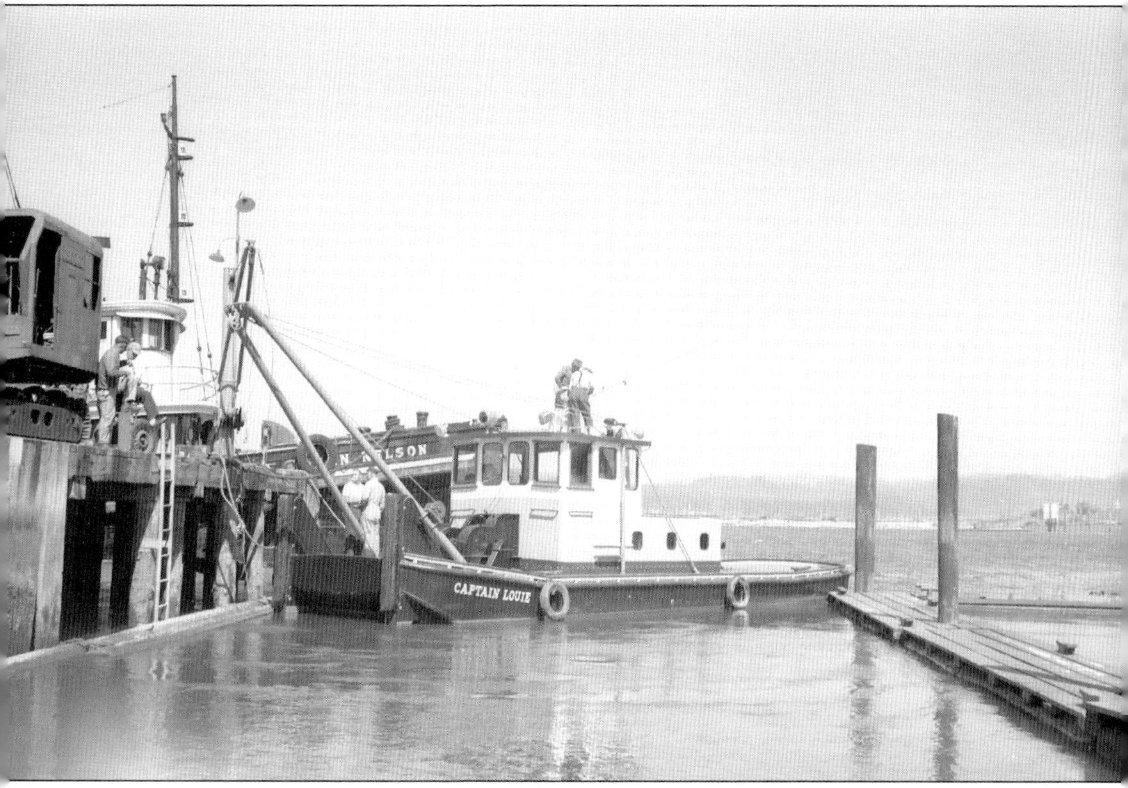

Louis "Captain Louie" Knutson established his own tugboat company, Knutson Towboat Company, in 1915. Knutson bought his first boat, had her converted to tow logs, and named her *Koos*. The *Koos* was followed by the *Koos No. 2*, which was built in 1924. Knutson Towboat Company expanded operations in 1940. Honoring the founder of Knutson Towboat Company, the 43-foot, 1,750-horsepower tug *Captain Louie* was launched in 1961. The *Captain Louie* was the first steel vessel built by the Hillstrom Shipbuilding Company. The Hillstrom Shipbuilding Company was started in North Bend by Bill Hillstrom in 1940, moved to 912 North Front Street in Coos Bay after the war, and closed in 1979. (CHMM 009-16.276A.)

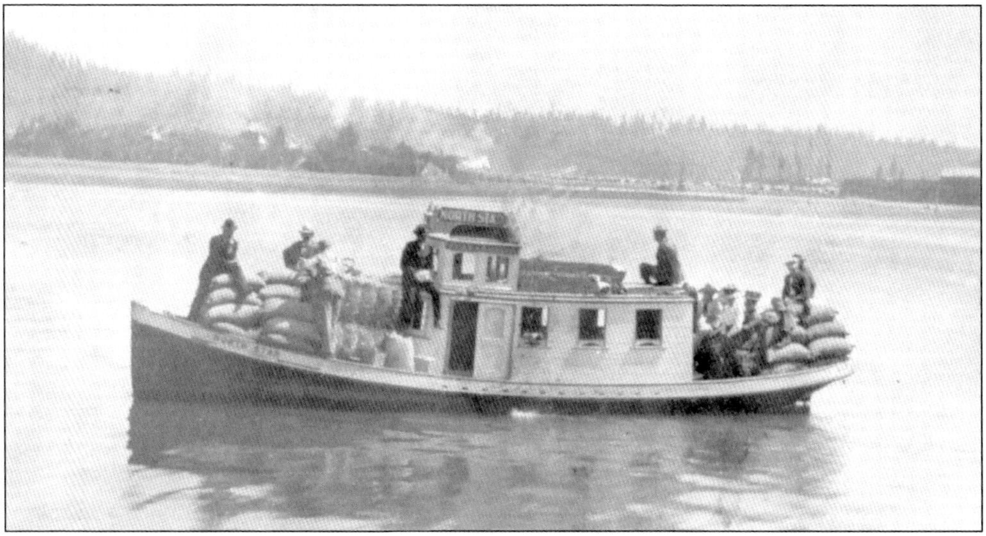

One of Eastside's boat builders was Max Timmerman, who specialized in gasoline launches. The first built was the *North Star* in 1905. In total, Timmerman built 12 launches from 1907 to 1913. They included the *Dispatch*, *Bonita*, *City of Coos Bay*, *Dixie*, *Wolverine*, *Hercules*, *Mae*, *Coaster*, *Turtle*, *Bear*, and *Big Chief*. (CHMM 961-128b.)

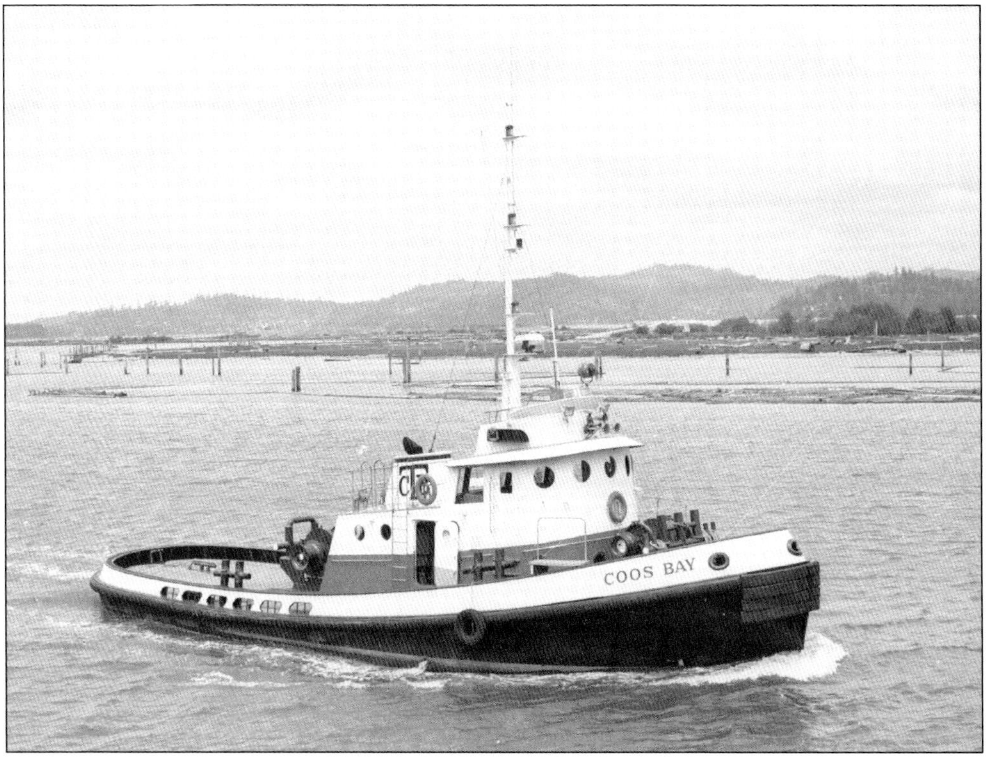

In later years, the shipbuilders of Coos Bay transitioned from wood to steel vessels. On March 25, 1969, the steel tug *Coos Bay* was launched from the Hillstrom Shipbuilding yard. Built for the Coos Bay Towboat Company, the *Coos Bay* was used by the Coos Bay Pilots Association as a pilot boat. (CHMM 009-16.163.)

Six

Serving the Community

Binding a community together and serving the public has always been the role of fraternities, civic groups, unions, and clubs. The people in Coos Bay were no exception. Whether it was physical attributes, nationality, employment, creed, or other events that brought them together, the like-minded citizens of Coos Bay bonded to provide a wide range of services to their community.

Over the years, there was hardly a secret or benevolent society of national origin that was not represented in Coos Bay. Many of the local organizations were in high standing at both state and national levels. The town was abuzz with social activity. Groups were meeting almost every night, and many would meet on the same night. The organizations were deemed beneficial to the community as a whole because of their service.

Some lodges have disappeared with time, while others have remained in service for many years. Perhaps the first gathering of like-minded citizens was conducted by Mrs. Vandervort of Empire City. Mrs. Vandervort was a consistent and earnest Christian and helped organize the first prayer meeting ever held in Coos County in the late 1850s. Mrs. Vandervort, like her father Henry Luse, was an earnest advocate of temperance. Through her efforts, which were aided by her father, a temperance organization was established. With the aid of Mrs. Smith, the temperance society was merged into a Good Templars lodge.

The International Order of Odd Fellows was one of the first lodges organized in Empire City. In 1877, the Odd Fellows hall, 30 by 60 feet and two stories high, was erected on the corner of First and B Streets. Another early lodge was the Chadwick Lodge, AF&AM, which was established in 1876. Another lodge, this one for women, was the Mama Rebecca No. 20. In Marshfield, early lodges included the Sunset Lodge of the International Order of Odd Fellows, which was established 1875, and the Masonic Blanco Lodge, which was formed in 1876.

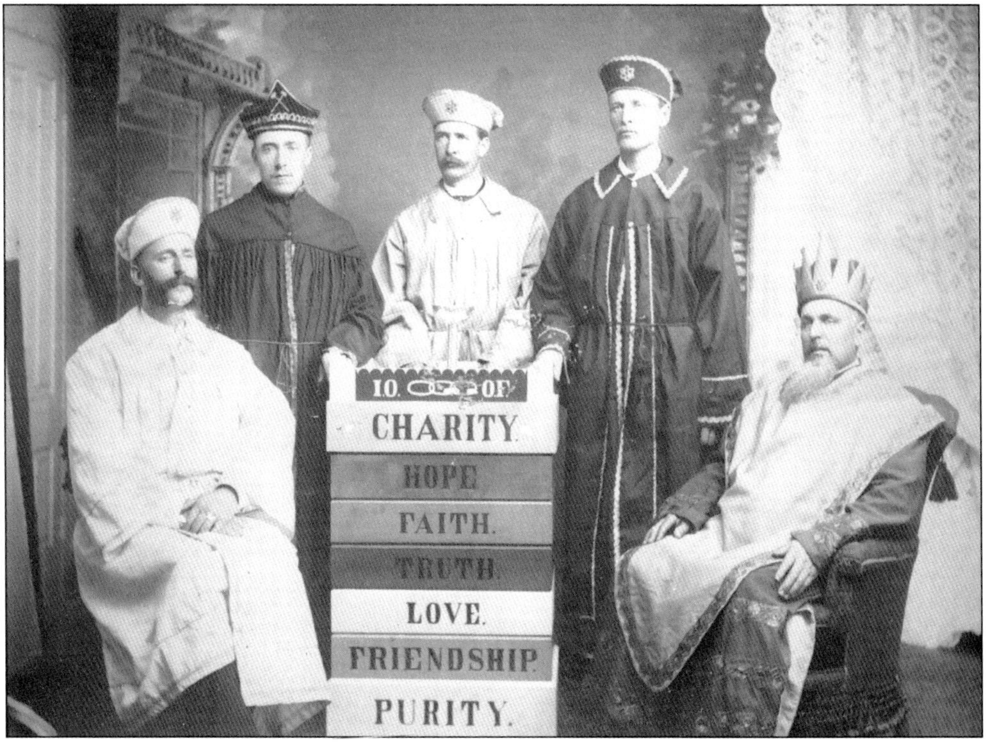

The dedication of the Independent Order of Odd Fellows hall was conducted on October 26, 1889. Pictured at the ceremony are W.B. Curtis, Chris Rasmussen, James Hill, Jacob Lando, and Thomas Hirst. On July 14, 1888, Charles H. Merchant sold a piece of hillside property to the Odd Fellows Cemetery Association for $350, creating what is now known as the Pioneer Cemetery. (CHMM 992-8-1217.)

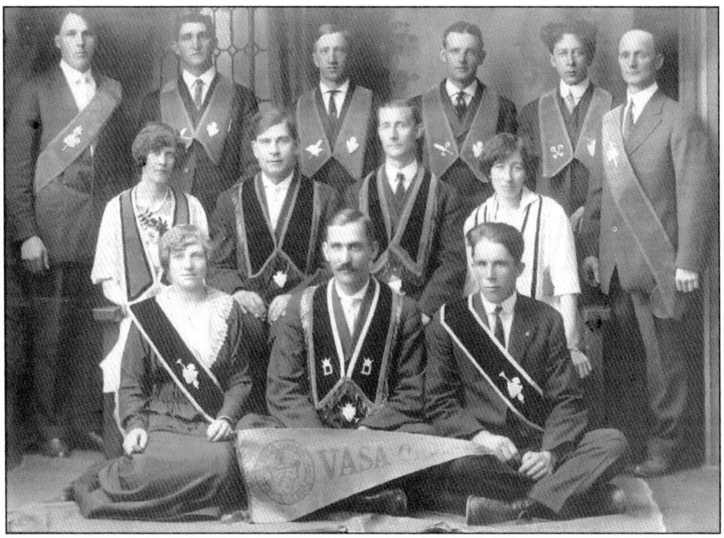

The Swedish society Linnea was one of the oldest Swedish societies in the Pacific Northwest. The officers of Marshfield's Lodge No. 269 are pictured in this 1915 photograph. The society not only provided social activities, it also helped those in need as well as providing employment information for the community. (CHMM 007-11.4701.)

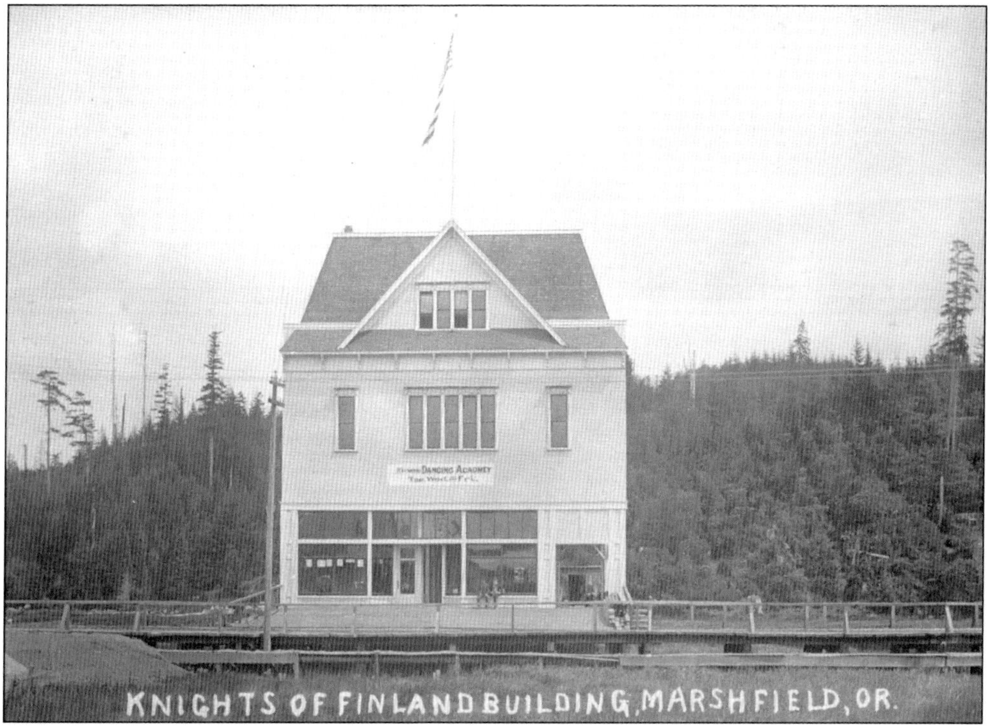

Local immigrant groups formed organizations to offer their members a vehicle for socializing with fellow countrymen. The Scandinavians were represented by the Knights of Finland, Suomi Lodge, Sons of Norway, Martha Lodge, Finnish Brotherhood, Ladies Finnish Society, and the International Order of Runeberg. The two major meeting places were the Suomi hall and the Knights of Finland building seen here. (CHMM 992-8-0993.)

Woodmen of the World was founded in Omaha, Nebraska, by Joseph Cullen Root on June 6, 1890. Root believed that Woodmen of the World members, through their local lodges, should be an active volunteer force within their communities, helping those in need. The Marshfield members of the Woodmen of the World are shown on November 5, 1904. (CHMM 982-68.)

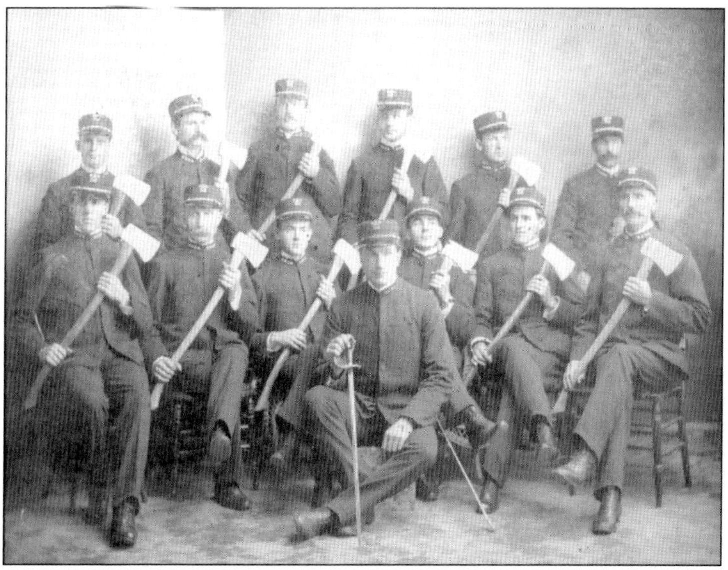

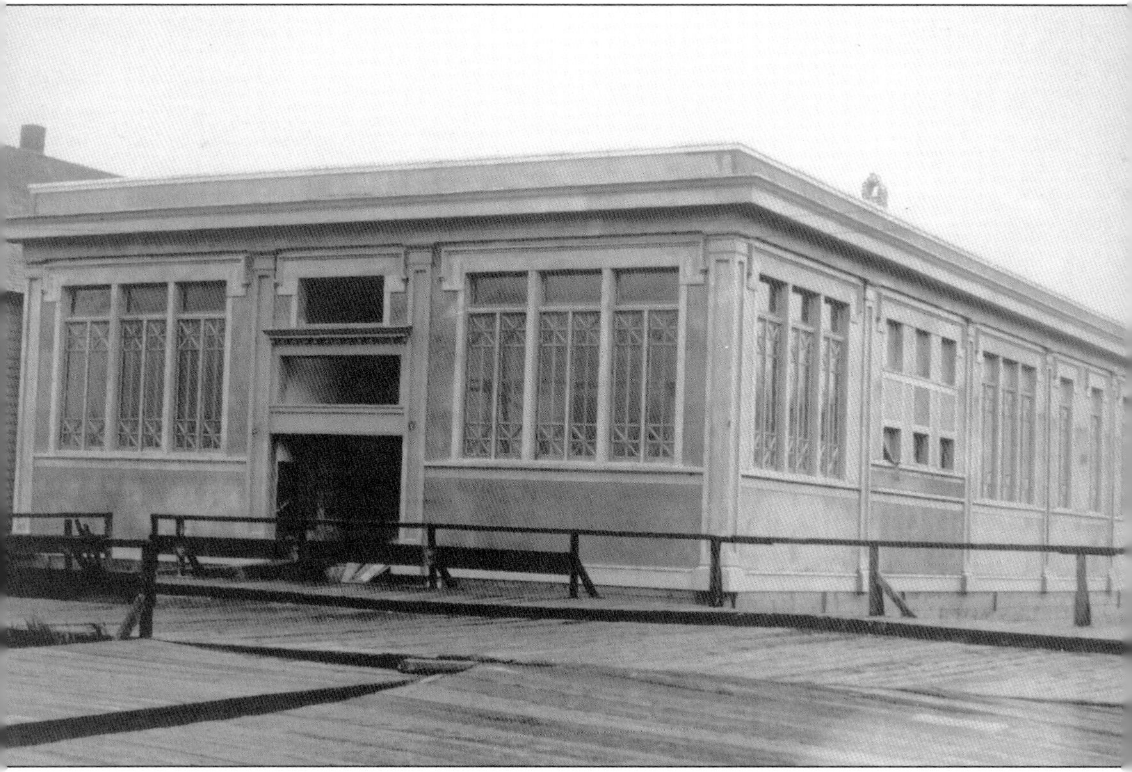

The Order of Knights of Pythias is an international fraternity that was founded on February 19, 1864, by Justus H. Rathbone. The order began during the Civil War, and its founder believed that it might do much to heal the wounds and allay the hatred of civil conflict. The primary objects of fraternal organizations are to promote friendship among men and to relieve suffering. Another object of the organization was the moral uplifting and purification of society. Strict morality, absolute truthfulness, honor, and integrity were thoroughly inculcated in the minds of its membership. Marshfield's Myrtle Lodge No. 3 of the Knights of Pythias was the oldest in the state of Oregon, having been formed in 1875. Local doctor C.B. Golden was the first grand chancellor in the state. The Knights of Pythias building was completed in 1921 at a cost of $15,000. (CHMM 992-8-0990.)

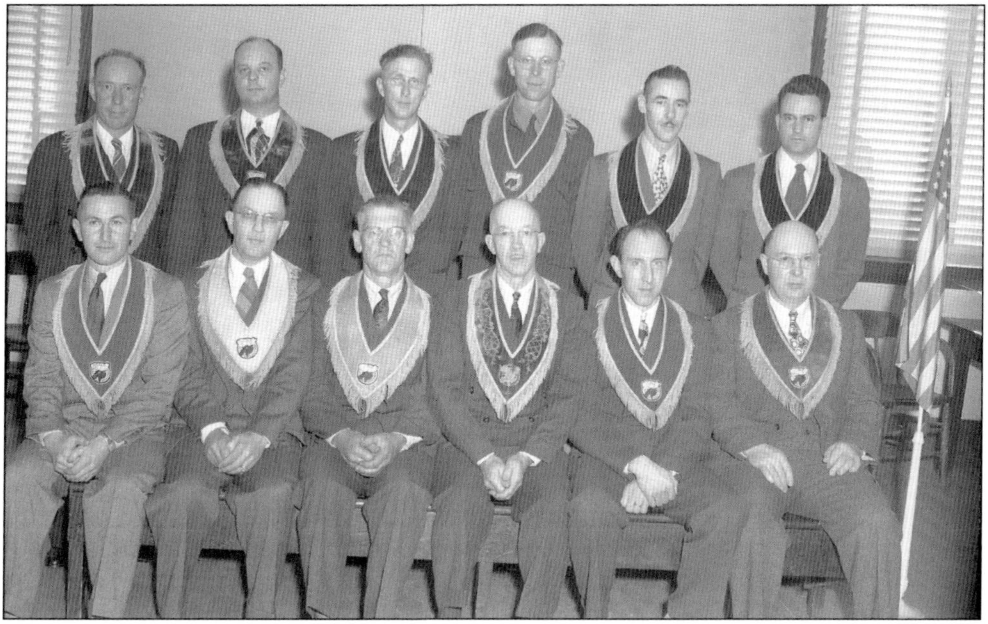

The Loyal Order of Moose is a fraternal and service organization that was founded nationally in 1888. Considered a family fraternity, the Moose Lodge has become an international organization of men and women who are dedicated to the care of young and old, to celebrating life, and to bringing communities closer together. On April 18, 1948, the Loyal Order of Moose, Marshfield Lodge was reactivated. (CHMM 995-1.2795.1.)

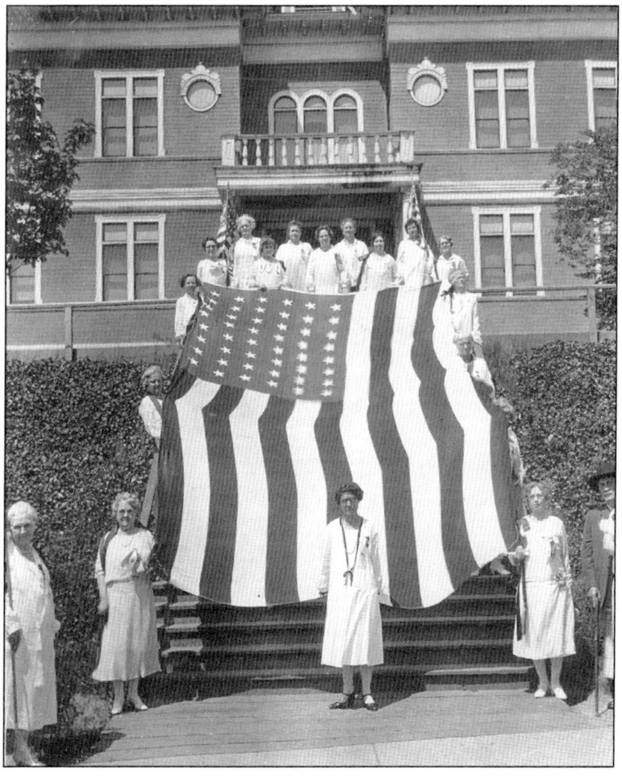

Named after Parisian composer Cecile Chaminade, the Marshfield Chaminade Club was formed in 1904 by Lydia Horsfall. At the time, the Chaminade Club was one of two exclusive clubs for women. The goal of the club was to further the general study and appreciation of music. In 1923, the members were photographed at Central School. (CHMM 988-P460.)

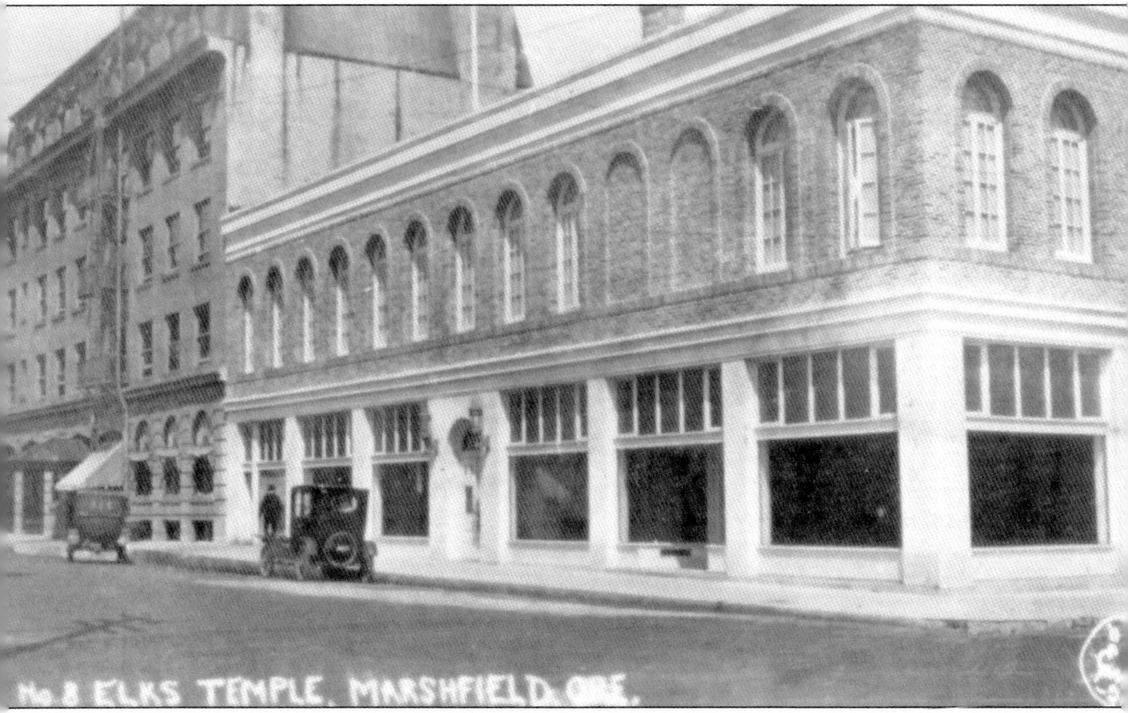

The Benevolent and Protective Order of the Elks was founded to promote and practice the four cardinal virtues of charity, justice, brotherly love, and fidelity. The Elks organization was founded in New York City on February 16, 1868, under the name "Jolly Corks" by 15 actors, entertainers, and others associated with the theater. In ensuing years, membership expanded to other professions. Marshfield Lodge No. 1160 of the Benevolent and Protective Order of the Elks was formed in 1909. The lodge included not only members from Marshfield but also members from western Douglas County, Curry County, and Coos County. The Elks temple was designed by William G. Chandler and was constructed in 1920 at a cost of $100,000. The grand opening of the temple was held September 5–6, 1920. The temple also served as a community center where many organizations would meet. (CHMM 962-44 c.)

On May 8, 1925, Ben Ostland organized and became president of Longfellow Club No. 1. Only men standing six feet or taller could be members. Their primary goal was to make life more comfortable for tall men. As Ostland traveled throughout the country, he promoted the club, and other cities quickly joined ranks, forming their own Longfellow clubs. To identify themselves, club members wore a giraffe pin on their lapel. (CHMM 960-182 c.)

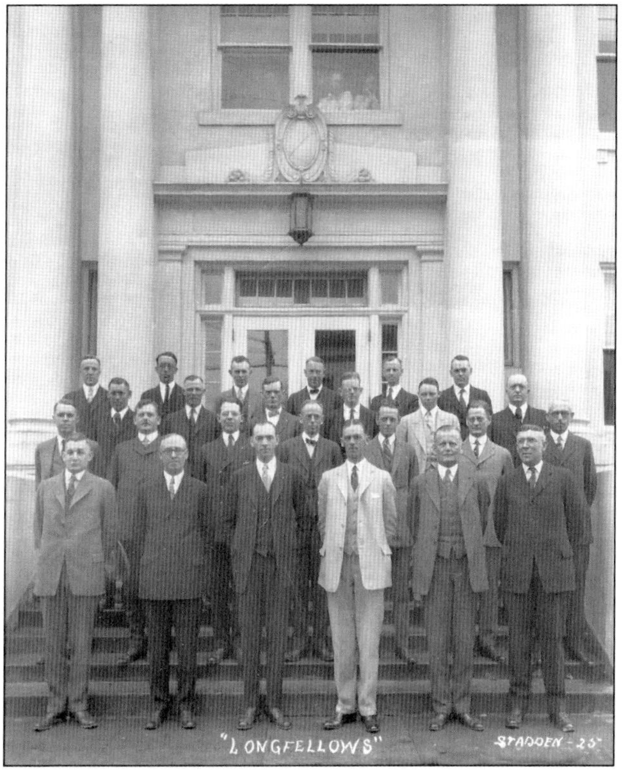

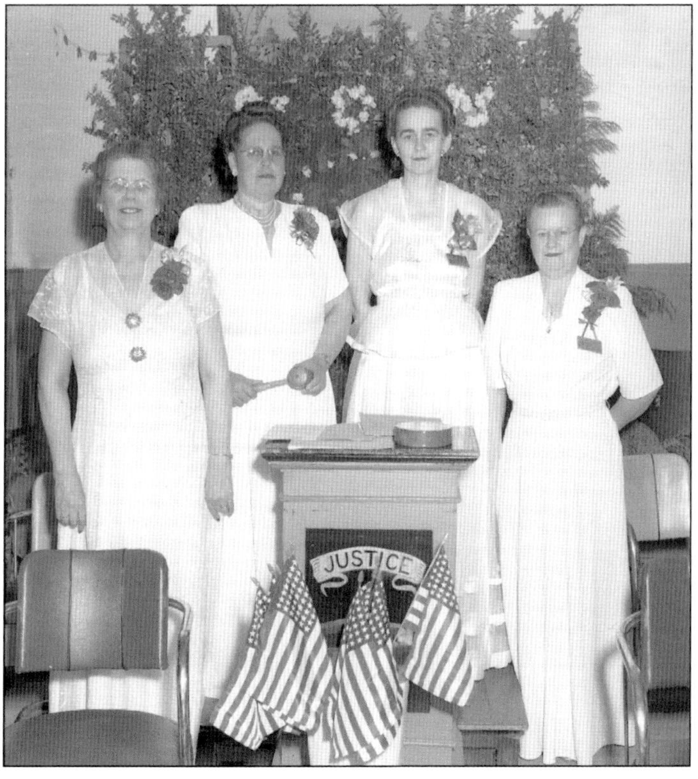

Founded by Joseph Cullen Root in 1897, Neighbors of Woodcraft was originally named Women of Woodcraft, and Neighbors of Woodcraft grew out of the Woodmen Circle. In 1917, Women of Woodcraft changed its name to Neighbors of Woodcraft to reflect the organization's acceptance of both men and women for membership. Here are the members of Coos Bay Circle No. 164. (CHMM 995-1.6506.)

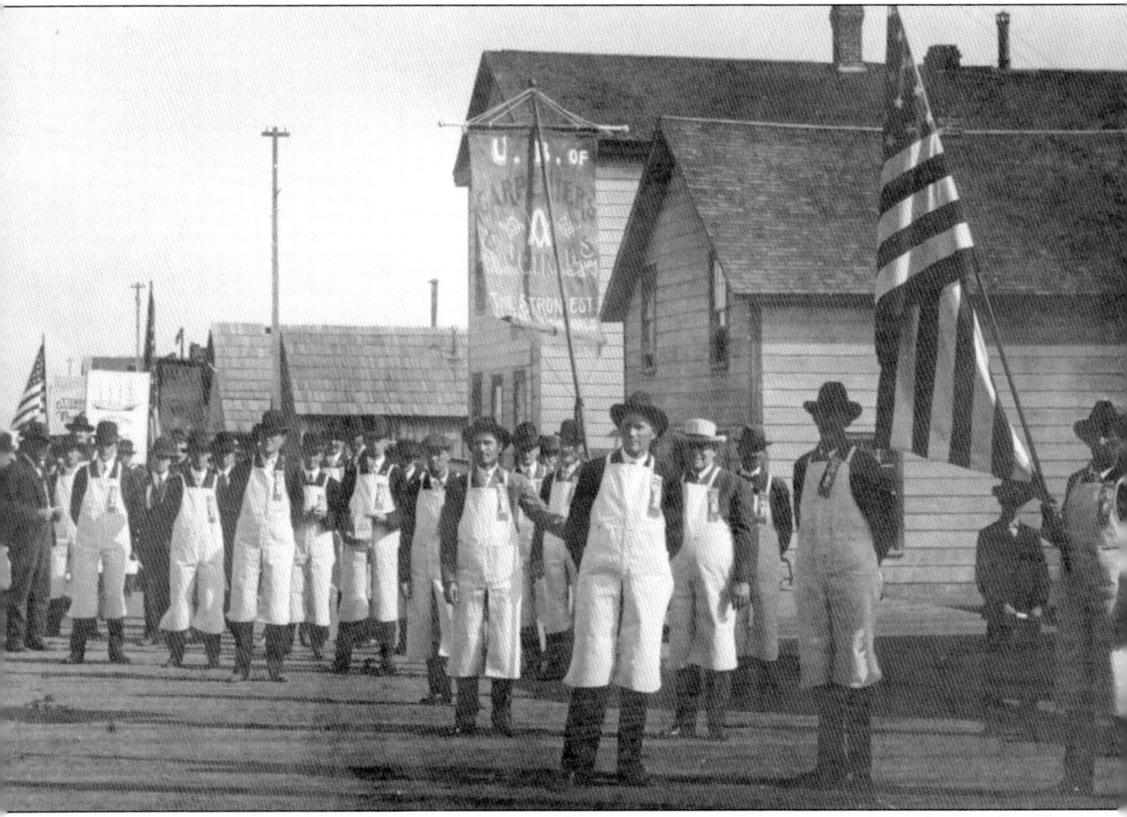

The United Brotherhood of Carpenters and Joiners of America is one of the largest building trade unions in the United States. The union was created in 1881 by a convention of carpenters' unions led by Peter J. McGuire. The Carpenters and Joiners' Union of Marshfield was organized on February 19, 1907, with a membership of 44. For dues of $5 per month, members were provided with accident benefits for total disability, strike benefits, funeral benefits, and workday benefits of eight hours with an average wage of $3.50 per day. Hard times fell upon union members in 1908. Though they were led to Marshfield by advertisements in the newspapers, there was no building going on. Migrating carpenters were warned to stay clear of Coos Bay. On a happier note, union members enjoyed a festive celebration, as this group is seen at the start of the Carpenters and Joiners' parade. (CHMM 995-D134.)

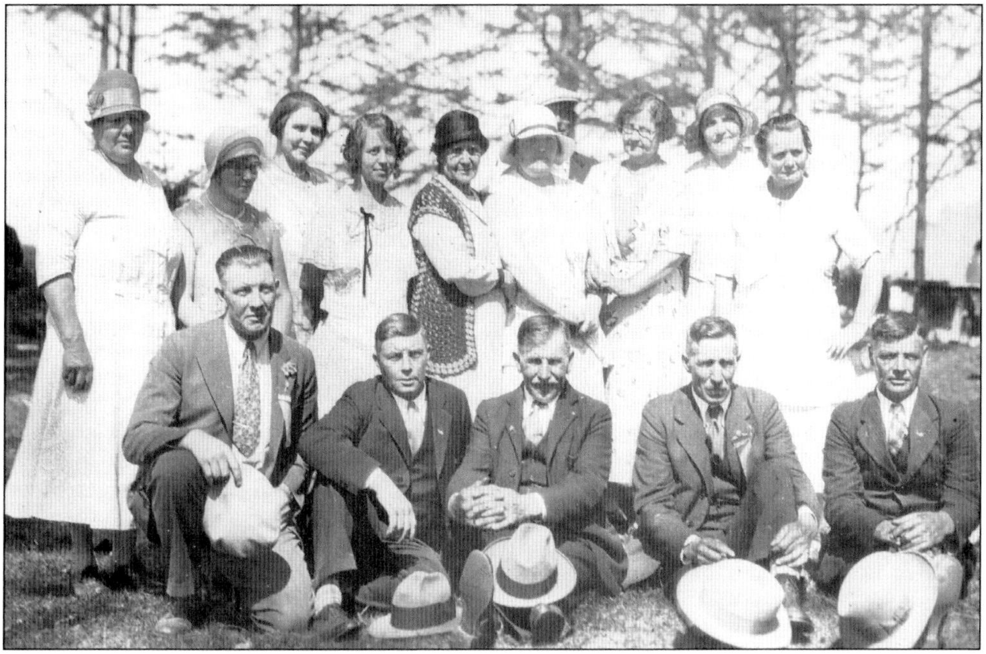

The Swedish organization Linnea was installed at Coos Bay in 1909 and was granted a national charter in 1913. Conducting many social activities, Linnea Lodge No. 2 was considered one of the liveliest on the bay. Membership grew to well over 100 members. Officers of the Linnea lodge are shown here in 1915. (CHMM 007-11.5015.)

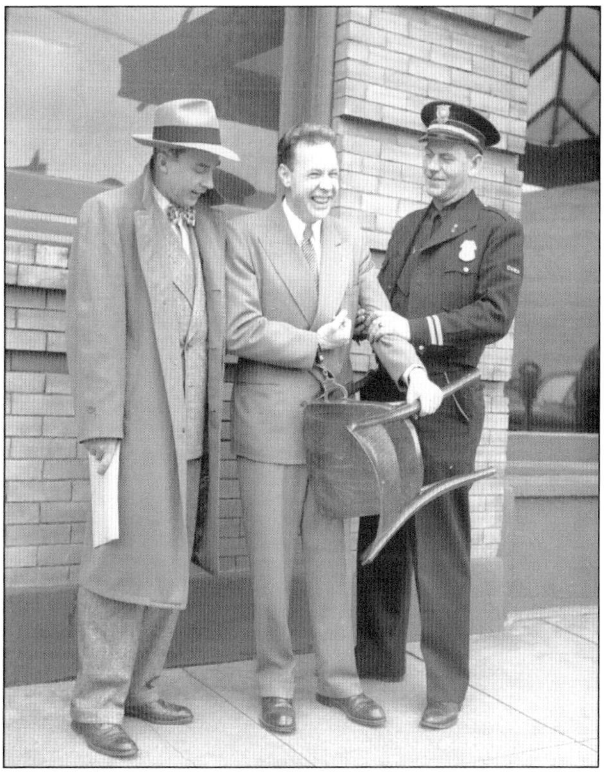

In February 1922, a group of business and professional men agreed to start a Rotary club, and Ben Chandler was elected the first president. In 1947, new Rotarian Ron Gamble learned quickly that one could not say no to Rotary. When Gamble hesitated to present a talk about himself, club members took matters in their own hands and called upon chief of police Leonard Nelson to take Gamble into custody. (CHMM 995-1.1991.)

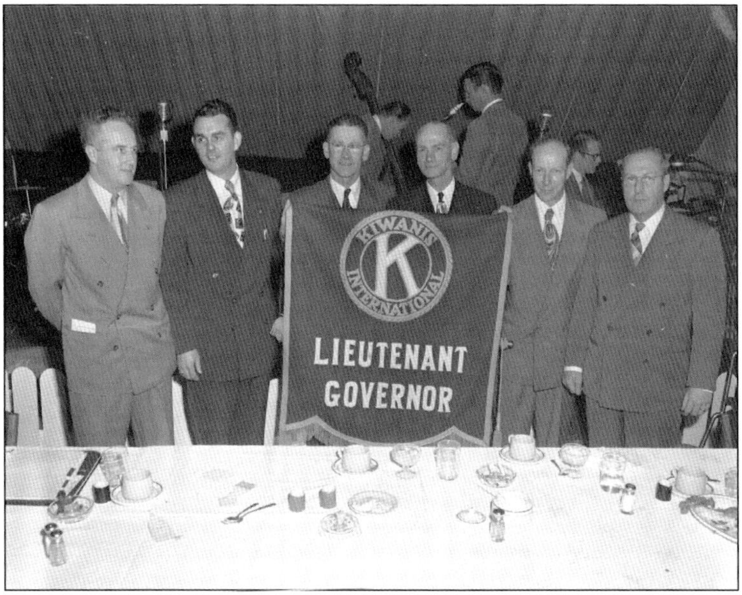

Kiwanis is a global organization of volunteers dedicated to changing the world one child and one community at a time. Members develop youth as leaders, build playgrounds, and raise funds for pediatric research. Kiwanis members help shelter the homeless, feed the hungry, mentor the disadvantaged, and care for the sick. (CHMM 995-1.8683.1.)

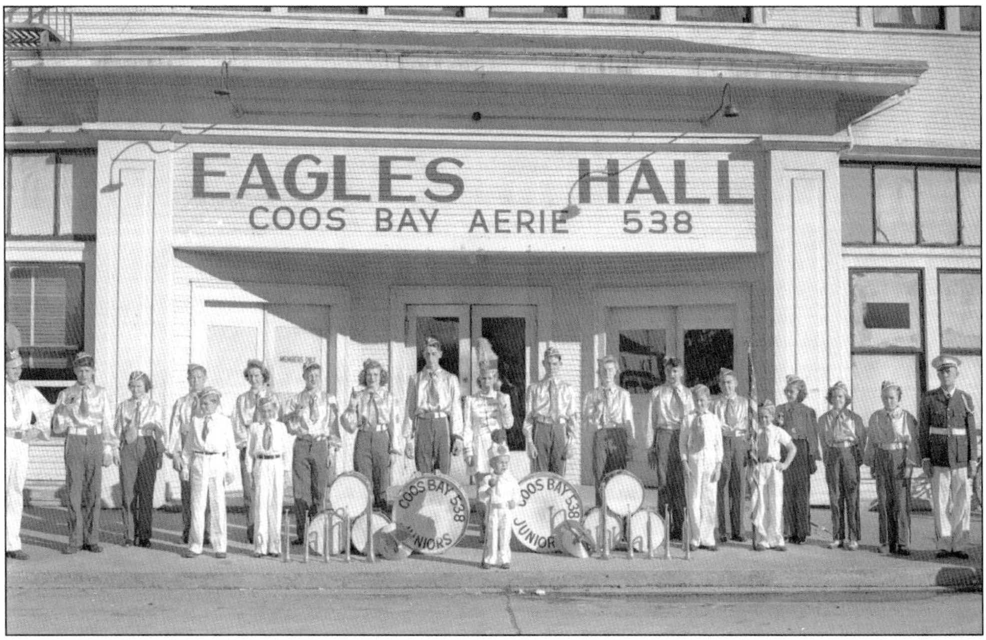

The Fraternal Order of Eagles was founded in February 1898 by six theater owners who formed the Order of Good Things. As numbers grew, members selected the bald eagle as the official emblem and changed the name to the Fraternal Order of Eagles. In Coos Bay, the Fraternal Order of Eagles Aerie 538 was chartered on November 22, 1903. (CHMM 992-N81.5.)

The 4-H (standing for head, heart, hands, and health) is a youth education program. The 4-H helps young people learn and grow through an intentional process that builds competence, confidence, connection, compassion, and character. The long-term vision of 4-H is for youth to experience economic and social success in adulthood while making positive contributions to their communities. On January 29, 1949, the Eastside Cooking Club initiated its first boy, Phil Shellaburger. (CHMM 995-1.5259.2.)

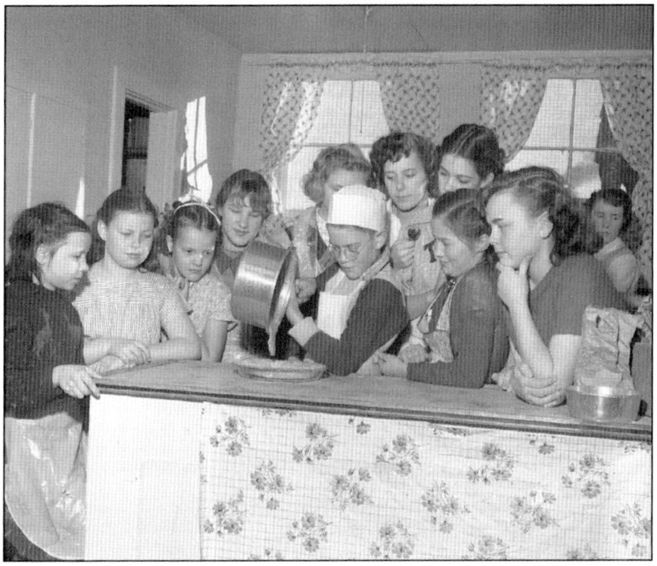

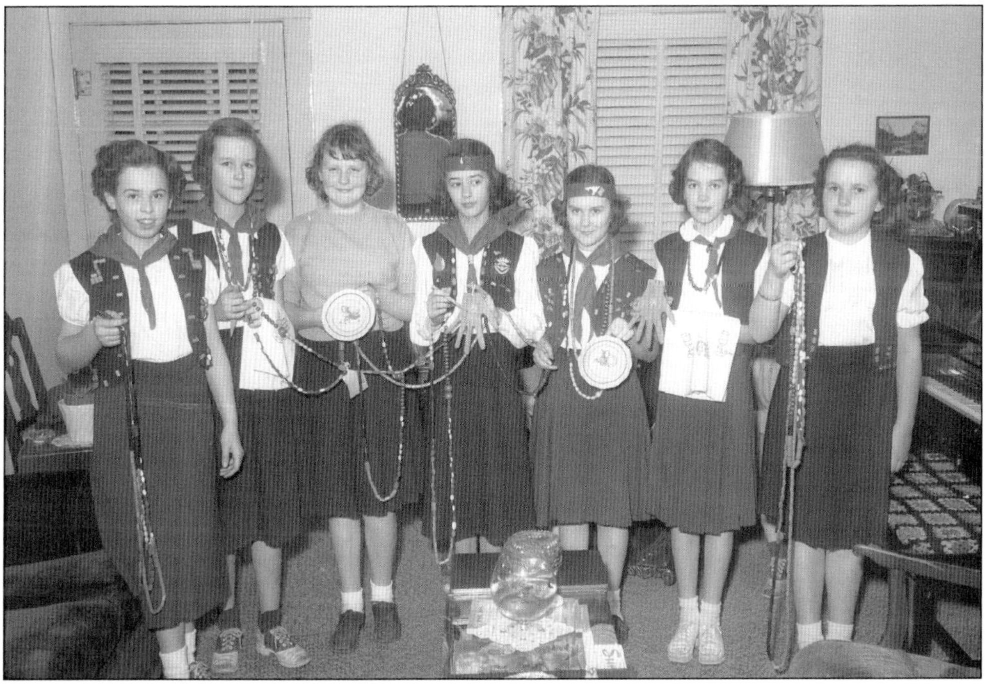

On February 16, 1950, local Campfire Girls set a fine record of achievement. The girls proudly displayed some of the honor beads they earned in Camp Fire since May 1949. Along with their honor beads, the girls showed some of their projects, achievements for which the beads were awarded and which represented work in home craft and citizenship. The girls were members of the Tanda group. (CHMM 995-1.8944.)

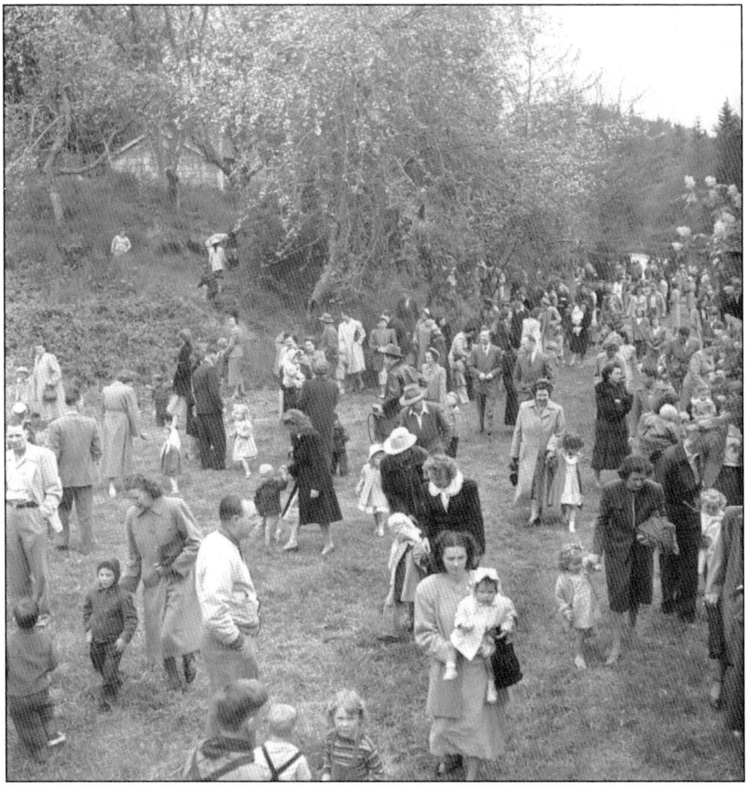

The mission of the Lions Club is to empower volunteers to serve their communities, meet humanitarian needs, encourage peace, and promote international understanding. The Lions Club of Coos Bay sponsored this annual Easter egg hunt at Mingus Park on April 18, 1946. (CHMM.)

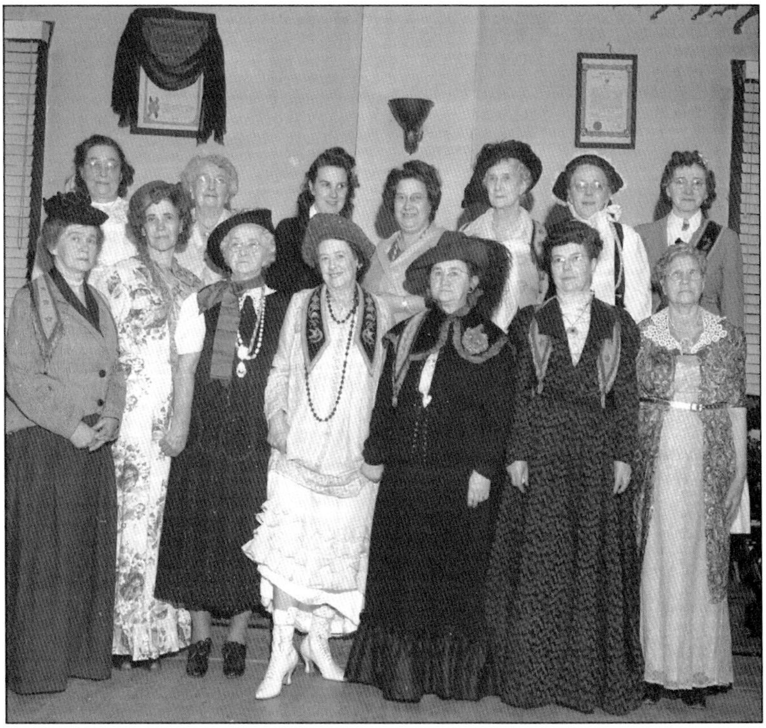

On March 4, 1949, the Star Rebekah Lodge of Coos Bay conducted an anniversary celebration of the institution. Celebrating their 62nd birthday are Mrs. William Hillstrom, Mrs. Tom Coke, Mrs. Noel Warden, Mrs. Jack McDonald, Mrs. Harry Lucas, and Mrs. H.A. Harris. (CHMM 995-1.5361.)

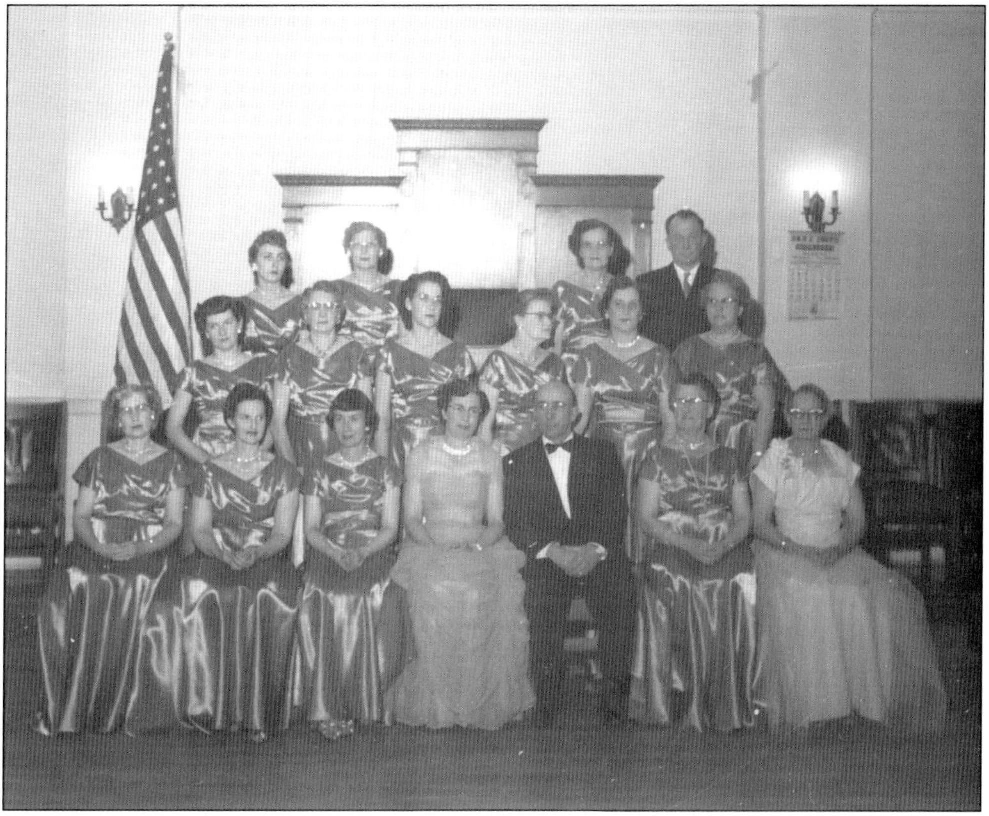

Considered the largest fraternal organization in the world, the Order of the Eastern Star is an organization to which both women and men may belong. The Eastern Star is a social order comprised of persons with spiritual values, but it is not a religion. In December 1953, the Coos Bay chapter celebrated its annual installation. (CHMM 992-N264.)

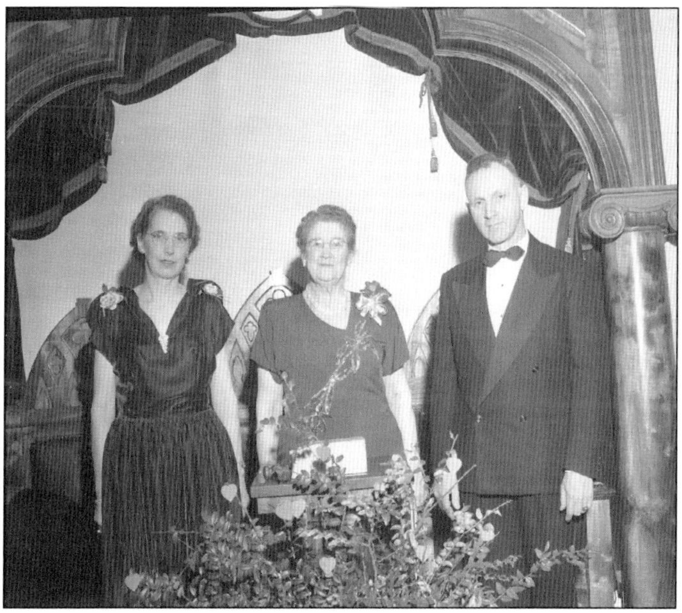

Dr. June Martin (center), longtime member of the Doric Chapter, Order of Eastern Star of Coos Bay, was given special honors at the chapter meeting on February 14, 1950. For several years, the meeting falling closest to her birthday has been designated "Doctor June Night." Other members pictured are W.L. Miller and Mrs. Earl Mathis, worthy patron and worthy matron. (CHMM 995-1.8900.2.)

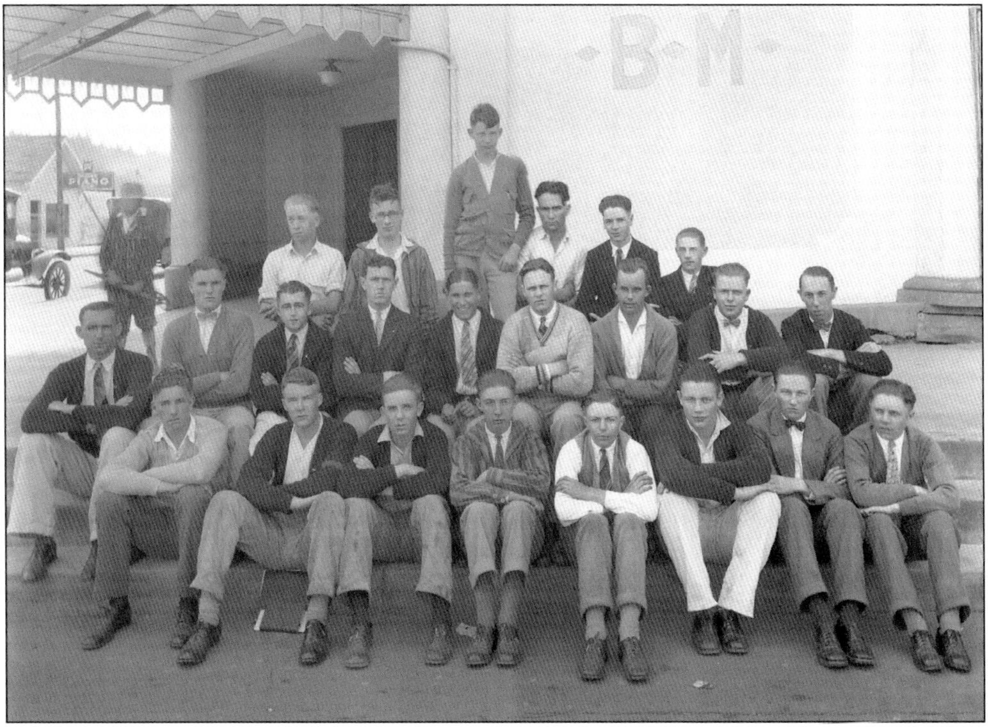

DeMolay is an organization dedicated to preparing young men to lead successful, happy, and productive lives. Open to young men between the ages 12 to 21, it develops civic awareness, personal responsibility, and leadership skills so vitally needed in society today. On May 25, 1926, the Marshfield chapter gathers above. (CHMM 987-S1009.)

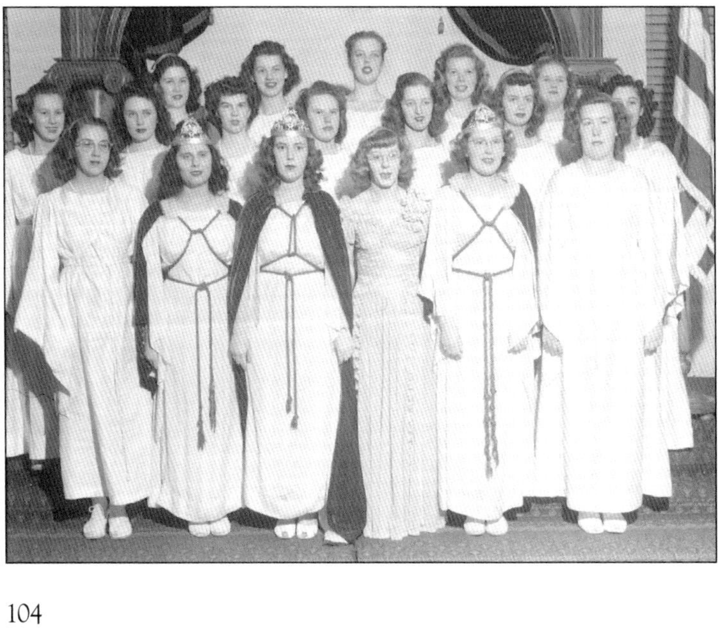

Membership in Job's Daughters consists of young ladies ages 11 to 20 who are related to Master Masons. The International Order of Job's Daughters teaches humility, patience, charity, public speaking, leadership, and many other lessons that are essential for their daily lives. On January 9, 1946, the Coos Bay Bethel Number 17 gathers at left. (CHMM 986-N697.)

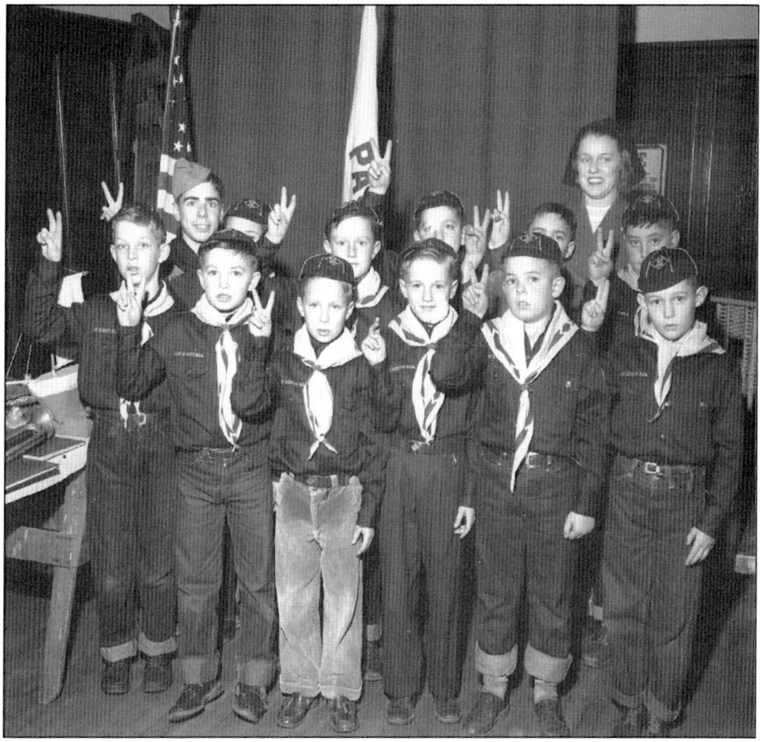

On Sunday, February 5, 1946, the induction of Coos Bay's newest Cub Scout den was featured at the end of a weeklong Cub-o-Rama. With the den were Den Mother Mrs. A.E. Hagan and Den Chief Jim Theiring. Cub Scouting, designed for boys who are in first through fifth grades, is a year-round family-oriented part of the Boy Scouts of America program. (CHMM 995-1.5314.2.)

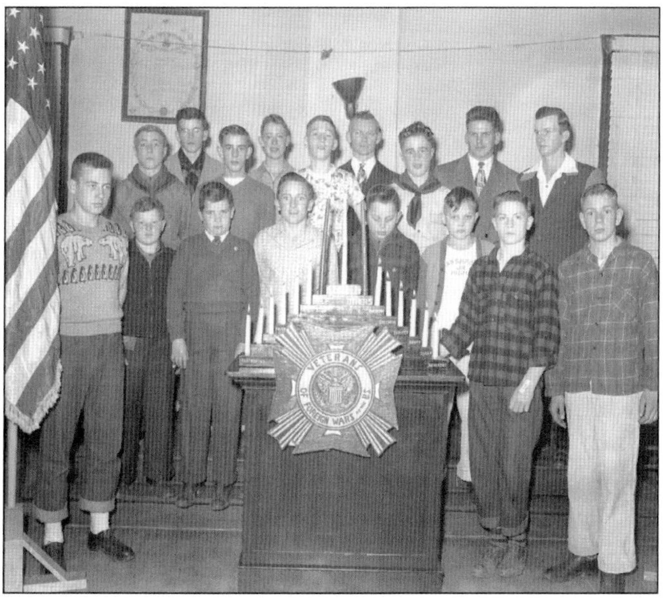

The Boy Scouts of America is one of the nation's largest and most prominent values-based youth development organizations. The Boy Scouts provide a program for young people that builds character, trains them in the responsibilities of participatory citizenship, and develops personal fitness. On February 26, 1947, members of the newly formed Englewood troop participate in a candlelight investiture ceremony before their Veterans of Foreign Wars sponsors. (CHMM 995-1.1999.)

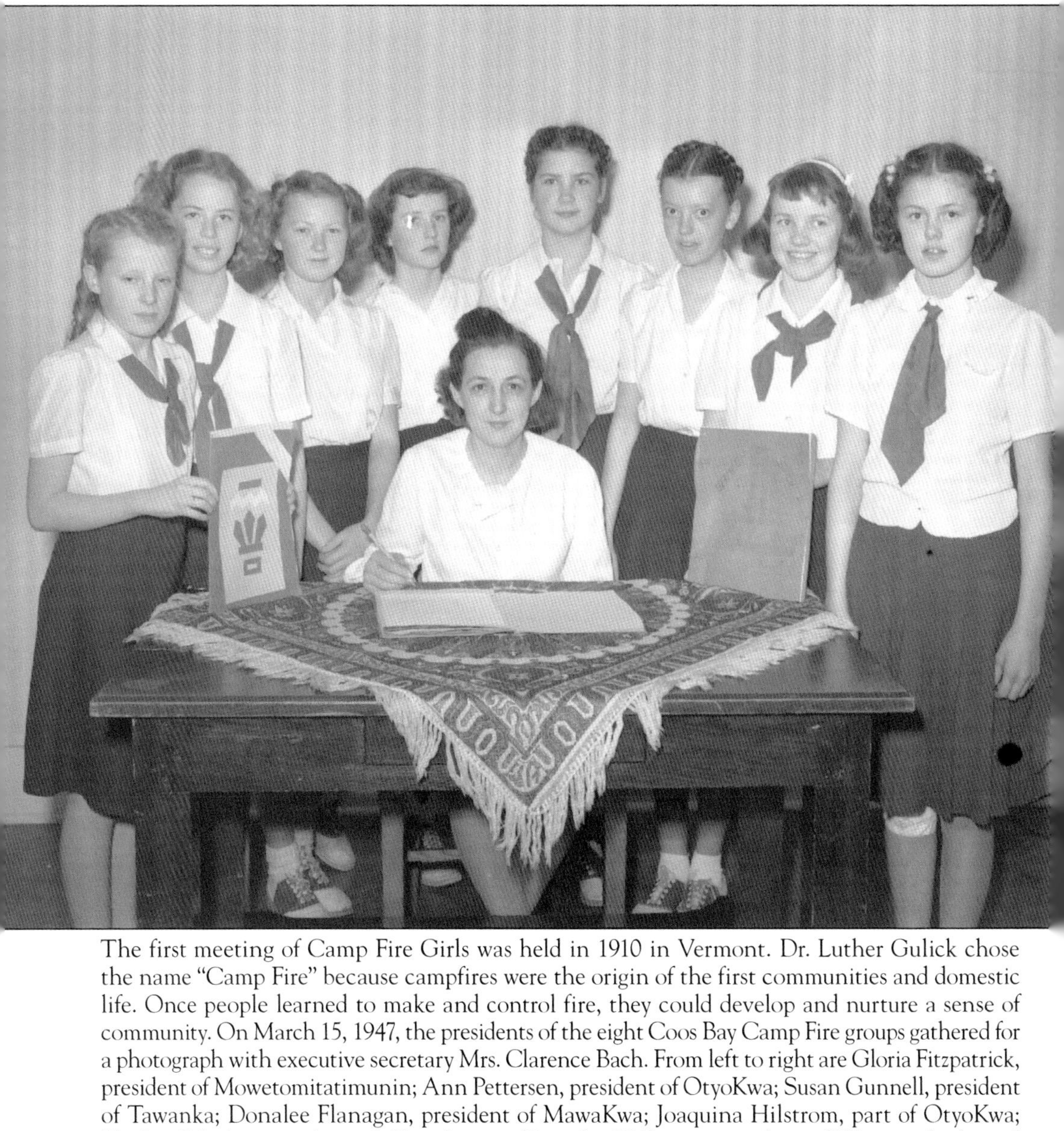

The first meeting of Camp Fire Girls was held in 1910 in Vermont. Dr. Luther Gulick chose the name "Camp Fire" because campfires were the origin of the first communities and domestic life. Once people learned to make and control fire, they could develop and nurture a sense of community. On March 15, 1947, the presidents of the eight Coos Bay Camp Fire groups gathered for a photograph with executive secretary Mrs. Clarence Bach. From left to right are Gloria Fitzpatrick, president of Mowetomitatimunin; Ann Pettersen, president of OtyoKwa; Susan Gunnell, president of Tawanka; Donalee Flanagan, president of MawaKwa; Joaquina Hilstrom, part of OtyoKwa; Shirley Schultz, president of Cheschamay; Dorothy Williams, president of Wetomachick; and Virginia Hazel, president of Oziku. In 1983, the Camp Fire Girls introduced a new coed program named Adventure. Designed for third- through fifth-graders, the program completed the task of program revisions focusing on the inclusion of boys. (CHMM 995-1.8944.)

Seven

Cause to Celebrate

Everybody loves a parade, especially in Coos Bay. Hardly an occasion went unnoticed, and the community gathered together to celebrate with a parade. Bands, floats, and members of civic groups rallied together to provide a day of entertainment. The history of local parades is unknown; however, the first photographed parade dates back to July 4, 1898. Parades alone were not the only reason the community banded together to celebrate. Carnivals of all types brought people together to have fun and participate in worthy causes. Festivals later took root and are important part of today's social activities.

The first known local community celebration occurred in Empire City. Every year near Christmas, a children's masquerade was held at the county courthouse. A tree was decorated, programs were presented, and treats and gifts were given to the children. By the beginning of the 20th century, the event turned into a grand masquerade ball for the adults.

Coos Bay even participated with other communities in special celebrations. One such case was during the 1928 Fourth of July celebration, dubbed "the Spirit of '28." The cities of Marshfield, Reedsport, and Winchester Bay joined to celebrate the uniting of the Roosevelt and Umpqua Highways. However, it was not the first time, nor the last, that communities rallied together to foster community pride during a celebration.

The first known weeklong celebration occurred in August 1953, when Empire held its centennial celebration. In conjunction with the Empire Centennial, the first annual Timberoo festival was held. A grand Timberoo parade began in Coos Bay and traveled to North Bend and then to the Empire "Y," where it joined the Empire Centennial parade.

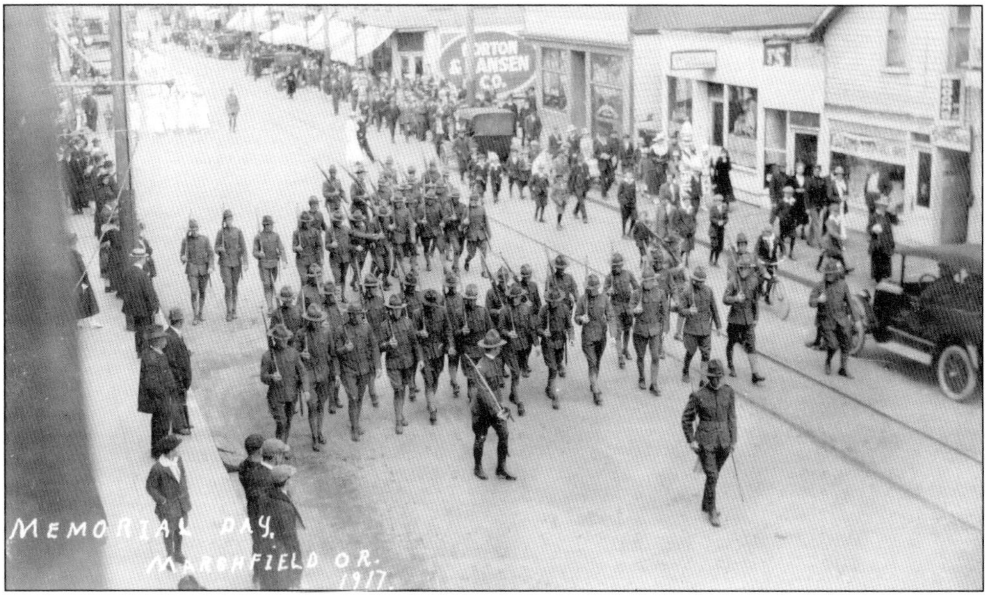

Memorial Day has always been one of the most celebrated holidays. In 1917, the community of Marshfield banded together to provide elaborate ceremonies. Not only was there a parade, there were also addresses and music at the Orpheum Theater. Ceremonies concluded at the Pioneer Cemetery with Company 11 of the Oregon National Guard firing a salute and the singing of the "Star Spangled Banner." (CHMM 006-27.31.)

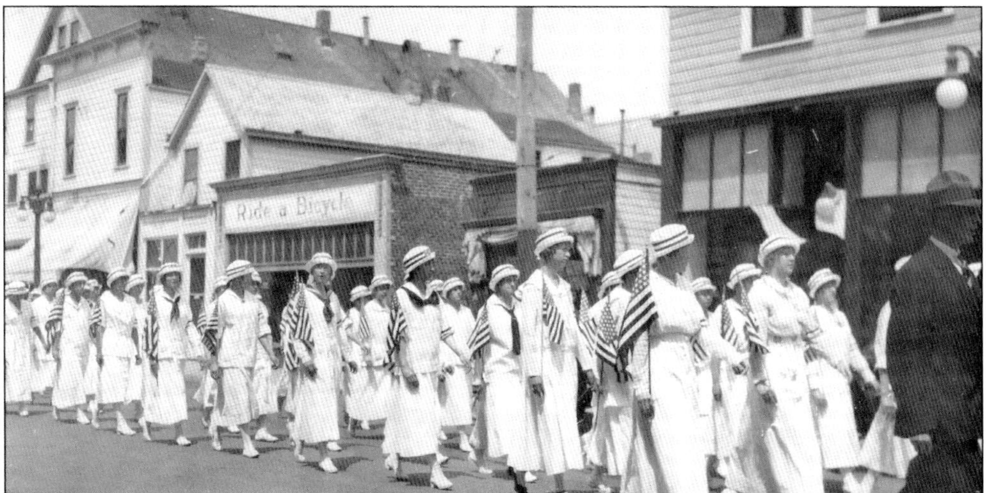

In the spirit of patriotism and loyalty to the country, Marshfield mayor R.A. Copple declared June 14, 1917, a city holiday to honor Flag Day. All businesses were encouraged to close between the hours of 1:00 and 4:00 p.m. to participate with the community to honor the country. During the parade, the Honor Guard Girls marched proudly displaying the nation's flag. (CHMM 980-36.3a.)

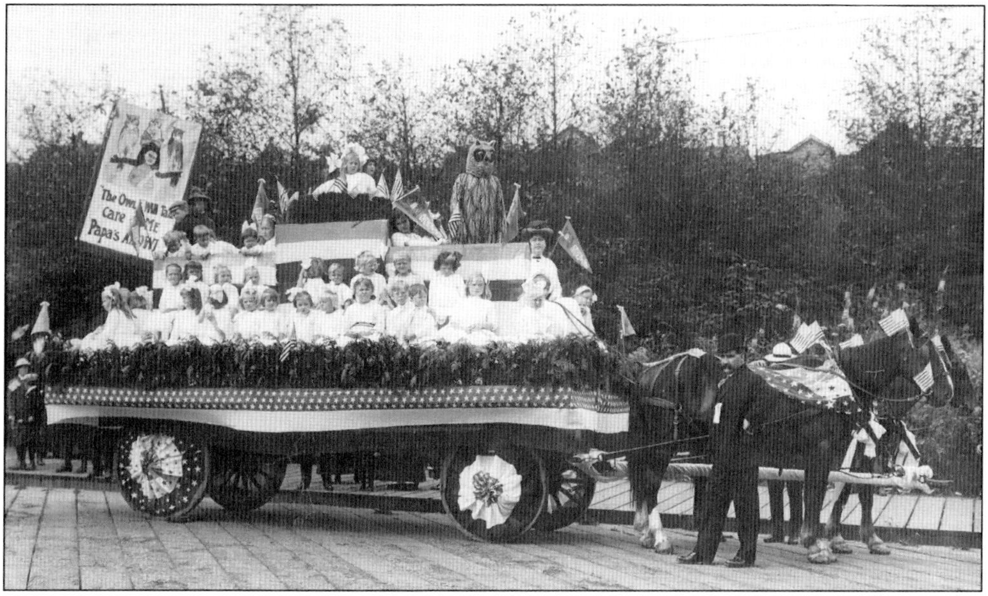

The first-place float winner of the 1913 Fourth of July parade was sponsored by Nest 1048 of the Order of the Owls. The float carried 62 children, an owl mascot, and a sign reading "the owl will take care of me, papa's an owl." (CHMM 989-P106.0.)

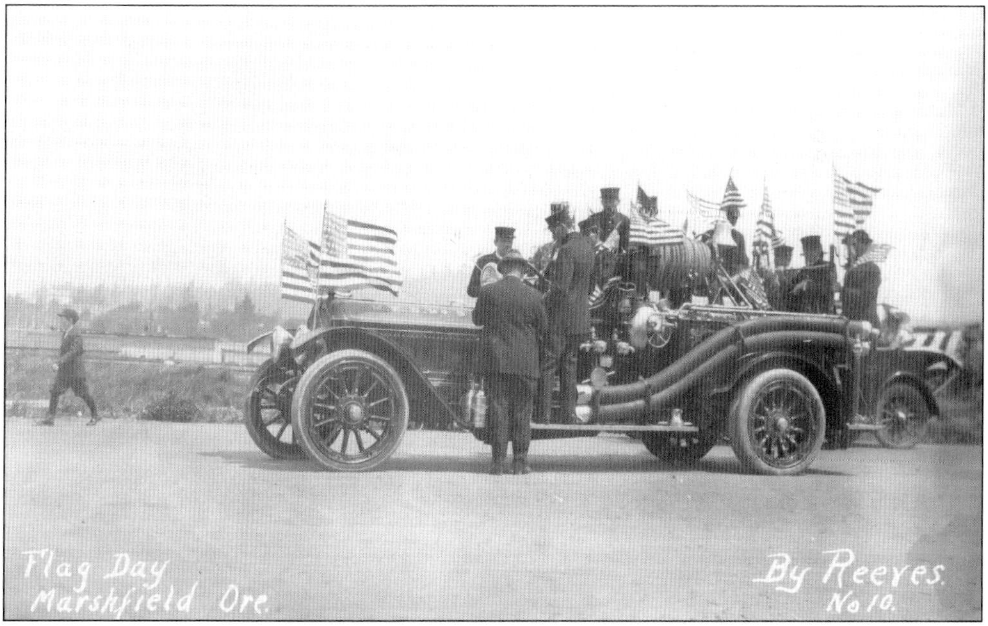

Spearheaded by the Marshfield Lodge of the Elks, Flag Day in 1917 was one of finest patriotic events held in the city. The parade formed at the armory on South Broadway. The automobile section of the parade was led by the fire department's engine, which was proudly decorated in the national colors. (CHMM 980-36.12)

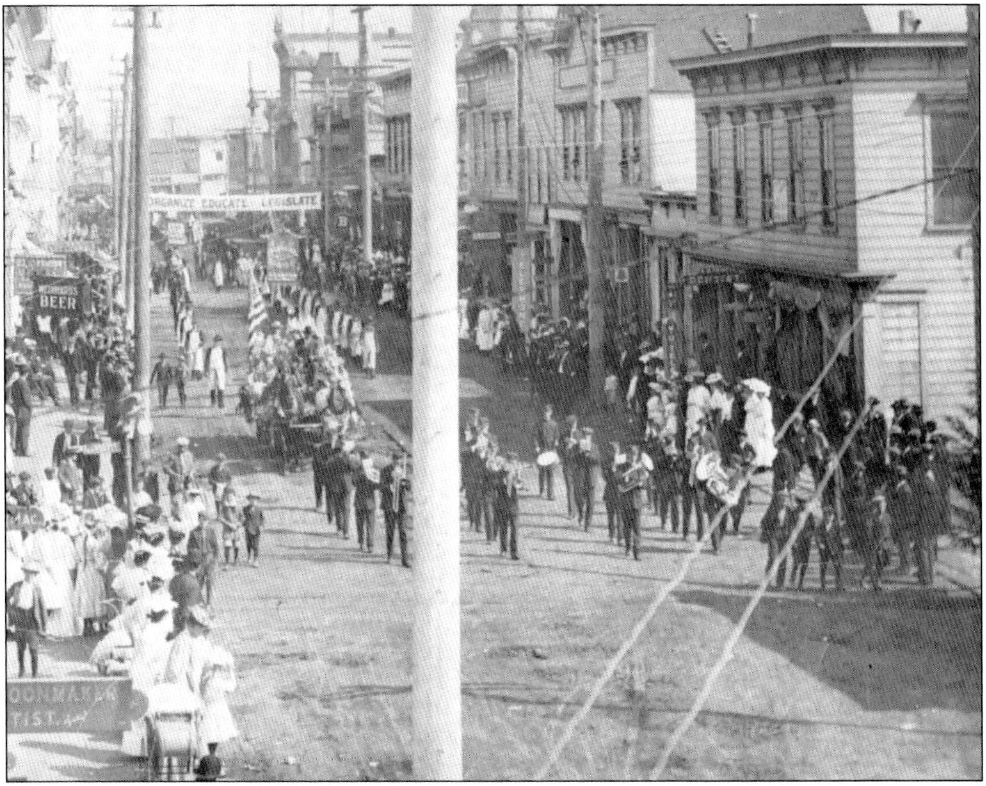

The Labor Day parade of 1918 was part of a cooperative day of celebration between the cities of North Bend and Marshfield. The parade assembled at Central Avenue and Front Street in Marshfield and concluded at Simpson Park in North Bend. The day of celebration also included exhibition drills from each company, a military ball at the Eagles hall, lunch, two dances, and tug-of-war contents between Marshfield and North Bend. (CHMM 978-1.6.)

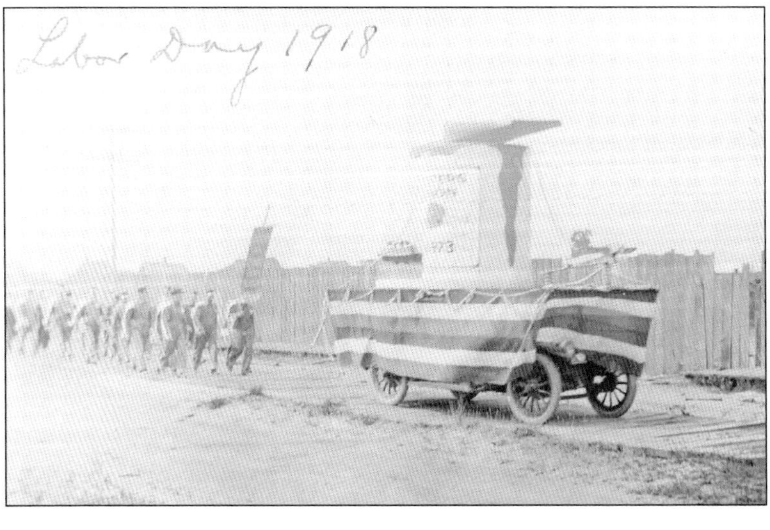

During the early days of the parades, they were not limited to just marching bands and military drill teams. Floats were an important part of the parade. One example was a float built by the local painters' union at the 1918 Labor Day parade. (CHMM 009-64.15.)

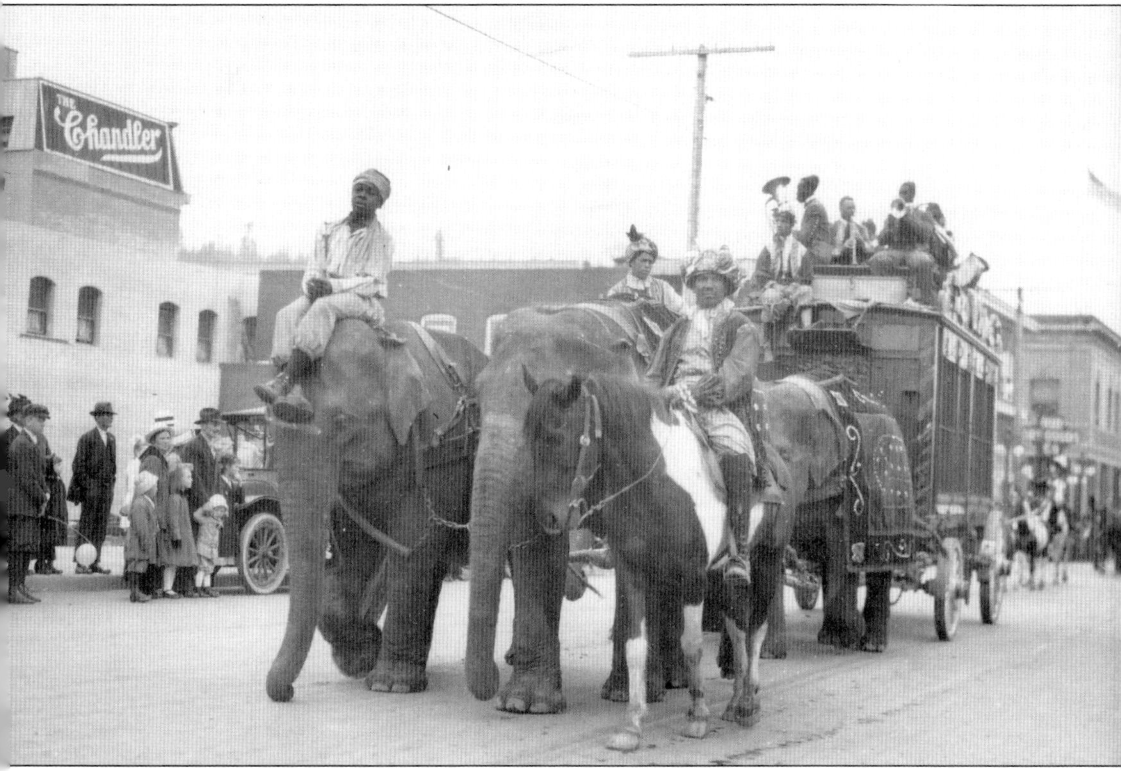

On May 8, 1917, the Al G. Barnes Circus came to town, and a most unusual parade was assembled. As early as 6:00 a.m., excited citizens lined the street just east of the post office to view the array of animals—ponies, caged wild beasts, elephants, and camels—that was proudly paraded down the streets of Marshfield. Across from the armory, a big tent was set up, tables were put out, and an early breakfast was provided for the circus employees. Al G. Barnes was known as a wizard animal educator who enjoyed making people happy. Barnes assembled from every known country animals of most every species and educated them in circus performing. Donkeys were taught to sing, elephants to play football, kangaroos to box and run races, and ostriches to dance. Fifty white lions were taught to ride galloping horses and leap through hoops of fire. The circus was described by the newspaper as clean and moral entertainment free from smut or suggestiveness. (CHMM 995-16.7 k.)

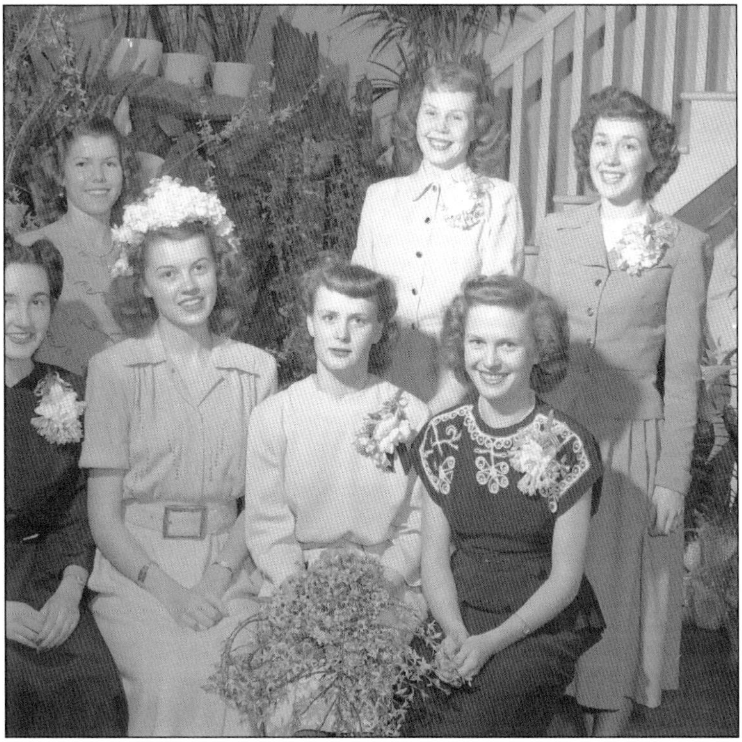

On May 7, 1947, Helen Schultz of Coos Bay was crowned Queen of May at the annual Bay May Festival, sponsored by the Business and Professional Women's Club of the Bay. Wearing a tiara of white carnations and orchid sweet peas, Shultz was accompanied by her maid of honor and princesses to form her court of honor. The purpose of the festival was to raise funds for two girls to attend an accredited nursing program. (CHMM 995-1.2686.1.)

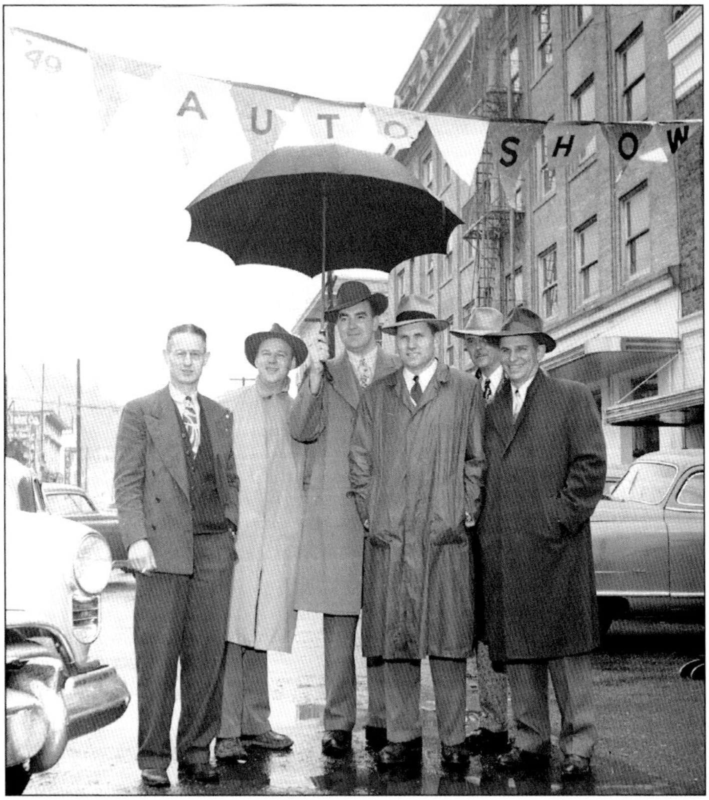

Despite the rainy weather, the annual retail trade show known as Spring Opening, held March 28, 1949, was a successful day. Crowds gathered for a day of shopping and activities, which included a parade and auto show, along with the unveiling and judging of the display windows. Celebrating the day were Clayton Driscoll, Ed. V. White, Pete Gray, Mr. Day, F.W. Linklater, and chairman A.H. Kohler. (CHMM 995-1.5651.2.)

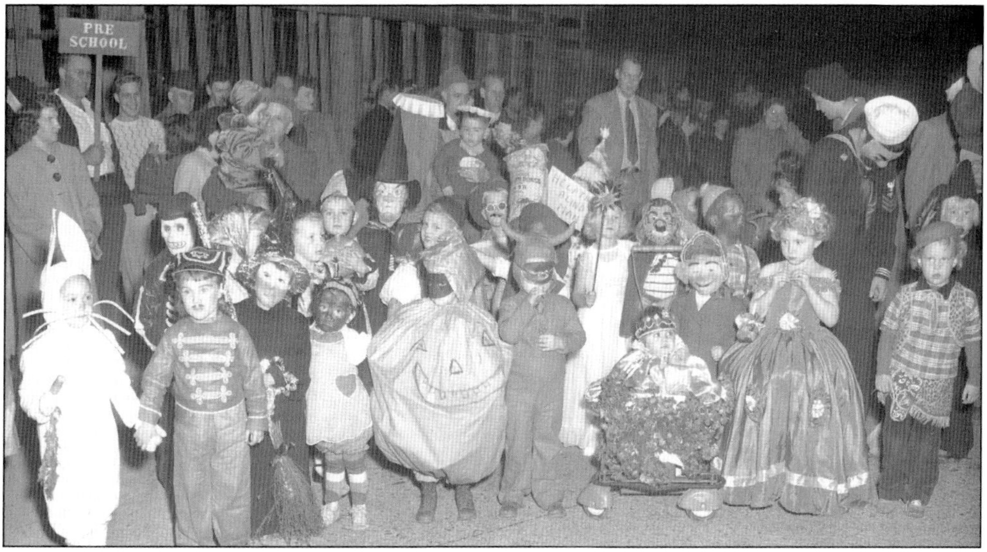

Not all parades were designed with the adults in mind. One special parade was geared for the children of Coos Bay. Preschoolers wore their finest 1949 Halloween costumes during the annual Neewollah celebration. Children were judged in such categories as prettiest, most patriotic, most comical, best pumpkin, and best witch. (CHMM 995-1.8093.)

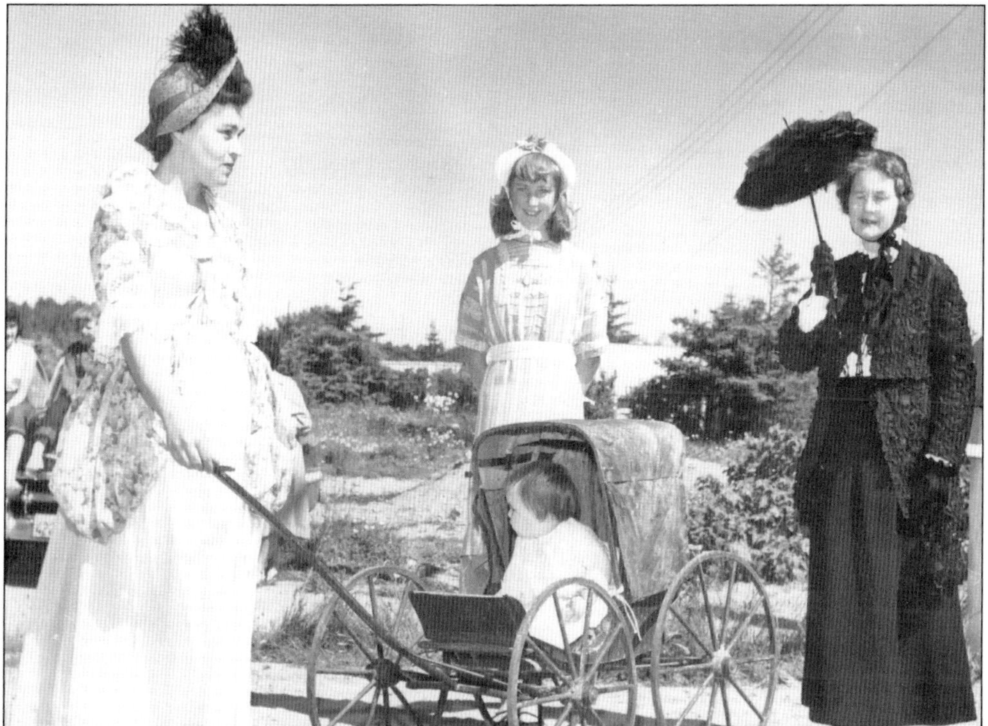

Debbie Hanson rides in a baby carriage that had traveled around the Horn in 1847, accompanied by Mrs. Gerald Hanson, Mrs. Dan Keating, and Bettina Baer. They were first-place winners in the individual category of the Empire Centennial Parade, held on August 7, 1953. (CHMM 973-77b.)

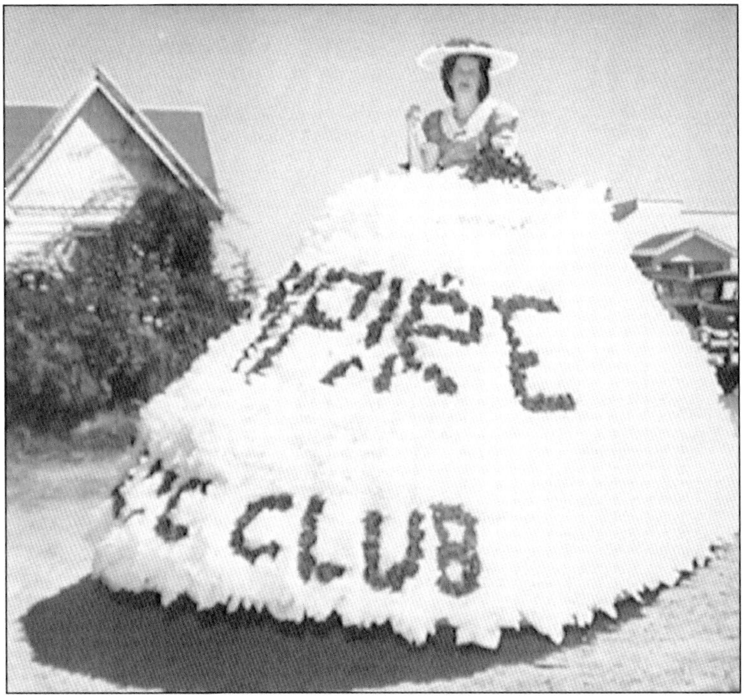

During the Empire Centennial Parade, the Empire Civic Club carried Wilma Richardson through the streets of Empire. The Empire Civic Club took third place in the organizations category of the parade. Other parade categories included individuals, drill teams, commercial, and horses. It was a good day for those who attended. (CHMM 996-P27.)

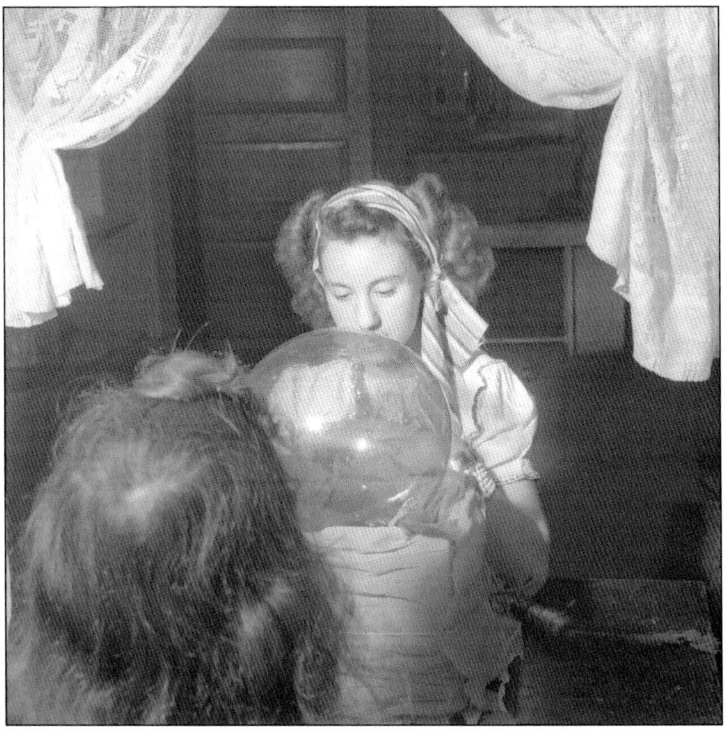

Filled with a wide array of activities, school carnivals are always fun events to attend. More than 600 people enjoyed the festivities at the annual Marshfield Junior High School Carnival held on March 13, 1947. Fortune-teller Colleen Macnab, using a Japanese fish float as her crystal ball, demonstrates her powers. (CHMM 995-1.1980.)

On April 30, 1949, in the presence of nearly 800 people, school superintendent J.B. Putman crowns Trudy Freemason queen and Dean Thurman king at the coronation ceremony of the Empire School Carnival. Also participating in the ceremony are crown bearers Janice Trott and Ronny Combs. (CHMM 995-1.6026.1.)

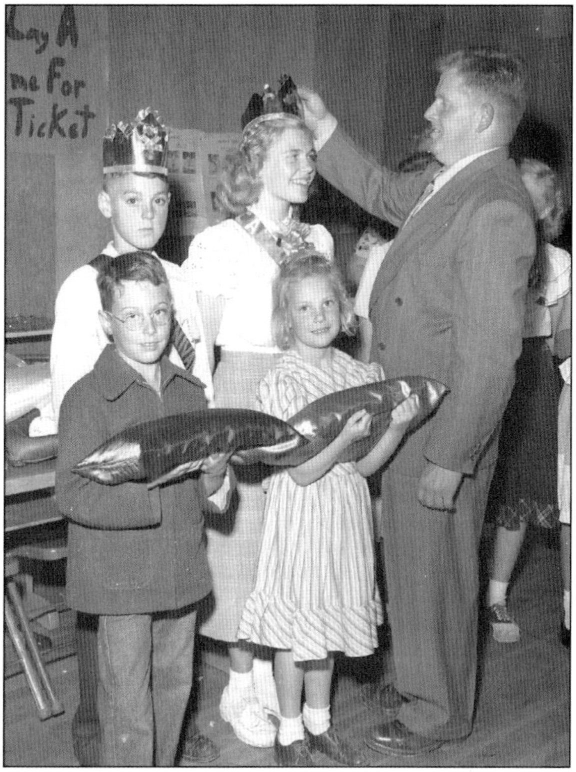

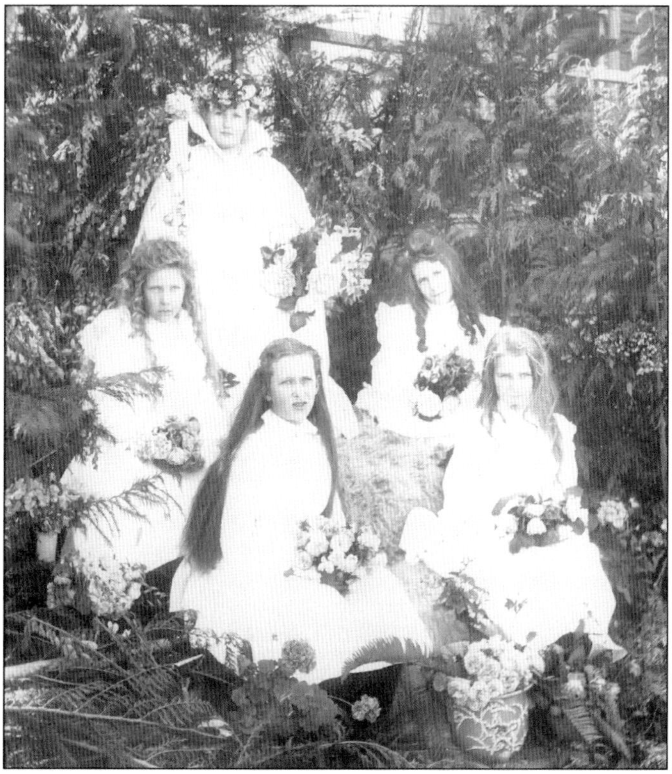

Carnivals were not limited to civic or school functions. The churches of the community also played an important role in carnival activities. Pictured with a group of young ladies, Henrietta Ferrey was crowned queen at the annual Methodist Church Children's Carnival in 1901. (CHMM 969-124 h.)

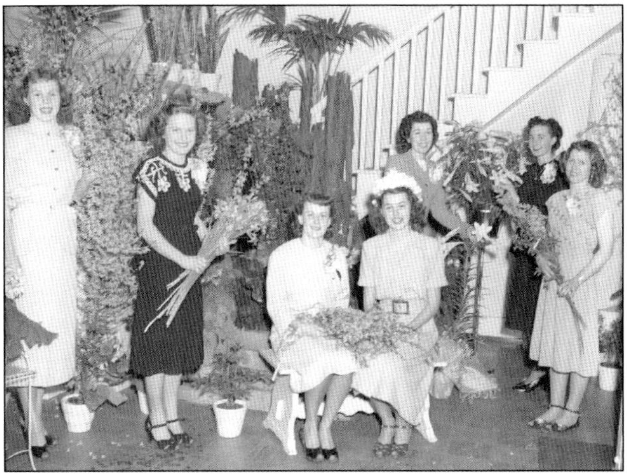

Wearing the tiara signifying that she is Queen of May, Helen Schultz, from Coos Bay, smiles happily for a *Coos Bay Times* photographer. She is surrounded by her maid of honor and princesses who formed her court of honor for the May Festival, which was sponsored annually by the Business and Professional Women's Club of the Bay. The purpose of the festival, held on May 7, 1948, was to raise funds for scholarships. (CHMM 995-1.2686.2.)

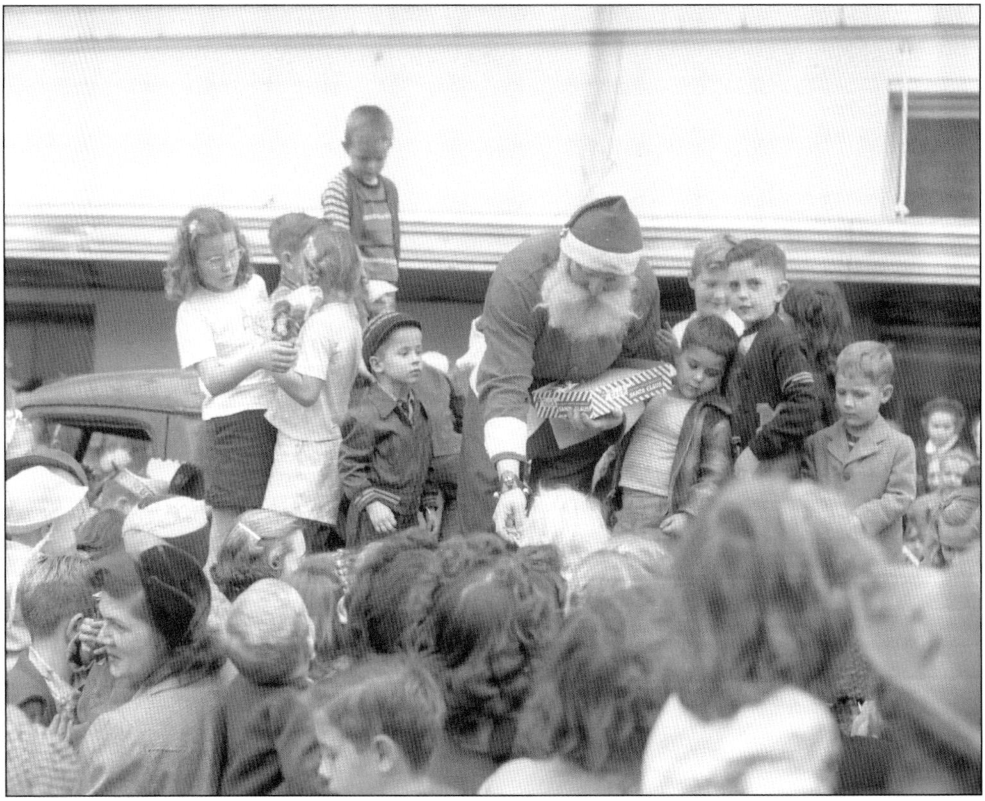

On November 29, 1952, at 9:30 a.m., Santa arrived in Coos Bay by a Coast Guard crash boat to launch the Christmas shopping season. Santa was then paraded through town by the fire department. From there, Santa mounted a specially constructed platform where he held private interviews with anyone who wanted to meet with him. (CHMM 995-1.12004.)

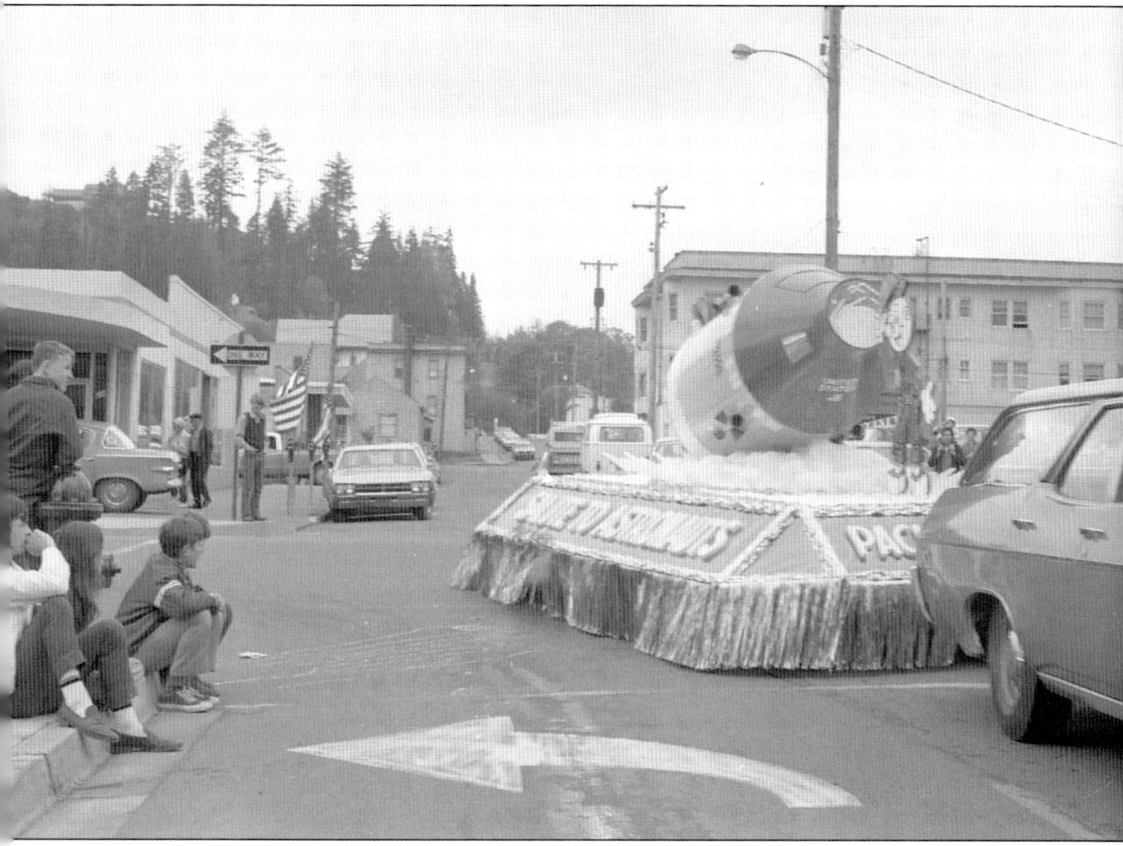

Stuart Roosa, command module pilot for Apollo 14, chose to have his official NASA "hometown parade" in Coos Bay. The connection began by chance in Bend, Oregon. Phil Waters and Bob Perkins of Coos Bay heard on the radio that astronauts would be in Bend and were interested to see what they were doing. During a lunch break, Stuart Roosa invited the two men to join him and the other astronauts. Phil and Bob returned the invitation and asked Stuart Roosa, Charlie Duke, and Joe Engle to ride with them in their air-conditioned car. The parade was the biggest ever held in Coos Bay and the highlight of "Stuart Roosa Days" in May 1971. Stuart Roosa Days was such a success that Coos Bay soon began its annual tradition of the Bay Area Fun Festival and parade. (CHMM 995-1.53094.2.)

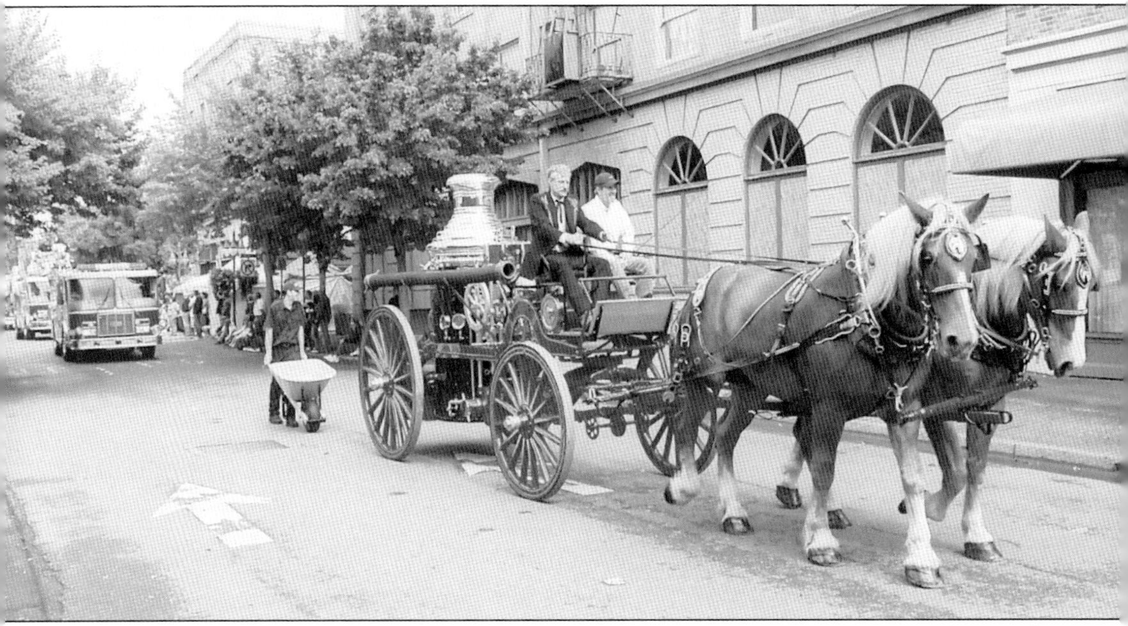

Established in 1973, the Bay Area Fun Festival has been going strong. During the parade on September 18, 2009, the Coos Bay Fire Department made the public debut of its restored steam pumper, a 1904 Nott fire engine. Driving the team of Belgian draft horses is Kerry Sweitz of Lincoln City. Riding next to him is Coos Bay mayor Jeff McKeown. The steam fire engine was used over 100 years ago by the Marshfield Fire Department. In 1910, the City of Marshfield purchased the engine from the Nott Fire Engine Co. in Minneapolis. The fire pumper has been retained by the fire department every since it was first purchased. It is now owned by the Volunteer Fire Fighters Association, and major restoration by the association began in October 2008. By the time of the Fun Festival parade in 2009, the engine was deemed road-ready and was 90- to 95-percent complete in its restoration. (The *World*.)

Eight

The Coos Bay Years

Coos Bay has transformed itself into a modern progressive city. Lost are the days of a strong timber influence. Today, Coos Bay relies on health care, tourism, and educational services for its strong employment opportunities. Coos Bay has grown not only in land mass but also in population. Coos Bay's population as of the 2010 census was 15,967. Spread out through the districts of Eastside, Englewood, and Empire, local residents enjoy low population density and more of a rural feel than that of a city.

Coos Bay is home to Southwestern Oregon Community College. The college was formed in a tax district election in May 1961 that originally included Coos, northern Curry, and western Douglas and Lane Counties. Within a year, Curry and Douglas Counties opted to leave the district. However, on July 1, 1995, Curry County rejoined the district following a successful annexation vote by its residents.

Coos Bay has even extended its hand abroad by developing a sister city in Japan. In 1982, the cities of Coos Bay and Choschi, Japan, began looking to establish a sister-city relationship. In June 1982, the City of Coos Bay received a letter of introduction to the City of Choschi. Sixty-three miles from Tokyo, Choschi is known for its production of soy sauce and is the second largest fishing harbor in Japan.

February 10, 1983, was the date chosen for the official signing of the agreement, which coincided with Choschi's 50th-anniversary celebration. Council member Jack Varra and his wife, Barbara, represented the City of Coos Bay in the two-and-one-half-hour signing ceremony to establish Coos Bay and Choschi as sister cities.

Not forgetting the importance of Marshfield, the City of Coos Bay formed the Old Marshfield Historic District, which was adopted by the city council on February 16, 1999. The district extends from Market Street to Curtis Avenue and from the waterfront to city hall.

With the rich histories and diversity of Eastside, Empire, and Englewood, along with the heritage of Marshfield, Coos Bay has developed into a modern progressive city that people are proud to call home.

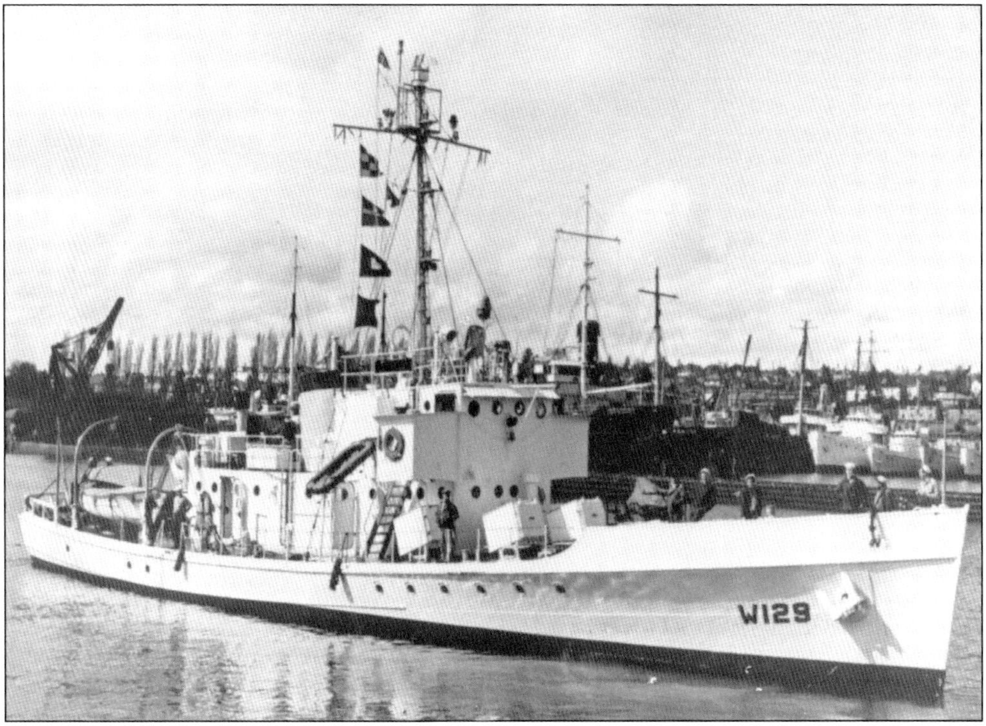

With a complement of two officers, one warrant officer, and 25 men, the 125-foot US Coast Guard cutter *Bonham* was stationed at Coos Bay from 1946 to 1959. Used for law enforcement and search and rescue, the *Bonham* was decommissioned in 1959 and sold to Sea Food Storage, Inc., in Petersburg, Alaska, where she was renamed *Polar Star*. The *Bonham* was built in 1927. (CHMM 991-20.17.)

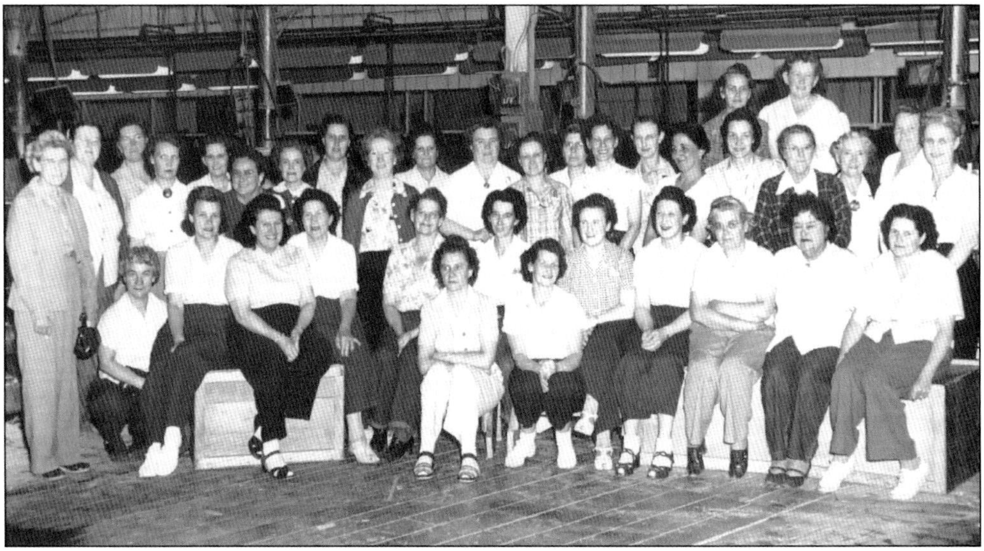

In 1949, the Grandmothers Club of the Evans Products Company was an important component of the labor force. Of the 1,200 employed at Evans Products, 800 were women. Paid the same as their male counterparts, the women were assigned as panel graders for the battery separators. The company also made venetian blinds, chairs, tables, and plywood. (CHMM 987-5.15.)

A new form of outdoor entertainment began to take shape on December 22, 1949, with the installation of a large motion picture screen on Ocean Boulevard. The screen, measuring 52 square feet according to the newspaper, was erected by Coos Bay Trucking Company with a large crane. Built to accommodate 500 vehicles, the new Motor Vu Theatre had its grand opening on June 7, 1950. (CHMM 995-1.8411.1.)

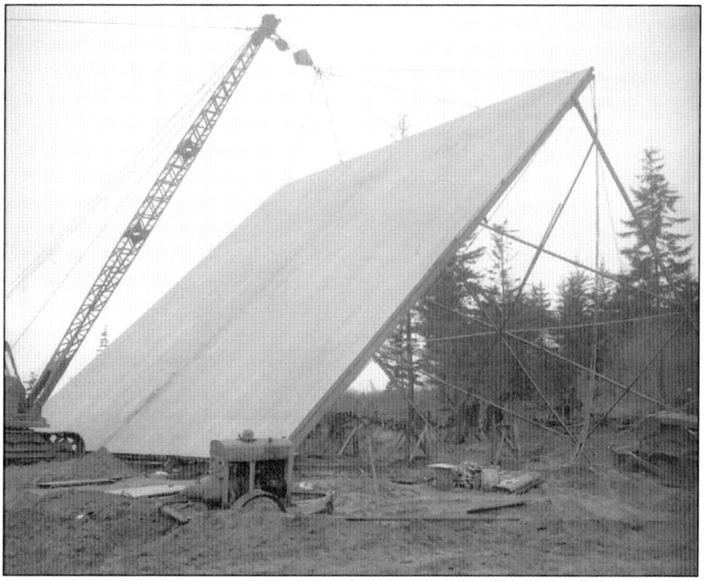

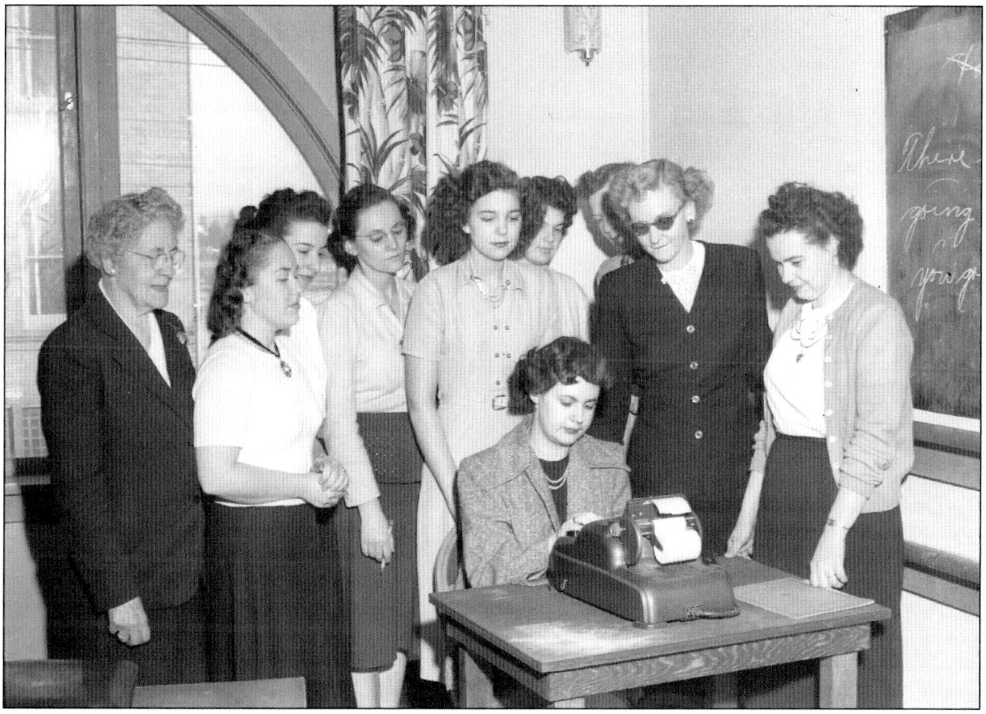

Established in 1950, the Coos Bay Business College provided students the opportunity to receive courses in business. Pictured are students receiving instruction in the use of adding machines with college director Margaret de Sarminto and instructor Eloise Roderick. (CHMM 995-1.9097.)

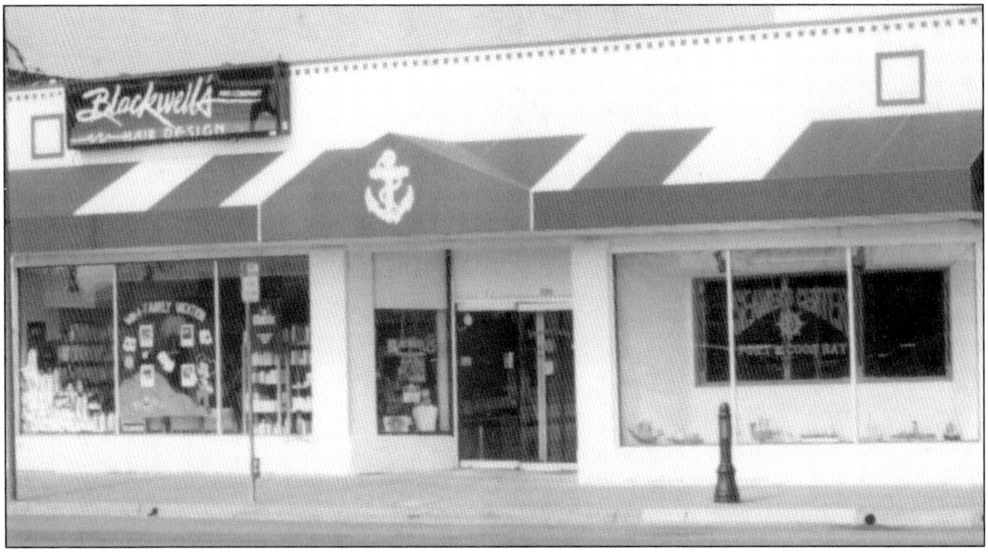

Hospitality has always been a goal for the citizens of Coos Bay. In order to provide a welcome to the seamen who docked at Coos Bay, various churches, the International Longshoremen's Union, Warehousemen's Local No. 12, the United Way, and others established the Seamen's Center in 1963. Described as one of the most desired centers to visit, the center was closed in 2002 due to a lack of ships coming to port. (CHMM 008-1.273.)

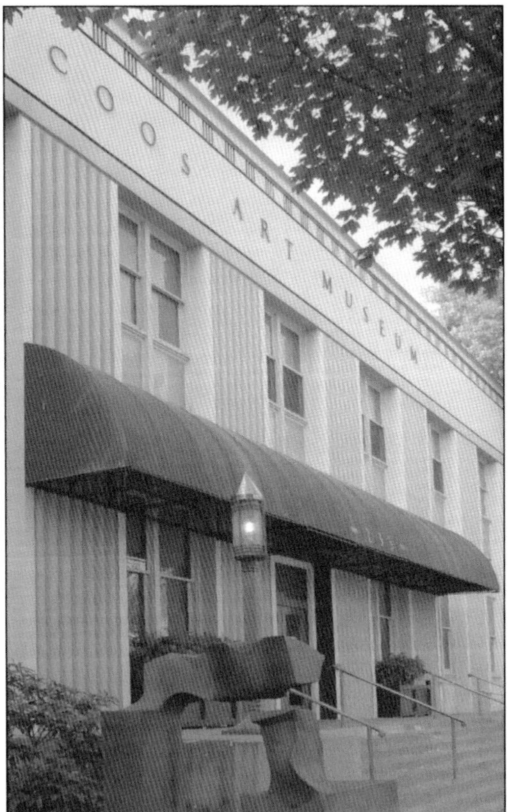

Coos Art Museum is the cornerstone of visual arts on Oregon's southern coast. Established in 1966, the Coos Art Museum is the third oldest art museum in Oregon. Since 1984, the museum has been located in the former federal building, which was built in 1936. This renovated Art Deco building contains six galleries and annually presents from 12 to 25 changing original and touring exhibitions, including exhibits from its 541-piece permanent collection. (Mike Holm.)

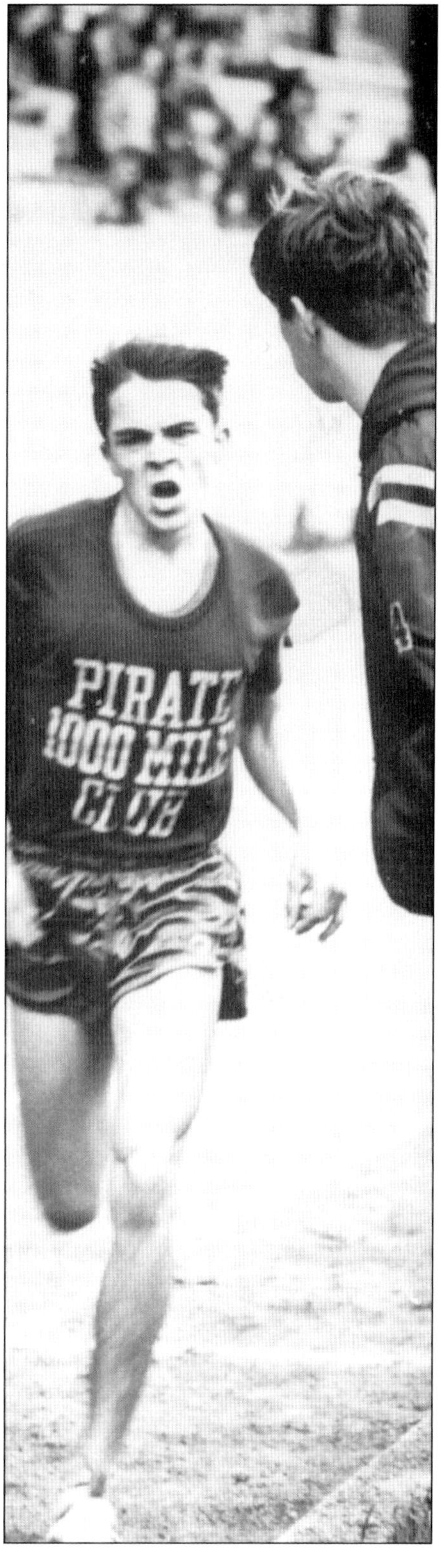

Track legend Steve Roland "Pre" Prefontaine was a native son of Coos Bay. Prior to his death in 1975 at age 24, Prefontaine set 14 track records. Born in 1951, Prefontaine discovered his gift for running fast and far as a student at Marshfield High School. He was undefeated in cross-country track as a junior and a senior. As a senior at Marshfield High School, he broke the two-mile American record. Prefontaine won seven NCAA championships while running for the University of Oregon from 1969 to 1973. Coos Bay honors its native son every September with the popular Prefontaine Memorial Run, a challenging 10-kilometer event that follows the route of one of his regular training courses. Three feature films have documented Prefontaine's life and career: the documentary *Fire on the Track: The Steve Prefontaine Story* (1995) and two Hollywood movies, *Prefontaine* (1996) and *Without Limits* (1998). (Marshfield High School Yearbook.)

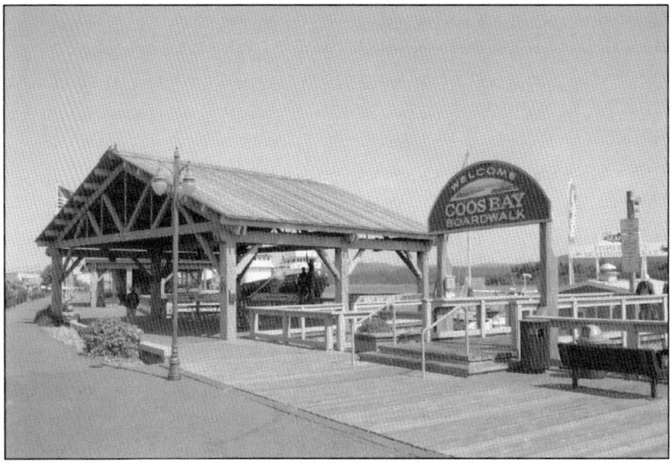

In 1986, the City of Coos Bay began plans to build a boardwalk featuring a working waterfront. Located at the boardwalk are interpretive signs explaining the significance of the Coos Bay estuary and other natural features. The boardwalk has featured several tall ships and is the site of Santa's annual arrival by tug each Friday after Thanksgiving. (CHMM.)

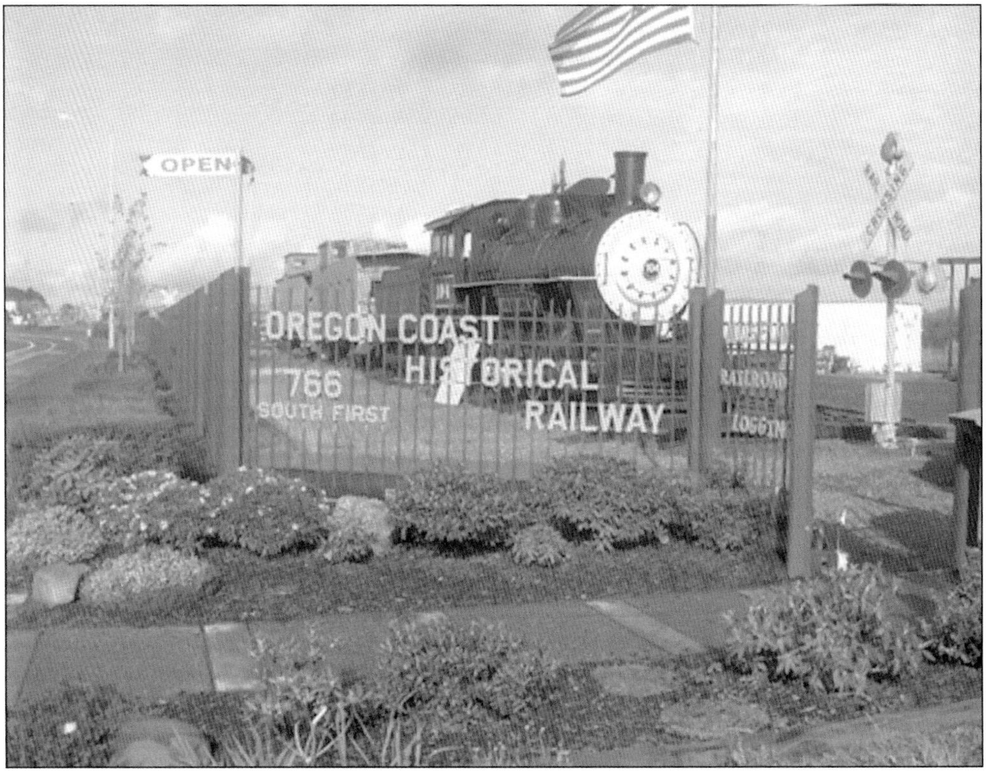

The Oregon Coast Historical Railway has been operating a display area and small museum in Coos Bay since 2001. The centerpiece is the 1922 Baldwin steam locomotive No. 104 and its tender, which worked for many decades in local forests. The museum has hundreds of artifacts and photographs. The museum's goals have been to preserve this vital part of the region's economic and cultural history and to work closely with other local museums. (Tom Baake.)

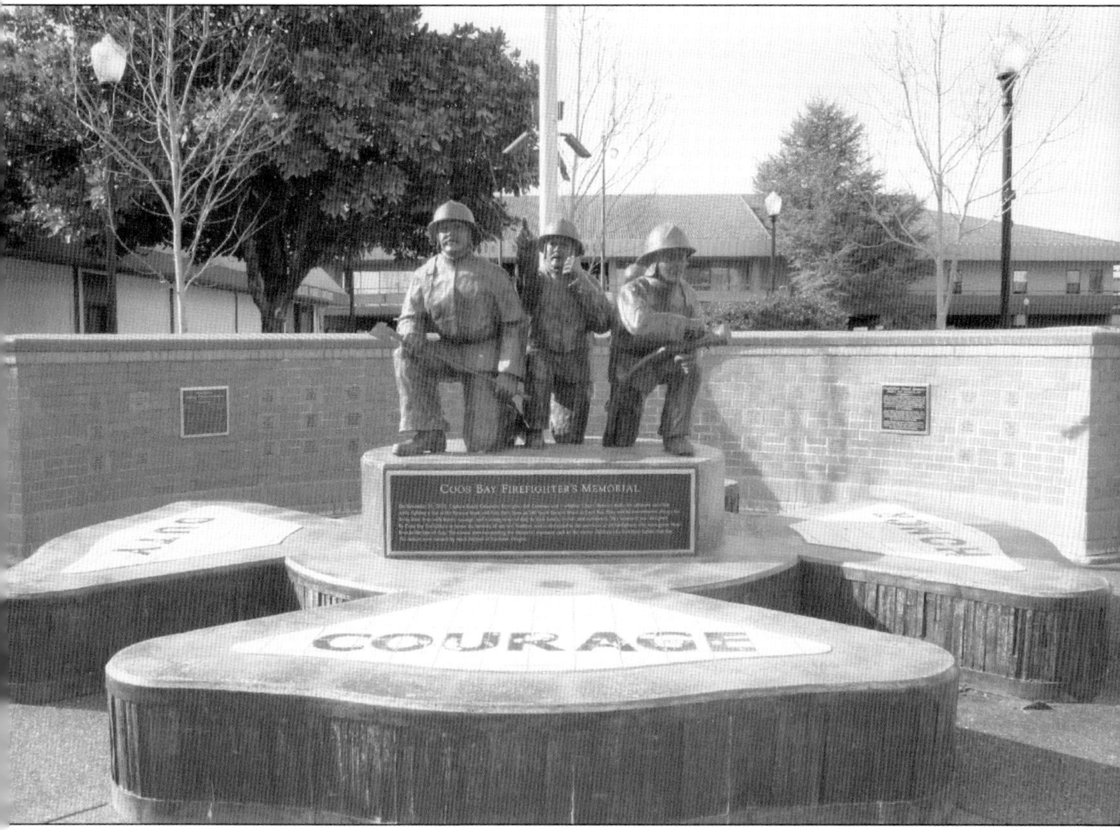

On November 25, 2002, three fire fighters died in the line of duty in Coos Bay after the roof collapsed on the Farwest Truck and Auto Parts at 340 South Second Street. Capt. Randall "Randy" Carpenter, age 46, firefighter Robert "Chuck" Hanners, age 33, and firefighter Jeffery "Jeff" E. Common, age 30, died in the collapse. The site in front of city hall was approved by the council on June 28, 2005, and the ground-breaking ceremony took place on March 21, 2006. The memorial was designed by Coos Bay firefighters to honor the memory of their lost brothers and was dedicated to the sacrifices of all firefighters who have given their lives in the line of duty. The site includes life-size statues of the three men, a remembrance wall, 11 trees that each represent one of the children left without a father, and three walkways lined with engraved bricks. At 1:00 p.m. on November 25, 2006, the Pipes & Drums Honor Guard started a procession led by the Coos Bay, North Bend, and Charleston firefighters to the dedication ceremony. (CHMM.)

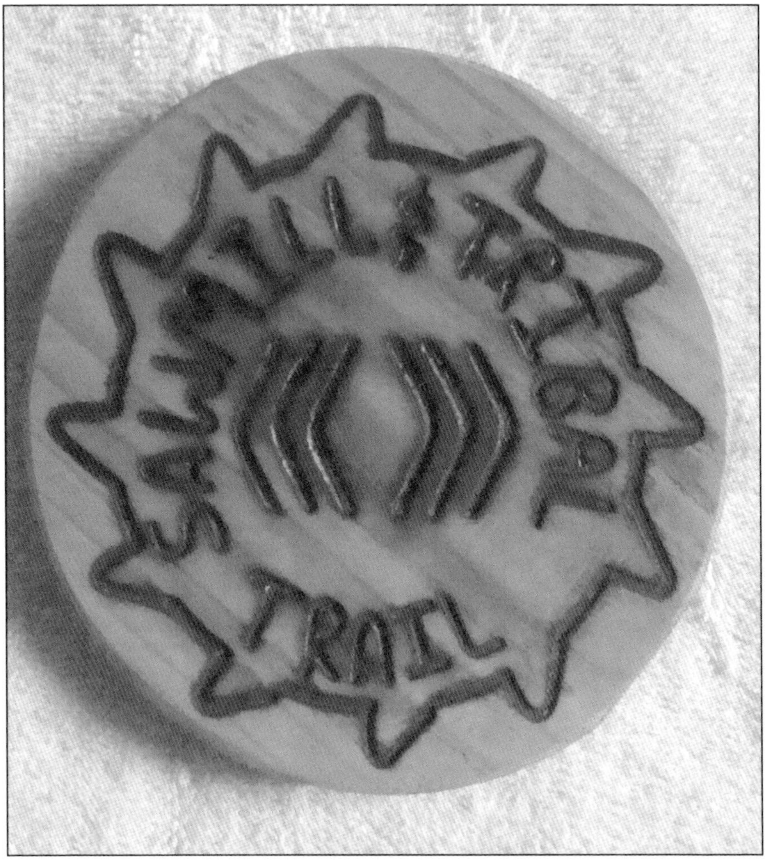

In 2009, the Sawmill & Tribal Trail Advisory Team undertook a project to approximate the 1859 route from North Bend to Empire. The 5.6-mile trail begins near the old Simpson Sawmill site at Ferry Road Park and ends near the old Luse Sawmill site at the Hollering Place. The First Peoples plant and tree usage is marked in John Topits Park. Hikers along the Oregon Coast Trail can also use this trail. (Tom Greaves.)

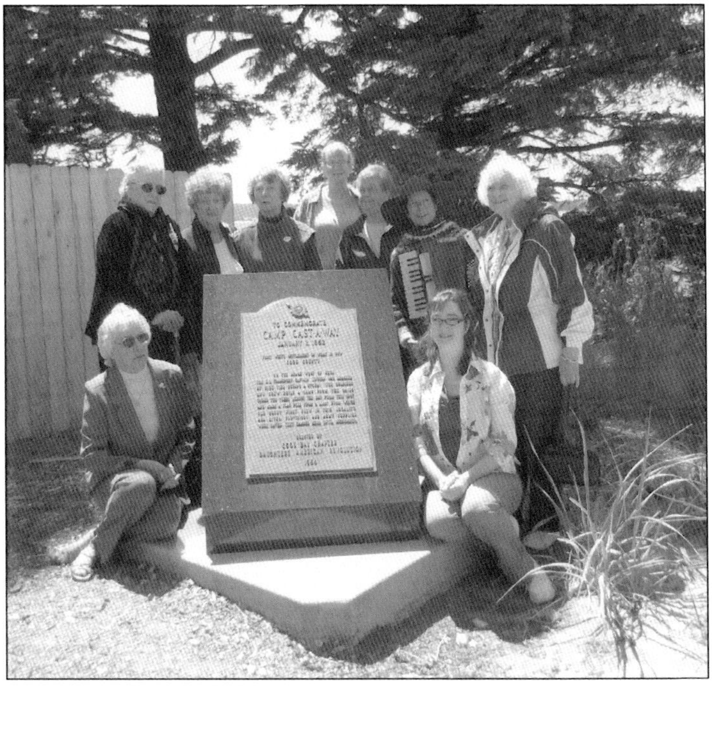

During the Empire Clamboree festivities of June 25, 2011, the Daughters of the American Revolution rededicated the Camp Castaway plaque at the Empire Wayside. The grounding of the military transport *Captain Lincoln* and establishment of Camp Castaway brought attention to the bay and opened the door to the development of the bay area by white settlers. The first dedication of the plaque occurred in Empire on February 14, 1956, with an address by Mrs. Albert H. Powers. (CCB.)

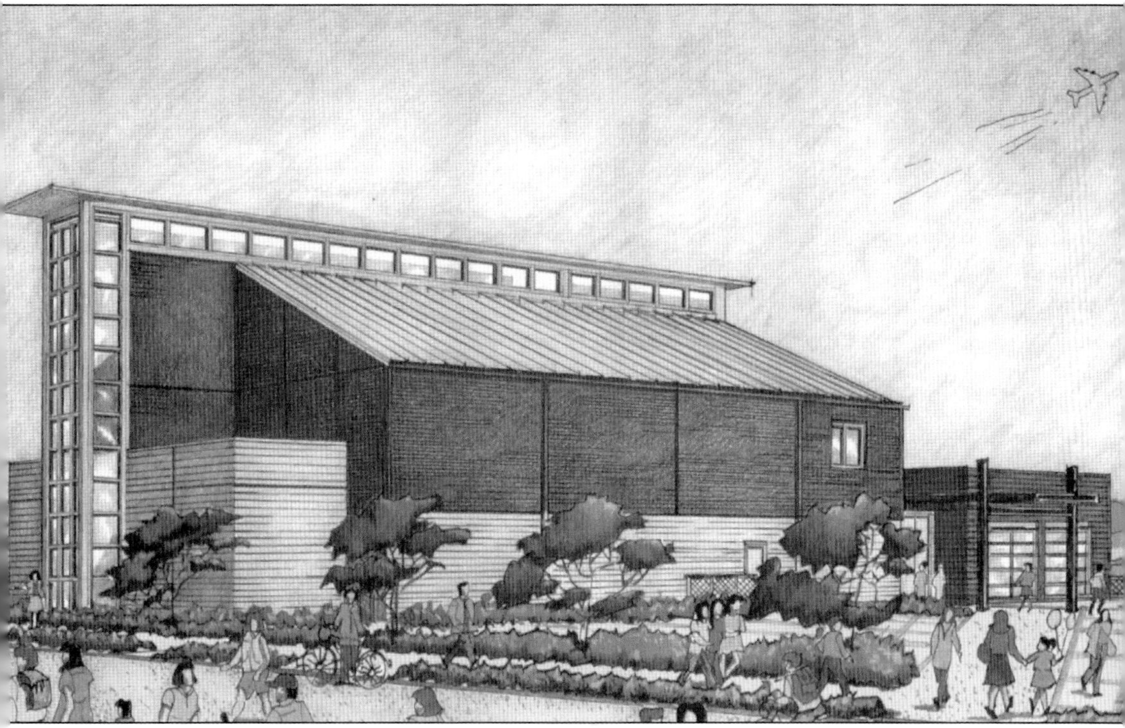

The Coos County Historical Society was formed in 1891. Its Coos Historical & Maritime Museum in the North Bend–Coos Bay area is the source of many images in this book. Its collections include more than 250,000 images and more than 45,000 artifacts pertaining to the cultural history of Oregon's south coast. Museum field trips, events, exhibits, and award-winning education programs are undertaken in partnership with tribes or area nonprofit organizations and provide an excellent orientation to the history of this somewhat remote area.

Currently, the Coos Historical & Maritime Museum is raising funds for the construction of a new waterfront facility in Coos Bay to improve its capacity for service. The museum has outgrown the building it has occupied since 1958. The new 11,000-square-foot building and adjacent plaza are designed for a range of community services. In addition to supporting existing and planned programs and activities, the facility will greatly expand opportunities for innovative partnerships and cultural events.

The museum thanks the author for donating all of royalties from this book to the new facility project.

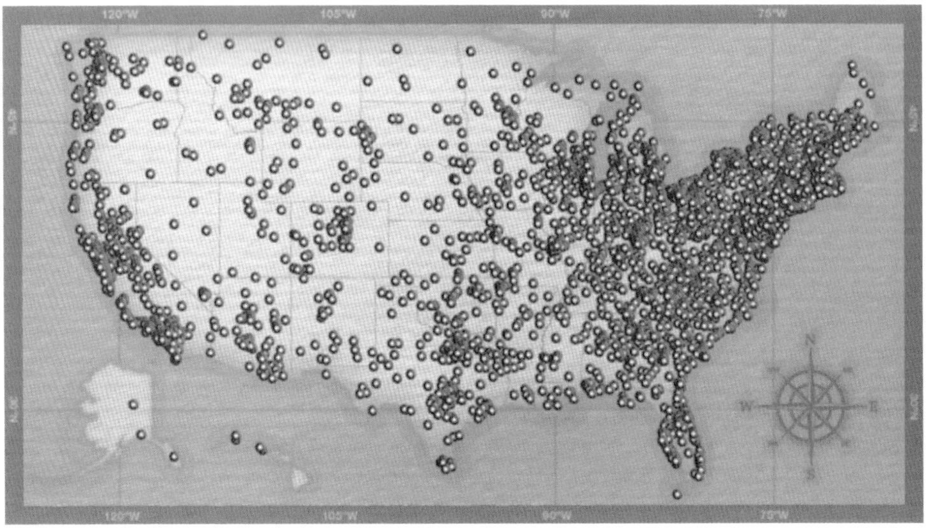

Consistent with our mission to preserve history on a local level, this book was printed in South Carolina on American-made paper and manufactured entirely in the United States. Products carrying the accredited Forest Stewardship Council (FSC) label are printed on 100 percent FSC-certified paper.

MADE IN THE USA